Mission to Rural America

Tamers of Death: The History of the Alexian Brothers 1300-1789. Volume I. New York, Seabury Press, 1976.

The Ministry of Healing: The History of the Alexian Brothers, 1789 to Present. Volume II. New York, Seabury Press, 1978.

Faith and Fraternalism: The History of the Knights of Columbus 1882-1982. New York, Harper & Row, 1982.

Tradition and Transformation in Catholic Culture, The Priests of Saint Sulpice in the United States from 1791 to the Present. New York, Macmillan, 1988.

General Editor: *Makers of the American Catholic Community: Historical Studies of the American People in the United States 1789-1989,* six-volumes. New York, Macmillan, 1989.

MISSION TO RURAL AMERICA

The Story of W. Howard Bishop, Founder of Glenmary

Christopher J. Kauffman

Paulist Press
New York/Mahwah, N.J.

155500

Book Design by Nighthawk Design.

Copyright © 1991 by The Home Missioners of America and
The Home Mission Sisters of America, Inc.

Kauffman, Christopher J., 1936-
    Mission to rural America: the story of W. Howard Bishop, founder of Glenmary/by
Christopher J. Kauffman.
        p.   cm.
    Includes bibliographical references and index.
    ISBN 0-8091-3213-3
        1. Bishop, William Howard, 1885-1953. 2. Catholic Church—United States—
Clergy—Biography.   3. Glenmary Home Missioners—History.   I. Title.
BX4705.B523K38   1991
    271'.79—dc20
    [B]   90-21934
                                                                              CIP

Published by Paulist Press
997 Macarthur Boulevard
Mahwah, N.J. 07430

Printed and bound in the United States of America

CONTENTS

PREFACE   ix

INTRODUCTION   1

Part I The Baltimore Years   7

1   Prologue: The Baltimore Church   9

2   The Young Priest   18

3   The Rural Pastor, 1917–1922   43

4   The Catholic Rural Movement   59

5   Leader of the Rural Church, 1928–1936   75

Part II The Cincinnati Years, 1937–1953   101

6   The Origins of the Home Missioners   105

7   The Foundation Years, 1937–1939   134

8   The Men Missioners, 1939–1946   156

9   The Women Missioners, 1939–1946   184

10   Post-War Developments   200

11   The Final Years, 1950–1953   219

EPILOGUE: THE LEGACY OF HOWARD BISHOP   237

NOTES   261

INDEX   286

To Justus George Lawler, in gratitude
for his friendship, inspiration, humor,
and for his skillful cultivation of irony

PREFACE

To journey through the rural landscape with W. Howard Bishop has been a stimulating intellectual and personal experience. I am very grateful to Colman Barry, O.S.B., John Tracy Ellis, James Hennesey, S.J. and John Padberg, S.J. for introducing me to the Glenmary Home Missioners.

During my travels with Howard Bishop I received support from the Glenmary archivists. I wish to thank Loretta Ernst and Don H. Buske of the archives for their kind assistance during these past three years. Ms. Ernst, who worked for Howard Bishop for nearly twenty years, was a particularly valuable resource person. Ms. Peggy Schreiber, secretary to Father Frank Ruff, kindly assisted me during my research visits to Glenmary. To the following archivists I extend my sincere thanks: Charles Elston of Marquette University, Fr. John Harrington, M.M. of Maryknoll, John Farina of the Paulist Fathers' Archives, Brother Michael Grace, S.J. of the archives of Loyola University in Chicago, Sister Felicitas Powers, R.S.M. of the archives of the diocese of Savannah, Paul Thomas of the archives of the archdiocese of Baltimore, Sister Mary Philip Trauth, S.N.D. of the diocese of Covington, Wendy Schlereth of the University of Notre Dame, and Anthony Zito and Sister Ann Crowley, S.N.D. of the archives of the Catholic University of America. Many thanks to David Siemsen and the library staff at St. Mary's Seminary and University for their kindnesses.

Among the many Glenmary women and men missioners I wish to particularly thank those who made my many visits to Cincinnati enjoyable experiences: Brothers Thomas Kelly and Terry O'Rourke, and Fathers Francois Pellissier and Richard Kreimer. Fathers Frank Ruff, Robert Dalton and James Kelly and Sisters Christine Beckett and Rosemary Esterkamp combined hospitality and valuable advice on the preparation of my manuscript. I am also grateful to Fathers Robert Berson, John Marquardt and Louis McNeil for their careful reading of the manuscript and to Father Daniel Dorsey for sharing his S.T.L. thesis on the charism of Father Howard Bishop.

Essential to my research were the transcripts of oral interviews conducted by Fathers Joseph Gartner and James Kelly. To these men and to many women and men Home Missioners whom I personally interviewed I extend my gratitude. Because of their insight on the life and times of Howard Bishop I gained a "feel" for the founder and the Glenmary story.

I am indebted to colleagues who proofread the text for historical accuracy and rhetorical cohesiveness; John W. Bowen, S.S., Joseph P. Chinnici, O.F.M., Thomas W. Spalding, C.F.X. and Joseph M. White read the manuscript with interest and concern for detail.

For several years my office has been lodged in the Sulpician Archives in Baltimore. To the archivist, John Bowen, to the provincial, Gerald Brown, and to the provincial secretary, William J. Lee, I extend my hearty thanks for their hospitality and friendship. I am indeed grateful to Dr. James Buckley and the Theology Department of Loyola College for their hospitality. Many thanks to Ms. Beverly Simpson, who typed the manuscript history of the Sulpician Fathers in the United States with great skill and even greater patience and who also typed the first three chapters of this biography.

I am also grateful for the assistance of Ms. Lisa M. Flaherty who placed the entire manuscript on a word processor with professional skill, personal concern and a cheery disposition.

I am profoundly grateful to be the husband of Helen Schaberg and the father of Jane, Christopher and Kathryn Ann. To adequately express my feelings toward my family I borrow the lyrics of a favorite song: "love, you are love, far greater than any metaphor could ever, ever be."

INTRODUCTION

Howard Bishop is a shadowy figure on the religious landscape of twentieth century America. His historical image, gleaned from his diary, correspondence, homilies, spiritual reflections, and many interviews with those who knew him, adds some substance to the shadow, but bringing him to life entails a radical openness to the person behind the documents. Unfortunately, just as one appears to grasp his character or personality, other documents reveal a contradictory image of the man. As Walt Whitman observed, the human condition abounds in contradictions because we all contain multitudes.

In the preface to his life of John Henry Newman, Henri Bremond indirectly comforts the biographer frustrated with contradictions. "But he resembles nobody; this is what I wish to come to. Biographers will have enough trouble to show how he is like himself, enough trouble to recognize him amid the surprises and contradiction which await them in this life and thought."[1]

As I have immersed myself in the relevant documents I have attempted to be open to surprises and contradictions, not as signs of elusive qualities but rather as representative of the human condition. In the process I have discovered Howard Bishop to be a romantic idealist, a dreamer, a practical administrator, a man who had frequent losses of memory, and was very self-conscious, shy, assertive, tenacious, strong-willed, stubborn, inattentive to his surroundings, quick-tempered, authoritarian, sensitive to criticism, paternalistic, approachable, never censorious, a man of simple tastes, an anti-modern ruralist, a modern office manager, an anti-capitalist distributist, a capitalist investor, a strong advocate of Catholic parochial education in rural areas, an ardent opponent of Catholic schools in the Glenmary missions, a New Dealer, an impassioned anti-communist, a closed-minded superior who was capable of reordering priorities late in life, a backward-looking conservative, and a prescient, prophetic liberal. Many of these characteristics were integrated into his development from young curate to superior general of a religious community, but some remain as unresolved contradictions that reveal Howard Bishop's humanity.

Because one must cultivate the skills of critical analysis and subjective empathy, writing biography entails a recurring circular process of descending from the high points of objectivity into the valleys of subjectivity and climbing back upward to gain a distanced perspective. In order to achieve a "feel" for the past and to discern the *Zeitgeist*, historians must also engage in that repetitive process. However, because biographers roam around the interiority of a single person the process is more specifically focused and there is a temptation for the biographer to over-identify with the subject of his study. Moreover, the process may be more strained for the biographer than for the historian. In either case students of the past must continuously struggle against the intervention of biases in their narrative. My principles of integration in this biography are based upon an awareness of the pre-understanding I bring to the documents. I am a postconciliar Catholic whose sense of the religious dimension of life was nurtured by the Benedictines of St. John's University in Minnesota during the immediate pre-conciliar period. Stated simply, my hermeneutic is that the documents form a bridge between Bishop and me, no full re-presentations of him are disclosed by the texts, and my narrative is not an entirely clear reflection of his life story. By drawing upon my own experience as analogous to his and by allowing him to speak for himself in the liberal use of direct quotes my narrative has struggled against the flaws inherent in any attempt to recreate the past.

Howard Bishop's diary, which he started with his ordination to the priesthood, is the major span of the bridge between himself and his biographer. It offers the contemporary reader insight into how he perceived himself as person, priest, pastor, founder and superior general. With only infrequent explicit notations about his feelings, his close friends and his family, the diary charts the journey of a priest and reveals both the rough routine of a country pastor and the dogged determination to pass on the faith in ever widening spheres of pastoral interest. After the foundation of Glenmary the entries become more detailed. Twenty-two years of living alone gave way to the close connectedness of community life.

The diary reflects his problems with dealing with others in an authority situation. Indeed, his self-image as founder, infused with a response to the movement of the Holy Spirit, brought out the best as well as the worst aspects of his personality. At times his diary appears as if he were writing specifically for the future biographer, but then a series of self-deprecating remarks engenders the conclusion that the diary was intended to be a personal rather than a public record. One is left with the impression that this was a man who was most comfortable in what he perceived as the sacred space of rural life where the hand of providence was most real. There in the simplicity of life and the beauty of nature were the actual graces impelling the community to live the good life in contrast to the complex, mechanistic forms of life and the capitalistic greed of urban individualism. To broadcast the good news of the sanctity of rural life and to redeem the country-side for Catholicity was Howard Bishop's mission in St. Louis Parish, in the Archdiocesan League of the Little Flower that he founded in 1923, in the National Catholic Rural Life Conference, and in Glenmary.

Hence, this is primarily the biography of a priest. Part I, the Baltimore years, is organized into chapters that feature particular spheres of pastoral activity, curate, pastor, Catholic rural leader, etc. The focus of Part II, the Cincinnati years, is upon him as founder and superior general of the Home Missioners of America. The chapters are organized around the relationship between Howard Bishop and a particular development in the life of the Society. Besides his diary, his homilies, public addresses, published writings, and personal correspondence form the core of the resource material for both parts.

Howard Bishop's Anglo-Saxon family background precluded strong expression of feelings. He was of a Catholic tradition that was rural, privatized and free from the influences of the immigrant church. He was close to the heritage of Maryland Catholicism with its strong attachment to the American republican ethos, particularly its principles of religious liberty and separation of church and state.

Woven throughout this narrative is the strong American identity of Howard Bishop and his Society. His romantic image of rural life was articulated within the heritage of the Jeffersonian myth of the yeoman farmer, buttressed by the cooperationist tendencies of Catholicity. In his role as a pastor and as a Catholic rural activist he did not rely upon the ready-made formulas of country priests anxious to move to the city. Rather he developed his own unique set of priorities based upon practical experience. He was inordinately open to the needs of rural people and responded with a creativity reflecting the contemporary trends toward organization and professionalization.

The thesis of this biography is that to fulfill his mission Howard Bishop evolved from a simple pastor to a founder because he shifted from indirect to direct evangelization of rural America. As pastor he considered all the inhabitants of Howard County, not just the Catholics, to be members of his parish. In that sense he had a self-image as a rural missionary, one who evangelized through parish organizations open to all. As president of the National Catholic Rural Life Conference his pastoral vision expanded beyond parish and archdiocese. He gradually realized that individual efforts of evangelization were doomed by their temporary and defensive strategies, and that rural America would only be converted through an organized collective offensive effort by a group of priests, brothers, and sisters dedicated to building the kingdom in the countrysides of the nation.

Toward the end of his life he revived a strategy of indirect evangelization that stressed Glenmary's role as a moral leaven in the mission areas. To achieve his goals he became single-minded and extremely tenacious. Moved by the low-conversion statistics and the intense social, economic and moral needs of rural people, Bishop adopted a more practical missiology.

Though ostensibly a rather aloof person he was an impassioned missionary sensitive to the movement of the Holy Spirit in his life and in the lives of the people he served. Though at times a very difficult person to deal with, he was nevertheless a man deeply motivated to improve his own effectiveness in spreading Catholicity throughout the countryside. The following words by Newman capture the general direction of the life of Howard Bishop.

> Now what I mean is this: that they who are living religiously, have from time to time truths they did not know before, or had no need to consider, brought before them forcibly; truths which involve duties, which are in fact precepts, and claim obedience. In this and

such like warp, Christ calls us now. There is nothing miraculous or extraordinary in his dealings with us. He works through our natural faculties and circumstances in life. Still what happens to us in providence is in all essential respects what His voice was to those whom He addressed when on earth: Whether He commands by a visible presence, or by a voice, or by our consciences, it matters not, so that we feel it to be a command.[2]

PART I

The Baltimore Years

CHAPTER 1

Prologue: The Baltimore Church

I

American Catholics developed their identities through various influences, such as ethnic groups, parishes, the dominance of a particular religious community in the educational experience (e.g. "Jesuit-trained" or "the product of the Visitation academy"), and, least influentially, the abstract notion of diocese. Of course persons "in religion," that is, nuns, brothers and priests, might have two or more identities. They would refer to their religious community and parish or school and, because they would be more likely to situate themselves in diocesan structures, they tended to identify themselves as of the archdiocese of Baltimore, Philadelphia, etc. As the unofficial primatial see, Baltimore elicited stronger loyalties than most dioceses; this was particularly true during the period of 1878–1921 when James Gibbons was archbishop.

In 1915, the year Howard Bishop was ordained, there were 275 secular priests and nearly 270,000 Catholics in the archdiocese. There were 48 churches in Baltimore and 25 in Washington, while there was a total of 144 churches with resident priests. With one priest for every 1,000 Catholics this may seem to be a very low ratio of priests to people, but in 1987 there were only 256 secular priests for a Catholic population of 441,000 and the demands upon priests today are far greater than those of 1915 when the professionalization of the clergy was in its infancy and Catholic culture was more supportive of the priesthood than is today's highly atomized Catholic society.[1]

From the origins of the church in Baltimore there had been an influential Anglo-American minority. Such names as the Carrolls, Brents, Schrivers, Jenkinses, McSherrys and Boones represent the social dominance of that minority. Under the leadership of the first bishop, John Carroll (1789-1815), most of the early Catholics were enlightened in the sense that they had embraced the principles of religious liberty and the separation of church and state as positive features of the new republic. They implicitly believed that Catholicism was in a more beneficial environment in the United States than in the traditionalist social structures of Europe.[2]

John England, bishop of Charleston, South Carolina (1820–1844), expanded the Carroll legacy. Not only did he extol the harmony between Catholicism and American democracy and build upon Carroll's conciliar notion of episcopal collegiality, but he wrote and implemented a diocesan constitution based upon the principle of shared authority among bishop, clergy, religious, and laity.[3]

However, in subsequent years the continuous migration of Catholic peoples from Europe and the episodic manifestations of nativism and anti-Catholicism fostered a new separatism and the development of a protective canopy under which Catholics formed their sense of peoplehood.[4]

Isaac Hecker, the founder of the Paulist Fathers, and a few other church leaders were in continuity with the Carroll–England tradition.[5] But by the 1880s some Catholic leaders were so opposed to the Protestant dominated culture that in order to preserve the faith they tended toward a strong separatist position, as if Catholicism and American society were inherently incompatible. In contrast to, and frequently in conflict with, the "preservationists" were the descendants of the Carroll tradition, greatly influenced by Hecker's identification of American culture with the movement of the Holy Spirit and with the mutual transformation of the Catholic Church and American society.

A preservationist–transformationist dialectic developed. On the one hand, preservationists opposed the Knights of Labor as a secret society dedicated to undermining law and order, opposed public schools as a secular, pseudo-religious institution, opposed the establishment of The Catholic University of America in Washington, D.C., and opposed sharing public meetings with leaders of Protestant denominations. The transformationists became identified with Americanism because they extolled the legitimacy of organized labor, the public school, etc., and displayed an expansive posture toward the principles of religious liberty, separation of church and state, and religious denominationalism. Several German bishops were preservationist and were allied with conservative anti-Americanist Irish bishops such as Michael Augustine Corrigan of New York and Bernard McQuaid of Rochester, New York. The Americanists were led by Archbishop John Ireland of St. Paul, Bishop John J. Keane, and Bishop Denis O'Connell, first rector of the American College in Rome. Cardinal Gibbons was a moderate Americanist, but Alphonse Magnien, the Sulpician superior of St. Mary's Seminary in Baltimore and a close confidant of Gibbons and the other leaders, was considered "the heart and head" of the Americanist movement.[6]

In an important sermon delivered on January 4, 1902, Cardinal Gibbons reviewed "the history and progress of the Catholic Church" during the course of the nineteenth century. He elaborated on his own Americanist leanings and his identity with the tradition of John Carroll. "I regard the selection of John Carroll as a most providential event for the welfare of the American Church." Gibbons considered the first bishop to have been in "sympathy and harmony with the genius of the new Republic. . . . He was a man of sterling piety and enlightened zeal." These qualities, combined with his "consummate tact . . . courteous manners . . . and unfailing charity" won him the respect of the Protestant majority. Gibbons manifested these same characteristics and was viewed by persons of all religious traditions as a prelate who was in harmony with the genius of the contemporary republic. Gibbons celebrated the immigrant contributions of Catholic life, and he particularly stressed the dominance of the Irish-American heritage. ". . . no country has contributed more efficiently to the establishment and growth of the Catholic religion among us than faithful Ireland."[7]

Born in Baltimore in 1834 but raised in Ireland, Gibbons in this same sermon betrayed a bias against the immigrants from "Germany, Bohemia, Poland and other parts of Eastern Europe . . . [who] have inherited the national traits of their warlike ancestors . . . [of] the fifth and sixth centuries . . . [who] invaded Southern Europe." Though these groups possessed "warlike traits" they were also "conspicuous for their thrift and industry, and for their sturdy devotion to the cause of Catholic education." Gibbons appears to have been entirely ignorant of the very strong ethnic separatism of each of these groups of eastern European Catholics. He generalized on the region of their settlement as "chiefly on our western prairie lands" and then mistakenly stated that "they have become speedily assimilated with the native population, animated by the patriotism of American citizens, and cherishing an ardent love for the faith of their fathers."[8] Except for the last remark on faith this was the sort of statement which engendered strong anti-Irish sentiments among Germans, Poles and others who did not wish to assimilate and indeed were champions of preservationist causes.

Gibbons' commentary on the latter groups consumed eighteen lines of his typed sermon; the French received twenty-five lines. Educated by the Sulpicians, the vast majority of whom were born and trained in France, Gibbons extolled the contribution of French missionaries who carried "the torch of faith in one hand, the torch of science in the other." With imagery in stark opposition to the realities of ethnic rivalry, Gibbons concluded with the analogy that just as every nation had contributed a block of marble to the Washington Monument in the nation's capital, "so have the various countries of the continent contributed a column to the edifice of Catholic faith in the United States. And as these marble slabs of the monument are chastened and whitened by time and the action of the climate, so they appear as if cut from the same quarry, in like manner the various nations congregated in this country are assimilated into one homogeneous mass by religious training and social intercourse, so as to form one [American] body in Christ."[9]

Though Gibbons' rendition of the Catholic melting pot was replete with idealism, the administration of his archdiocese was guided by realism. There were national parishes and other accommodations to ethnicity. However, he wished to be identified as an Americanist, one who consciously pursued strong assimilationist policies. Unlike John Ireland or John Keane, Gibbons did not strongly articulate the spirituality of Americanism with its emphasis upon the religious character and the providential design inherent in the dynamic of American society. But the Americanist bishops relied upon Gibbons to represent their cause in Rome.

Dated January 1899, Pope Leo XIII's apostolic letter condemning "Americanism" (*Testem Benevolentiae*) listed several errors, including the notions that the church should adjust its structure and dogma to fit the demands of modern civilization, that one should form one's conscience according to the prompting of the Holy Spirit and to natural truth and virtue, and that the active religious life was preferable to the spirituality of the religious cloister. Pope Leo considered Americanism to be a tendency rather than an organized movement based on heretical tenets. Understandably, the preservationists viewed the encyclical as a vindication of their views on the incompatibility of modern American culture and Catholic tradition. The transformationists considered Americanism to be a "phantom heresy."[10] In fact, there was a distinctive Americanist impulse that animated many leading Catholic laymen in education and journalism as well as many members of the hierarchy and the clergy. There was, therefore, an Americanist movement that viewed the religious and cultural developments in the United States as paradigmatic of a new era in church and society. If the church was to remain vital, then a new apologetic must be forged in accord with the science of evolution, the sociological notions of development, and the activist, pragmatic character of the times. John Ireland hinted at the new apologetic: "Today we need the Christian gentleman and the Christian citizen; an honest ballot and social decorum will do more for God's glory and the salvation of souls than midnight flagellations and compostellan pilgrimages."[11]

The anti-Americanist encyclical had a sedative effect upon the movement, but individual participants such as Ireland and Gibbons continued to have a strong impact upon the next generation. If one views Americanism as derived from experiences in the young nation, then one discerns forms of Americanism in such diverse manifestations as new missionary movements, including Maryknoll, in the modern organizational character of the movement of eucharistic piety, in the lay activism of the retreat movement, and in the structure and spirit of the National Catholic Welfare Conference (N.C.W.C.).[12] The thought of Hecker, Ireland and Keane represent the maturation of the seeds sown by John Carroll and John England; it was up to subsequent generations to nurture an American church derived from a blend of Catholic tradition and American experience. The latter included the idealism of new-world vision, the pragmatism of constructing a culture in pioneer conditions, a loose social structure continuously challenged by waves of immigrants, and a strong sense that these characteristics formed a unique character, one which European Catholics did not fully understand. However, French liberal Catholics were attracted to the Americanists. Since the 1870 proclamation of papal infallibility shattered Gallicanism, the French embraced the transformationist ethos of the American liberals. Many progressive Sulpicians in the United States, such as Alphonse Magnien and John Hogan, provided an Americanist bridge from the United States to Europe.[13]

II

The Gibbons church was in a sense reminiscent of the enlightened character of Baltimore's first bishop, John Carroll. Both bishops were at ease with pluralism and religious liberty; both extolled the inherent value of the American republic and exhibited strong patriotism. They also shared a national perspective and a disinterest in the details of administration; if modernization of a diocese entails a rationalization of the administrative offices, then Gibbons was almost as pre-modern as Carroll.[14] Obviously the demands of the urban church of the late nineteenth century distinguished the Gibbons era from that of John Carroll and deeply affected the way Gibbons perceived the role of the clergy. In his 1896 work *The Ambassador of Christ*, Gibbons elaborated on the theological and ministerial character of the clergy. In the preface the Baltimore prelate placed the historical patterns of nativism and anti-Catholicism within the context of his views on the American character. He referred to the spasmodic outbursts of religious fanaticism as the "steady and increasing tide of opposition," and the "earnest antagonism, prompted by honest, though misguided zeal in the cause of Christianity. . . ." However, he concluded that "rabid bigotry is not a plant that flourishes on Columbian soil. Those ebullitions [sic] of unreasoning hatred toward the Catholic Church are not congenial to the American character. They are generally aroused and fomented by aliens as yet ill-acquainted with our constitutions. . . ."[15]

This book by Gibbons was published during a period when the American Protective Association was generating anti-Catholic bigotry throughout the nation. Though the A.P.A. membership ignored the principles of the first amendment to the Constitution, they were certainly not alien agitators; rather they identified Catholicism as an alien religion tied to the papal monarchy in the Vatican. It was characteristically irenic of Gibbons to conclude that anti-Catholic bigotry was un-American as well as to point out that anti-Catholicism frequently had the positive effect of cementing loyalty to the church. "Americans are fundamentally a religious people . . . [who] spend millions annually in the erection of churches, and in the maintenance of home and foreign missions. . . ." Gibbons went on to comment on the attributes of the Americans. "The American people possess, also, in a marked degree the natural virtues that are the indispensable basis of supernatural life. They are gifted with a high order of intelligence; they are self-poised and deliberate; they are of industrious and temperate habits; they are frank, manly and ingenuous. They have a deep sense of justice and fair play; they are brave and generous; and they usually have the courage of their convictions."[6] He did not juxtapose the American and the European character, but he did say that while Catholicism "adapts itself to every form of government, it has a special adaptability to our political system and to the genius of the American people." Gibbons interpreted the role of the Catholic Church in American society as one of a mediator between the "extremes of undue severity and excessive laxity," and between "the rights of capital and the claims of labor."[7] He viewed Catholicism as "eminently the Church of the people. . . . She appeals to their enlightened self-interest and moral sense and she endeavors to control them by religious sanctions." In short, he, like John Ireland and other Americanists, identified the American character with the highest plane of human development, and the Catholic Church in the United States as on an equally high plane of religious development. It followed, therefore, that the Catholic clergy must be paragons of natural virtues in accord with the American character, and representatives of the supernatural virtues embodied in the priesthood. Hence, according to Gibbons, the priest should display "Truth and Sincerity of Character," possess "Self Respect and Human Respect," exude "Charity and Politeness" and "Humility." The ideal priest cherished "Silence and Solitude" as the conditions for a "Studious Life." The Catholic clergy should be well acquainted not only with the sacred sciences but also with the Greek, Latin and English classics and the "Study of Men and the Times."

The American priest must be eminently practical as well; he must be a good extemporaneous preacher, a catechist, an instructor of converts, an administrator of Sunday schools and parochial schools, a leader of congregational singing, and above all a minister of the sacraments. Gibbons' stress upon a learned clergy, no doubt derived from his experience at the Sulpician seminaries in Baltimore, St. Charles' and St. Mary's, led him to exclaim that "there is no spectacle more deplorable . . . than that of an ignorant and torpid clergy. . . . Piety in a priest, though indispensable, can never be an adequate substitute for learning. . . . Knowledge without piety may, indeed, make a churchman vain and ignorant; but piety without knowledge renders him an unprofitable servant."[18]

The spirituality of the priesthood was a topic Gibbons did not directly address. Though he did state that the priest is "another Christ," particularly evident in his role in administering the sacraments, he strongly emphasized the active, ministerial life of the priest. The spiritual exercises of the seminary were expected to become habitual, especially mental prayer before the blessed sacrament. In accord with the practical bent of the American character and the ever-increasing demands of the parishes, Gibbons affirmed that spirituality is primarily manifested in priestly ministry rather than in private reflection. The founder of the priests of St. Sulpice devised a three-part formula for mental prayer: Jesus in my eyes (adoration), Jesus in my heart (communion), and Jesus in my hands (cooperation). The Americans implicitly reversed the order as if it were only through action/cooperation that the priest achieved a sense of communion and grateful adoration.[19]

III

The administration of Michael J. Curley, archbishop of Baltimore from 1922 to 1947, was in direct opposition to that of James Gibbons. Born in Ireland and educated at the Propaganda Fide in preparation for his missionary work in Florida, Curley was appointed bishop of St. Augustine in 1914 at the age of thirty-four. Monsignor Giovanni Bonzano, his former professor and apostolic delegate to the United States, was instrumental in Curley's appointment to St. Augustine and Baltimore. In contrast to the irenicism of Gibbons, Curley struggled militantly against the forces of nativism and anti-Catholicism. He marshaled the laity and told them to "be neither squeamish nor weak-kneed in the matter of stating their Faith. . . . We never gain anything by being apologetic and we have no reason to be."[20]

To prepare Catholics to better stand their ground and defend the faith, Curley placed priority upon building Catholic schools, and he centralized school authority in an archdiocesan office of education. Organization, centralization, and institutional expansion were characteristic of Curley's administration. This rationalization and modernization of the institutional church was a profound departure from the style of the Gibbons era. Because Curley's policies aimed at building Catholic structures parallel to those of secular society, the church in Baltimore became more American in organization but more separatist in religion. While Curley's predecessor decried ethnic particularism, he fostered national parishes. In contrast to the immigrant or Americanist styles of public Catholicism, Curley's was a triumphalist ghetto church, separate and superior.[21] It was in this church that the future founder of Glenmary was to carry out much of his ministry.

CHAPTER 2

The Young Priest

William Howard Bishop was born on December 19, 1885 in a little wooden cottage at the intersection of 23rd Street and Pennsylvania Avenue, in the northwest quadrant of Washington, D.C. His siblings were Mary Edna (1875–1921), John Knowles (1878–1923), Frances Eleanor (1880–1920), Grace Ethel (1882–1962), and the only one younger than himself, Harry Aloysius (1888–1979). His father, Francis Besant ("Bannie") Bishop (1853–1916), was born near Fayetteville, North Carolina, and his mother Eleanor Teresa Knowles was born and raised in Delco, North Carolina. Both parents were well educated.

Howard Bishop's paternal grandfather died in 1892; his obituary implies that he was a businessman of the small-town middle class. "He was a warm-hearted, generous man, ever ready to respond to the wants of the poor and needy. He never sought benevolences but was content to be kind for the love of doing good." The family was Protestant in background but was not active in church. "He was a Baptist by sentiment," so said the author of the obituary. "Though he was not a member of the church, he professed faith in Christ as his personal savior, and one who knew him well and had conversed with him on religion believed him to be a devout Christian."[1]

Howard's father, Francis Bishop, was a physician who had studied medicine at the University of Maryland, located in Baltimore. According to Grace Bishop, Eleanor Knowles, the only daughter in a staunchly Catholic family, did not view Francis' Protestant background as an obstacle to their eventual marriage, but her parents attempted to keep them apart. Francis did gradually drift toward the Catholic Church, no doubt edified by Eleanor's manifestations of faith. According to family tradition Francis was instructed in the

Catholic faith by Cardinal Gibbons, and the cardinal also presided at the wedding of Eleanor and Francis.² It was when Gibbons was vicar-apostolic of North Carolina, residing in Wilmington, that he witnessed the Knowles-Bishop marriage in 1872 before being translated to the see of Richmond later that year. As a wedding gift, Gibbons presented them with a family Bible.

By the time Howard was in primary school the family had moved into a sixteen-room house at 1913 I Street, N.W. Just about that time he became very ill with pneumonia. "The doctor didn't expect him to live," recalled his sister Grace. "After the priest had visited a number of times, one day he was speaking to mother . . . and he told her that [Howard] had never committed a mortal sin. I think his whole life was like that." The family lore includes stories of Howard's Protestant aunt praying for his health, and prophesying that Howard would live and become a priest. Though no one mentioned this to Howard, it appears that after his health was restored he would frequently be the "priest" in childhood play-acting in the home. "I think anyone would look at him, even as a child, and say he'll be a priest some day."³

The large home on I Street was in St. Matthew's Parish, which became the cathedral of the District of Columbia. The pastor was Thomas Sim Lee; after 1922 Edward L. Buckey was pastor. Though the parish had a rather large school, 140 pupils in 1892, staffed by the Sisters of the Holy Cross and the Christian Brothers, the Bishop children attended public schools and, on Saturdays, religious instruction classes at the parish.⁴ After graduating from Force primary school Howard went to Central High School. His brother Francis recalled that Howard was a good but not a brilliant student. However, his sister Grace commented that "he was very brilliant in his classes at school. . . . I know his teachers were very proud of him."⁵

Howard was artistic and his brother John became a professional artist and photographer. During his senior year (1905–06) Howard was editor of the school paper. Because poor health precluded regular class attendance during primary school, Howard turned twenty in December of 1905 during his last year in high school. His intellectual maturity was evident in his writing. In a brief account of a debate between Central and Western High Schools, he criticized both teams for their "faulty presentation."⁶ An editorial on "School Honesty" was severely critical of the "unauthorized use of ponies in translating and use of oral or written promptings in examinations." He doubted that those who engaged in these abuses even seriously considered the "moral or practical question involved." Howard built his case on how deception is at the core of such behavior. Not only has the student deceived teachers but he "has deceived himself" as well. The dishonest student relies upon the "need for a mental crutch" and fosters "mental indolence." Howard concludes with the remark: "There is no short road to learning and he who sticks to the beaten path of study, earning slow and steady progress by honest toil is flying on the wings of the wind, compared with the lad who lies awake nights planning to shorten his week by trickery."[7]

In his last editorial Howard became reflective. After noting that it is impossible to please everyone, he said that in the course of the year he hoped that most of the readers were satisfied with the quality of *The Review*. Apparently, some students had criticized him for composing strongly opinionated editorials. "Of those who impend honest motions, and attack the upholding of right by a school paper, we have nothing to say. Their very abuses are a vindication of the cause they assail. To the rest of the school and to this group of detractors we wish a happy and prosperous future, the one in doing what is right and the other in making right more attractive to fair minds by their vigorous but fallacious arguments against it."

Perhaps Howard had alienated some readers because he would not be swept up by the quest for victory on Central's athletic field. "As for the year, it has been far from a failure for Central. We have tasted heavily of victory and defeat without defaming the one or rejecting the good lesson of the other. What more can be said for any school? Life itself is a mixture of victory and defeat which we must make the most of by learning the proper uses of each. The school that has no defeats is as bad off as the school that wins no victories; it sees only one side of life. . . . When a school gets so hungry for victory that no laws of propriety and common sense can restrain them once the prize is won, it is high time the school in question reflect upon its future."[8] This is not the writing of a conformist nor of the typical high school student seeking to gain the respect of his peers.

Nicknamed Shelly by his fellow students, Howard was portrayed in the school's 1905 yearbook as "a born politician and proofreader. He possesses a terrible temper, kept under control by a sweet disposition and an excellent appetite. Altho [sic] he has no bad habits, abhorring moonlight nights and cozy corners, he has admirably guided the

Roines [a high school club, perhaps a literary group] through the perils and pitfalls of a senior year."[9] Never has Howard's character been so succinctly described: tactful yet critical, short-tempered yet endearing, aloof from the crowd yet a leader of his peers. He was an idealist with a strong sense of duty. He went out of his way to assume responsibilities in the home and easily absorbed the rules of the household. His social life was no different from his brother's; they both attended dances, and Howard displayed a fondness for a young classmate named Ruth.

The social life of the family took place among the political elite. Dr. Bishop's patients included several congressmen, senators, and judges. Chief Justice Edward White was an occasional guest for dinner, and upon Howard's ordination he and Mrs. White presented him with a chalice engraved with their names at its base. International affairs and politics were frequently discussed at the family dinner. Francis reported that Dr. Bishop was a Republican, which for a North Carolinian meant that he was a moderate on the race issue. Though Francis said that his father was "unbiased," he proceeded to say: "He was very fond of the old type of negro, very kind to them."[10] Within the context of race relations in the gilded age, a patronizing attitude was considered by many to be as open to blacks as one could be without being radical.

Howard's oldest sister, Edna, married John W. Daniel, son of a United States senator from Virginia. It was a home wedding, and since Daniel was not a Catholic, "the officiating clergyman [Rev. Thomas F. Lee of St. Matthew's] read the short service of the Catholic Church." The newspaper account of the wedding celebration continues with detailed descriptions of the decor of the house and the gowns of the bridal party. It referred to the "well known physician, Dr. Bishop" and in general conveys the impression that the Bishops of I Street were an ascending family on the social ladder of the nation's capital.[11]

In a family photograph taken when Howard was a young man in his twenties it is quite apparent that he was a Knowles while his brother Francis was a Bishop. Howard was indeed quite close to his mother whom he called "Honey." Eleanor Knowles Bishop was the major religious influence in the home. She taught the children their prayers which of course included the rosary. It was said that she had a good sense of humor, a trait reflected in Howard as throughout his life he always enjoyed periods of story-telling. In the family photograph Howard is the only Bishop not facing the camera. Indeed, it almost appears as if he is daydreaming, completely oblivious to the formality of the occasion.[12]

In accord with the patriarchal character of a southern family, the Bishop girls did not attend college, but it was expected that the boys would continue their studies beyond high school. John Knowles Bishop studied art and photography. Harry studied at Yale and attended medical school at the University of Maryland. Howard had shown a strong interest in the study of journalism, and when he indicated his desire to attend Harvard College, his family supported him. From the fall of 1906 to the summer of 1908 he was enrolled at Harvard. He decided to take a year off, working as a map salesman for Underwood and Underwood, and then, as he later recalled, he would "return to college better prepared financially and physically to continue my course."[13]

Preoccupation with finances and health is a persistent pattern throughout his life. Of course his severe illness at an early age and the lateral curvature of his lower spine, which developed during his teens and caused one leg to be shorter than the other, had been major factors in his concern over health. Though he would never complain to others, he later confided to his diary the severe discomforts he experienced. However, Howard's financial preoccupation is not so easily explained. Certainly the family was affluent, but perhaps Dr. Bishop expected his sons to assume partial responsibility for their education as a means of achieving maturity. Howard was very parsimonious but this may have been one factor in his drive to achieve personal independence.

A year before he died, Howard Bishop reflected on his early experiences of a vocation to the priesthood. During and after his illness, the parish priest and several members of the family were praying that Howard would indeed have such a vocation. The young man felt that "they were trying to stack the cards against . . . [me]." He recollected that he had "detested the idea of becoming a priest," but admitted that his "conscience continued to prick him concerning the subject." While at Harvard his spiritual director was the chaplain of St. Paul's Catholic Club. Upon his suggestion, Howard made a three-day retreat at a Trappist monastery in Rhode Island. When he told the retreat master that he felt he did not have a vocation to the priesthood, the Trappist agreed, much to the distress of Howard's spiritual director.[14]

During his year away from college Howard Bishop more seriously considered his vocation to the priesthood. He consulted the pastor of St. Matthew's, Edward L. Buckey, and sometime during the winter of 1909 Buckey and Bishop visited St. Mary's Seminary in Baltimore and met with Edward R. Dyer, S.S., the first American superior of the seminary. However, it was not until August 11, 1909 that Bishop wrote to Dyer asking him for a seminary catalogue and information on the opening of the fall term. He told Dyer that he had been "talking the matter over with Father Buckey . . . who advises me to get started in some institution this year." Howard was "not yet settled as to [his] vocation," but he felt the need to take a "definite step which would be more agreeable than the uncertainty I have been laboring under so long."[15] Six weeks later he still had not decided to enter the seminary and wished to talk with Dyer. The visit with the superior resulted in a flurry of last-minute activity and formal letters from his pastor and from Cardinal Gibbons so that Howard could enter St. Mary's a week later.

Few students without minor seminary education were as prepared for the seminary as was Howard Bishop. In a letter to Dyer he listed his academic courses which included two years at Harvard—six years of Latin, four of Greek, six of English, mathematics to geometry and trigonometry, five courses in history, and language skills in French and German.[16] Approaching his twenty-fourth birthday he was somewhat older than his first-philosophy classmates. Moreover, his public school background, his Anglo-American heritage, and his Harvard experience set him apart from the typical seminarian of the period, i.e. parochial school education, Irish or German-American heritage, and thoroughly immersed in the devotional Catholicism characteristic of the ethnic enclaves in urban Catholic life. According to the catalogue, St. Mary's Seminary "is a place of Novitiate, wherein clerical candidates examine their vocation, acquire the science and virtues" to prepare them for the priesthood. The moral qualifications of the student were to be well-formed and have the desire of studying for the priesthood "uninfluenced by human or worldly notions but accompanied by disposition of mind and heart well in harmony with the Ecclesiastical spirit and wishes of the community."[17]

Howard began seminary life September 11, 1909 as one of 235 stu-

dents at the seminary on Paca Street. The traditional three-day retreat began on September 11. One of the most significant conferences
of Howard's first year was "The Trials and Consolations of the Missionary in North Carolina" by Father Thomas F. Price, well-known
for his rural mission work, and later as co-founder of Maryknoll.
Howard's mother had attended school with Price in Wilmington;
Howard had met him when the missionary visited the Bishop home. It
is coincidental that, besides Price, Father J. Swint (later bishop of
Wheeling) addressed the students on "Missions to Non-Catholics,"
a mark of the Glenmary charism some thirty years later. Archbishop John Ireland, Bishops John Lancaster Spalding and Camillus
Maes, and several other dignitaries visited the Sulpician seminary
that year.[18]

Joseph Bruneau, S.S., superior of the philosophy division of the
seminary, was a mission-oriented Sulpician who had been close to
James Anthony Walsh, the co-founder of Maryknoll, during his later
years at Boston's St. John's Seminary. As superior, Bruneau was responsible for evaluating students. For the first two years of philosophy Bruneau wrote of Howard Bishop's first term: "ordinary intelligence, slow, writes well, conscientious, regular"; second term: "not
yet familiar with ceremonies . . . good intelligence, intellectual curios-
ity." Over a two-year period philosophy students took courses in
logic, psychology, epistemology, ontology, cosmology, scripture,
church history, chant, chemistry, physics and geology. The philosophy was according to Thomas Aquinas but the Sulpicians were not
wedded to neo-Thomism. Bruneau's comments for Bishop's second
year were the same for both terms: "Serious, systematic, painstaking,
upright, careful, somewhat slow, esteemed."[19]

The persistence of the term "slow" connotes a methodical, rather
inhibited character; since Howard was a good student the term is not
a comment on his academic achievement.

During his second year of philosophy Howard presented a practice
homily on Luke 10:21, "Thou hast hidden these things from the wise
and prudent and revealed them to the little ones." According to his
outline, which became a part of his permanent file, he entitled the
homily "Gratitude to God for Divine Revelation." Bishop introduced
the topic by contrasting the rationalistic view of revelation with that
of the church. Then he focused on the "Necessity of Revelation"
which he said was proved by several factors, including the "frailty of

[the] human mind . . . [and] the nobility of non-Christian philosophers to attain even natural truths or religion without mixture of
error." He drew "an analogy of a journey to a distant land applied to
a soul's journey to salvation." Rather than stress the impact of revelation upon individual believers he related "pure religion" as the
"most effective safeguard of morals of a nation." Howard's concluding line illustrates that even at a relatively early period in his life he
was concerned about what became so significant to Glenmary, "Exhortation for prayer for separated brethren."[20]

The teachers' comments on the reverse side of the outline were
generally favorable. Bruneau's critique was the longest and is representative of the consensus: "voice clear, resonant, deliberate utter-
ance, a little exaggerated, very good to bring something home, just
the thing for big church, but well in ordinary circumstances to use
normal utterances generally . . . while delivery was so deliberate,
even a little stiff, it was animated, forceful, on account of earnestness,
interesting . . . promises to preach effectively." From this and other
remarks by Bruneau, one may surmise that Howard Bishop was a
good student, cautious, and industrious. At the completion of his
second year of philosophy in 1911, Bishop was awarded the Master of
Arts degree, Magna Cum Laude. Twenty-four classmates received
the B.A., and fifteen received the M.A.[21]

He must have been very dedicated to his religious duties, for had
he not been it would have been noted in his file. During summer
vacations, which he spent at the family's country home near Falls
Church, Virginia, he was expected to attend mass regularly and conduct himself in a manner appropriate to the clerical life. Attached to
the standardized form sent to the pastors who supervised seminarians' summer responsibilities, the acting pastor of St. James Church
in West Falls Church said that Howard Bishop "has shown marked
signs of the sacerdotal vocation. He is to be especially commended
for the great effort made to be present at the Holy Sacrifice, as he
lived many miles from Church and had to travel over rough and
lonesome roads."[22]

During Bishop's years as a theology student his record was free of
any negative comment on his religious exercises or his academic
work. This was not the case with regard to his courses on liturgy. He
was considered "almost too slow" and without any "aptitude for
ceremonies." Other professors remarked on his timidity and slow-

ness. One professor said that he was "intelligent, personal, not very deep—too stiff, something's strange—very good intentions." This was balanced by another's remark that Bishop was "a little stiff, [but it] wears off, [he has] a noble character." One professor also said that he was "a fine character" but added that he "never heard him laugh." Since no one ever said that Howard was morose or given to depressions, it is obvious that his behavior was not mercurial but rather steady, serious, and when he felt deep emotions he was hesitant about expressing such feelings to anyone. The last set of remarks on his academic record were all quite positive without any references to slowness, timidity, etc., except for his poor showing in the course in liturgy—"one of the slowest at ceremonies."[23]

As a public speaker Howard Bishop was not as slow as he was in ceremonies. In December of 1913, shortly after his twenty-eighth birthday, he delivered a required speech on "Child Labor in the United States." His outline for the talk was logical; he defined and described the extent of the problem, focused on its evil consequences, and advocated its abolition through the passage of state laws urged by the National Child Labor Committee. In his conclusion he exhorted "Catholic laymen to identify themselves with the movement initiated by that Committee." Of the ten professors assigned to evaluate the talk, only two criticized the style of delivery, while even they made it unanimous that it was a well prepared talk. Edward Dyer gave him the highest mark and underscored his comment: "good piece of work."[24]

From the vantage point of the future it appears more than coincidental that Howard Bishop chose a social-reform topic for his theology speech and a topic on revelation for his practice homily. In both talks he contextualized the themes within the national milieu, and in the conclusion to one he urged prayers for Protestants and in the other he challenged the laity to lead the church in social reform. Themes of triumphalism and Catholic separatism were conspicuously absent from his talks just as they were not a part of his family or educational experience.

According to a strand of oral tradition, Howard had a speech impediment and was allowed to visit a therapist who had him practice speaking with his mouth full of marbles. Apparently, it was a successful treatment as his speech subsequently conveyed only a hint of the problem. He also experienced ill health during his theology years. He was absent from classes on the average of eleven days during the 1911–12, 1912–13 academic years. The following year he spent three months (December–March) in the hospital for a severe foot problem. Almost immediately after he had returned to the seminary he received word that his mother was critically ill. While he seems to have considered his own physical malady as only a nuisance, he was deeply affected by his mother's condition. He confided in a letter that he had been simply incapable of writing or thinking under the circumstances "of his mother's illness."[25]

Howard's own hospitalization had an impact upon his studies. St. Mary's Seminary allowed exceptional fourth-year theologians to attend graduate school at Catholic University. The cooperative program originated from a variety of sources: over-crowding at the seminary; Dyer's concern that above average students be continuously challenged; the University's interest in developing enrollment in its graduate programs. (In 1919 the Sulpicians established a seminary in the orbit of the University which remained autonomous for nearly twenty years. It was officially absorbed into the University in 1938, and two years later the Sulpician Seminary became Theological College, a residence for diocesan seminarians attending classes at the University.) Because of his nearly four-month absence from regular studies the faculty was consulted on the question of his qualifications for fourth-year status and whether he should attend Catholic University. There was near unanimity on the issue of passing him on to the fourth-year course after an examination; most professors approved him for the University, although two recommended that he repeat his third year. He must have passed the exam, for he was officially allowed to attend the University, but was not recommended for ordination until he had finished the first term at the University. It had been the policy to ordain students prior to attendance at the University or at least by Christmas.

After Howard had been attending classes at the University for about two months he asked Dyer for ordination at Christmas time. Apparently Bishop had been ordained a deacon by this time because Dyer's reply was addressed to Reverend Mr. W. Howard Bishop. Dyer informed him that the faculty "did not approve of your ordination at Christmas, but would wish you to be ordained with your class or sometime at the end of the University year. They made a big stretch as to ordinary seminary requirements, and they think that they do not see sufficient reason to modify the conditions that were made."[26] Dyer's letter came as a "deep disappointment" to Bishop. He thought that he "had nearly fulfilled the requirements for ordination." His disappointment did not stem from spiritual frustration at the delay, but rather because he "was looking forward to a far more effective year with the worry of preparation behind rather than in front of me." These are not the considerations of a religious idealist but rather the characteristic concerns of a religiously motivated student who found preparations for ordination—i.e. learning the rubrics of the liturgy—a distraction from his academic work. He told Dyer that despite the fact that the faculty's decision "will make things quite difficult," he had "resolved to adjust myself to the conditions . . . and to accept the situation as the will of God in my behalf which must redound ultimately to my own good, however inconvenient it may seem at present."[27]

Father John Fenlon, S.S., superior of Divinity College at Caldwell Hall, where the priest graduate students resided, was the Sulpician director responsible for presenting Howard's official request to Cardinal Gibbons for ordination. As late as March 15, 1915, Howard did not know the exact date, which turned out to be twelve days later.[28] On Easter Sunday (March 27) Bishop Thomas J. Shahan, rector of the University, ordained W. Howard Bishop in the chapel of Caldwell Hall. The only evidence of his first days as a priest is a copy of his first sermon, preached at St. Theresa's Church, in the Anacosta area of the District. It is undated, but was delivered two weeks after his ordination, as it was on the second Sunday after Easter. Howard's topic for his homily was derived from the gospel, "I am the good shepherd." He opened with the juxtaposition of the hireling who flees at the first danger with the good shepherd who calls each sheep "by name" and "cheers and comforts them with words they understand and he does whatever his wit can suggest to lead them into safety and drive wolves away." The newly ordained priest identified the flock with the Catholic Church and referred to the "office" of the good shepherd having "passed on to . . . [Jesus'] apostles . . . and to their successors the bishops and priests of the Church of Christ even to the present day." The mission of the pope, bishops and priests is to feed the world "the food of sound doctrine and good morals" as well as to protect the sheep "from the ravaging wolves of error and hatred and sin." He then developed the analogy of the good shepherd to God's presence in the tabernacle: "He still feeds with His own Body and Blood." Bishop concluded with the remark that Jesus, the good shepherd, is still the flock's "Counselor . . . friend [and] Champion."[29]

Howard's ecclesiology was expressed in traditional, institutional terms, but he stressed a God who cheers and comforts, guides and befriends the people in the world rather than shelters them from a bad world. Of course there was "error, hatred and sin," but the world was not pitted in an external conflict with the church. Instead, the latter should be moved to guard the flock "with tender loving care" of the shepherd. Tenderness, comfort, and friendship may also be clues to Howard Bishop's own unconscious promptings as if he deeply needed Jesus to comfort and heal him, just as he must have attempted to form his priestly life on the model of the good shepherd.

Howard was still attending the University during this time. In June of 1915 he earned a Bachelor of Sacred Theology. Within the school he received excellent grades; for American History he received 95 and 90, History of Philosophy, 99 and 100, and for Elementary Sociology, 91 and 90. It appears from a later remark that Bishop intended to complete the S.T.D. at the University and perhaps teach.

Howard began a diary in 1915 shortly after he was ordained a priest at the age of thirty. There may have been earlier diaries but this is the only extant journal, one which was apparently prompted by his need to record the new experience of what was referred to as "the priestly state." Though entries for 1915 are infrequent, with months (August–December 1915) consuming only six typed pages, they are very personal and chatty notes. By selecting quotes from 1915 and the first six months of 1916 that reveal his self-perception, one may discern the interior life of Howard Bishop, the young priest. With periodic flashes of self-revelation, his first entry relates to his farewell homily to the Sisters of Notre Dame, in Northcliff, Maryland, where he was located prior to his September assignment at the Shrine of the Sacred Heart in the Mount Washington area of Baltimore County. "I told [the Sisters] from the altar that I had often felt at a loss to know what to say in my Sunday morning talks, for it seemed a contradiction that I should preach on Sunday to those who had been preaching to me by their good example all week."[30] Four days later Bishop wrote a long notation on the business acumen of his first pastor, Francis E. Craig,

former treasurer at the Sulpician seminary in Boston and also treasurer at St. Charles minor seminary in Catonsville. After noting that
the Sulpicians had attempted to convince Craig to leave parish ministry and return to them, Bishop confided to his diary, "Alas the poor
Sulps! Will they ever secure men who are wise enough in the ways of
the world to conduct their business as it should be conducted?"[31]

The priests of the Sacred Heart Parish were responsible for the
liturgies at Mount St. Agnes Convent of the Sisters of Mercy. In
contrast to his glowing tribute to the Notre Dame Sisters, Bishop
found himself at odds with this Mercy community. "The Sisters told
Father C. I was very slow saying Mass and wondered whether I was
scrupulous. . . . So I must be on my P's and Q's with them hereafter.
. . . But it doesn't matter much, they will have to take what they get
and be glad of it."[32] In late September of 1915 Bishop noted that he
had "been examined and X-rayed as to my spine and have decided
with the advice of my brother and my father [both physicians] to
submit to the strait-jacket imprisonment to which Dr. Reilly has sen-
tenced me for a year or more." This is the first reference to his spinal
curvature.

In early January he confided to his diary that he had subscribed to
a correspondence course in memory training and that he had "taken
this step without consulting anybody." It was not impulsive, however,
for he wrote that he had been considering it for "eight or ten years
past." As an accompaniment to the memory course was a book on
public speaking.[33] His poor memory had manifested itself in a variety
of ways. For example, on January 9, 1916, he forgot to place a host on
the paten and "forgot and drank both ablutions [the consecrated
wine] at early Mass."[34] Some two months later he wrote that his pastor had "passed some strong hints about men who are long saying
Mass, seeming to place them in the same category, as far as service to
the people is concerned, with a certain priest who has given much
scandal on account of drink."[35] Seven weeks prior to this confrontation, Bishop had just completed mass ("which was one of the longest I
have said, I think") when Craig "took occasion to administer a 'call
down' in the presence of the altar boys and I answered him in kind."
He then told his diary that "I am tired of having the watch held on me
while saying Mass. I am tired of being overreached, interfered with
and prevented in everything I am given to do. I am tired of being
ignored on all matters of real importance to the parish. In short, I

have been treated like an office boy long enough and intend to demand the consideration and confidence that are due to an assistant. He can never expect me to overcome my awkwardness and slowness as long as the ogre of distrust is staring me in the face."[36]

One other entry in his diary during the first year of his priesthood reveals his self-consciousness. He was scheduled to preach at the Mount St. Agnes community at a ceremony honoring students and guests on the feast of St. Agnes, January 21, 1916. Five days before the event Sister Superior "kindly offered to go over my sermon with me when it was ready for preaching." "This is the climax," wrote Bishop in his diary. "The first sign of distrust was when she told me how I should address the gathering. Not 'Dear friends,' she said, but 'Right Reverend Bishop, Reverend Fathers, Sisters and students. . . .' It is all over now. I have written cancelling the engagement."[37] However, "all difficulties having been satisfactorily explained," Bishop did preach on the feast day and received many compliments. He concluded the diary entry for that day, "Thank God it is done. *No more public appearances for me this year.*"[38]

These selective citations from his diary are clues to the personality of W. Howard Bishop. He turned to his diary as one would turn to a friend; it was also a safe place to express the wrath that he was unable to vent directly, particularly on his pastor, Father Craig. The diary allowed him the space to process the experiences of frustration at his shyness, clumsiness, absent-minded slips of memory, and his suspicion that those in authority tended to distrust him, a condition which engendered self-consciousness and diffidence. His revelations about the negative encounters with Craig and the Sisters of Mercy obviously point to his anxiety in dealing with conflict. Even when his experience was positive, such as his short chaplaincy of the community of the Sisters of Notre Dame, he was self-effacing; he considered himself unworthy to preach to those who were far more virtuous than he. One receives the impression that Bishop was a pre-occupied dreamer uncomfortable with persons in authority. However, he considered himself far more practical and worldly wise than his former seminary teachers and spiritual directors, the Sulpicians of St. Mary's Seminary in Baltimore. Also, he tended to work on what he perceived as weaknesses, through such means as his self-help courses in memory training and public speaking.

There are significant clues embedded in the style of his diary. Except for the occasional moment of anger, he would never depart from the formal titles of Mr., Mrs., Sister, Father, and Bishop. He never once identified a person as a classmate or personal friend, and since he never used first names it is difficult to discern the degree to which he was close to one person or another. However, he tended to drop in on families of the parish and was apparently warmly welcomed by them. He could express himself very openly in his diary, and perhaps by being so formal he was projecting a need to be respected by others as well as a need to remain relatively distant. He was such a private person that even when he was confiding in his diary he was remote and formal. The ideal of the priesthood articulated by Sulpicians was embodied in *alter Christus* and *esprit ecclésiastique*, terms that entailed a code of behavior which represented religious sanctity and social decorum. No doubt he absorbed the ethos of the Sulpician seminary, but his personality had been structured many years before his encounter with the Sulpicians.

When Bishop referred to his back problems the tone was rather clinical as if he had become accustomed to the discomfort. However, he never indicated that he viewed his malady in a religious perspective. Indeed his early diary does not reveal that he was on a spiritual journey during his first years as a priest. He may have experienced such a journey but his diary was far too formal to allow such expressions of spiritual intimacy. However, the formulas of popular devotional Catholicism such as pleas to St. Jude or St. Anthony were absent from his diary. Hence, we have no direct clues to his particular religious world view.

In the rectory the conflict between him and his pastor, Father Craig, deeply affected his identity as a priest. He noted in his diary for January 30, 1916 that he had "preached poorly prepared sermons on . . . Jesus calming the storm at sea" as if he could not be calmed from the storms of self-doubt as a preacher.[39] While he experienced problems with preaching and with celebrating the liturgy, he openly confronted the problem with Craig. In February of 1916 Howard approached Bishop Corrigan, auxiliary bishop of Baltimore, about his conflict with his pastor. Corrigan "advised me to say nothing but *work out my own Salvation by deeds that will convince the people and Craig of my worth.*"[40] (his italics) However, Howard did not place the struggle with Craig within the context of his "own salvation." In late March he "politely demanded a showdown. [I] told him I was doing my best and he need not look for any improvement. . . . If he wanted a change it was his privilege to take the means of getting it. He replied by shifting the burden to me. I could think it over . . . and if I preferred another place to my present one it could be arranged. I told him my answer was final then and there was no need to think it over. He must decide what to do again. He put it off."[41] On May 15, 1916 Bishop "called for another show-down with Craig on the question of whether he wants me to remain or not. He said he did unless I had found a place I liked better." He approached two influential priests of the archdiocese, including Edward Dyer, to represent his case to Cardinal Gibbons. After Craig expressed his desire for reaching a compromise, Bishop confided in his diary that "it is now my duty to stop those who agreed to intercede for me if they have not already gone too far."[42]

During his struggles with Craig, Bishop made an unusual notation in his diary of his "despondency."[43] Given his reticence to admit such a condition, even in the privacy of his diary, one may presume that such despondency was not infrequent. In a sermon preached on May 14, 1916, the day before he called for a "show-down with Craig," Bishop elaborated on the passage from John's gospel "A little while and you shall not see me and again a little while and you shall see me. Because I go to the Father." Rather than engage in exegesis, Bishop focused on how human despondency engenders a feeling that Christ has abandoned us. "For though Christ . . . now dwells in our Churches, nay, in our very hearts as often as we will let Him in, yet there are dark times in our lives, times that are full of disgust for the past and dread of the future, times that are full of bitterness and grief and yearning, when Jesus Christ seems utterly to have forsaken us. . . ." Such emotive language is the stuff of personal experience. Not uncoincidentally, Bishop lists the first "great calamity" that may cause such "dark times" as when "Some loved and trusted friend has turned traitor." Though Craig was not such a friend, Bishop certainly felt despondent by the betrayal of his pastor. As if he were projecting his own need, Bishop told his parishioners that "These are the times when we must show Christian heroism and fortitude, when we must believe and hope *in spite of ourselves.* . . . We must continue to love and believe, and hope and pray, *even against our own inclinations,* for we know the source of all consolation still lives though we cannot now feel *the warm glow of His presence.*"[44] (my italics) This is one of his few extant sermons that reveal his feelings of brokenness and alienation.

Indeed for him to use such existential language in either the diary
or in a sermon was quite rare. Hence, one concludes that this
priest, only a year after his ordination, had experienced deep disillusionment.

It was a very critical period for Howard. Besides his difficulties
with priestly duties and with Craig, he was adjusting to a series of
therapeutic braces for his curvature of the spine. Then on April 29,
1916 he received word of his father's illness. He wrote that when he
arrived home "only faint signs of recognition could be elicited from
him when I reached him. Said prayers for the dying and gave him
conditional absolution in afternoon. Went with him in an ambulance
to Emergency Hospital."[45] The next day his father died and two days
later Howard Bishop celebrated a solemn requiem mass but another
priest preached, as if it would have been too emotional for Howard to
do so. There was a conspicuously clinical tone to his diary citation for
the day, May 2, 1916. "Pa buried at Mt. Olivet Cemetery. . . . Chief
Justice White honored us with his presence. Was one of honorary
pall-bearers. R.I.P."[46] Dr. Bishop had requested that his funeral take
place at his former parish, St. Stephen's, because it was less pretentious than St. Matthew's. One obituary in a professional journal
included the comment that Dr. Bishop's "scientific discussions . . .
were always couched in simple terms without glittering generalities,
though clothed in the gentle courtesy of his southern breeding."[47]

Howard Bishop was also not one for "glittering generalities." Indeed he seldom generalized in his diary. Though his daily notations
were increasingly about one hundred words, they included detailed
references, such as the purchases of a particular number of clothes
hangers or greeting cards. His ordinary day was quite full and followed a rather set pattern. After morning mass he would frequently
go downtown on various business trips. He was always engaged in
reading literature, history, or spiritual books. He spent at least an
hour in preparation for teaching either catechism or social studies at
the parish school. He did take this position very seriously and periodically met with each of his students for discussion of his or her work
during the school day. He took daily naps and walks. After dinner at
the rectory he often visited families in the parish. He noted his many
visits to the Joneses, relatives of R. Sargent Shriver's father, Herbert.
On one occasion he found himself delighted with "their plainness
and simplicity which I could observe more as an 'old friend' than as

. . . an occasional guest. He never referred to a priest acquaintance as 'an old friend.' "[48] Seldom did he record the topics of conversation but occasionally he referred to prayers at the bedside of a sick child.

In response to his self-perceived weaknesses Howard pursued self-help remedies. In his struggle against wasting time he embarked on an efficiency course, which required written work and recording times spent on various projects. He noted that as a result of the first few lessons he had reduced by three minutes the time it took him to get dressed and ready for the day. Bishop kept a very detailed budget for the year which included twenty items from socks to alumni dues to Harvard. In the same vein he taught himself typing and practiced sometimes for more than an hour a day. He had a weekly one-hour tutorial in homiletics and scripture from a former seminary professor. Because he was determined to improve his understanding of the Bible, he frequently devoted more than an hour a day to reading and synopsizing a book of the Old Testament. Less often did he spend an hour in meditation before the blessed sacrament. He continued to experience memory problems with the liturgy; after a mistake at midnight mass of 1916 he resolved "to make my Mass the chief business of my life hereafter." His New Year's resolution of 1917 buttressed this promise: "I will endeavor by careful study of liturgy and ceremonies to make the Mass my chief preoccupation and care, the centre of my religious life in every sense, and will preach frequently upon the different phases of the sublime Sacrifice. This with the help of Almighty God and His Divine Son whom it is my privilege to receive and offer up daily."[49]

The Bishop-Craig conflict was never far below the surface at the rectory of the Shrine of the Sacred Heart. The pastor was busy with fund-raising and planning for a new church. In his diary, Bishop occasionally referred to his disagreements with Craig. At one point he had considered leaving parish life to attend the Paulist Mission House at The Catholic University of America.[50] Since the Mission House trained priests for rural mission life, from the vantage point of Glenmary this passing interest is very significant.

By visiting families in the parish he seems to have found some compensation from the tedium of the rectory. However, Craig "objected to my visiting in the parish." Such criticism elicited one of the infrequent emotional passages in his diary: "Felt miserable at heart over what had been said to me in the morning. It is not pleasant to be threatened with 'the Cardinal' for every little whipstitch. I was full of resentment."[51] Howard did not allow his emotion to show; later that day he "composed" himself and went to confession to Craig.[52] However, within the following two weeks he sought advice on a possible transfer to another parish; the priests with whom he confided, even Bishop Corrigan, supported such a move.[53] Finally, on February 2, 1917 he went to see Cardinal Gibbons and "asked for a change. This is a decisive step. God see me through. . . . I have had some misgivings as to the wisdom of this step . . . but have resolved to brush them aside and 'stand pat' no matter what [assignment] I get. Again, God help me."[54]

Gibbons had promised to transfer him by May. In the meantime, Bishop was sure that most parishioners were aware of the tensions in the rectory. "How could anybody help not knowing." It was not until September 8, 1917 that Gibbons "summoned" by phone Bishop and Craig to his residence. Later that day "His Eminence told me of my appointment to succeed John Liljencrants as pastor of St. Louis Parish in Clarksville, Maryland." Bishop was very pleased with the positive turn of events: "It must have been Providence who sent to me just the right man to advance my cause."[55]

The providential character of his appointment to St. Louis Parish was not only an answer to his prayer for a release from the authority of Craig but was also a response to his long-felt wish to serve in a rural parish. For many years he and his family had lived in the Bishop country home in Clifton, Virginia. A priest friend recalled Howard's romantic attachment to the land, a characteristic that flourished ten years later when he became a leader of the Catholic rural movement.[56] However, his immediate concern was to extend his farewell to the people of Mount Washington and to prepare to assume the responsibilities of a pastor.

On Sunday, September 9 Bishop informed the parishioners of his transfer to St. Louis Church. He and the people of Sacred Heart Parish had achieved mutual respect over their two years together: "I told them of my change, complimented them and thanked them. There was much sniffling and coughing through the rest of the Mass and I was just able to continue myself though I shed no tears." Bishop was ambivalent about such a display of emotion; he was moved by the overt display of affection but his deep sense of formality would not allow him to consider his own feelings as anything other than self-indulgence bordering on pride. Hence, at the next mass that day he presented the congregation "with a shorter version of the announcement made at early Mass without adding any touching details. Consequently very little weeping though I know they were all touched."[57]

Despite his conflict with Craig, Bishop had certainly achieved a strong self-image in his priestly ministry in the parish. He was confident that he had made a positive impact. His departing words of thanks and compliments were symbolic of his affirmative style of ministry. However, he could be negative with his parishioners who flagrantly failed to perform their duties. It was not uncommon for him to record in his diary a visit with a family who were not attending church. On one occasion he noted that "had to do my quarreling [with a couple who were falling away from church] before their non-Catholic relatives, but it was good natured and no harm was done."[58]

Bishop seldom relates "good natured" discussions with fellow priests or with sisters at the Mercy convent. His struggles with Craig derived not only from a personality conflict but also from Howard's deep sensitivity to any form of criticism, particularly from those in authority. His quick temper ignited when he felt someone was "talking down" to him or did not trust his abilities. Frequently the criticism he felt so deeply was in those areas of his life about which he was self-critical, such as his slowness in saying mass, his blundering, his faulty memory, his preaching, and public speaking in general. For example, when one of the sisters reminded him of the preface appropriate for a particular feast, he fumed in defensiveness. He instinctively felt persecuted precisely because he had experienced so many instances when he did forget something important and he felt embarrassed and hurt that others were aware of those characteristics that he considered to be weaknesses.

He was honest with himself. He admitted his failure to adequately prepare for a sermon, his blunders at the altar, and his hurt feelings in the conflict with Craig. Just as he was self-critical, so he experienced satisfaction in his priestly ministry. As if to compensate for his tendencies to daydream, to be extremely preoccupied and remote from the demands of the present, he became a very practical person with a penchant for focusing on details. The general rhythm of parish life—liturgies, parish school, administering the sacraments—combined with his routine of self-help projects and visits downtown and with parishioners, formed a very patterned existence. However, he did not perceive himself in narrow clerical terms. From his parents' associations and from their concern with issues of politics and culture he developed a variety of interests; he was in many ways quite cosmopolitan. Besides his reading, he attended public lectures and occasional dramatic and musical productions, and easily conversed on a wide range of issues. He did not nurture a clerical self-image but he was immersed in the life of the parish priest. Though he regularly visited with his family he seldom comments on them in his diary. His annual expenses of $460 included a payment of $50 to his home and $50 for train fares—Baltimore–Washington, D.C. He also allocated $50 for his vacation.[59]

The infrequent references to his spiritual, moral, and emotional life seem to symbolize his drive to live an uncomplicated life. His Anglo-American character, his development separate from the immigrant church, indeed from the institutional church, and the quiet yet charming southern-gentleman formality are the qualities which identify him; he was not a typical priest in the church in the United States. He seems to have understood his distinctiveness and may have even refined those characteristics which set him apart. Though his family had roots in North Carolina, he was of the Bishop family who lived in the large home on I Street in the nation's capital. He seemed to have been more at ease with lay people than with priests and he was very accommodating to Protestants. Howard was a man of fine abilities but he was definitely of an extraordinary character.

Howard Bishop's Catholic identity was derived from his parents' experiences in North Carolina and his own religious self-awareness as a Catholic in public schools and at Harvard. He was far removed from the burgeoning immigrant church with its strong devotionalism and emotional ties with European roots through language and culture. He therefore shared the Americanist vision of James Gibbons. Indeed, his Anglo-American heritage places him within the heritage of those early Catholics of Maryland who formed the church of John Carroll. The Shrine of the Sacred Heart in Mount Washington was a suburban parish of second and third generation immigrants most of whom were thoroughly Americanized families of Irish descent. The pastor, Father Craig, was a convert, while the Mercy Sisters were quite Americanized. Hence, Howard Bishop's experiences as a young priest were in accord with his own background. Of course, there were no recent immigrants in St. Louis Parish, Clarksville, where Bishop resided as pastor from 1917 to 1937. Indeed the Catholic families in the area comprised only sixty-nine households in 1934.

The young priest was very open to the general culture and tended to privatize specific religious beliefs. David O'Brien refers to this trait as a "republican style" of public Catholicism. First expressed in the church of John Carroll, this republican style stressed the Christian (vis-à-vis Catholic) component in the making of American society and fostered an enlightened and patriotic Catholic citizenry. The immigrant style was relatively closed to American society, ever conscious of its periodic outbursts of nativism and anti-Catholicism. As it nurtured the German, Italian, Polish and other ethnic Catholic sub-cultures, the immigrant style of public Catholicism related to public issues through local political parties that promised economic security and respected religious and ethnic diversity.[60]

The Americanists revived the republican style but imposed upon it a liberal imprint. John Ireland and James Gibbons embraced the American democratic ethos and extolled the inherently progressive spirit of the gilded age as if they were marks of divine providence. Conscious of the decline of Protestantism they were confident of the triumph of Catholicism in America, but rather than proclaim triumphalism the Americanists manifested an irenic attitude toward the compatibility of Catholicism and American culture.

As previously mentioned Howard Bishop's student homilies were on the role of religion in promoting a national moral climate and on the need for laws to foster child welfare, both of which illustrate his commitment to large religious and social issues. After ordination he continued his interest in social, political and historical issues. He was continuously reading books on these topics; he seldom engaged in spiritual reading. His diary notations touched upon religious topics infrequently. Instead they were related to his social life, his geography classes at the parish primary school, his favorite books and his personal problems with homilies, memorization and the liturgy.

As the product of the religious pluralism of public schools, Bishop's reserved personality and his preference for privacy compounded his inhibition to impose his religious views on his social life. His homilies tended to be moral exhortations rather than deeply spiritual explorations or scriptural exegesis. His public Catholicism was certainly more related to the open-minded republican style of Gibbons than the self-preoccupied character of immigrant Catholicism. As noted, Gibbons and Ireland were confident that the United States would gradually convert to Catholicism. In a sermon preached in April 1917, Howard Bishop focused on the conversion of America. In answer to those who criticized Catholics for pursuing such a course, Bishop concluded that they are right. "We deserve to follow Christ . . . [and] like Him we pray that we may all be one, that they may be one fold and one Shepherd." Catholics "desire to convert the world" but not "by underhand means, by stealth and by trickery and deceit. . . . We have Christ with us every day. Should we hesitate to show the world where He is to be found?" Bishop's means for conversion entailed prayer and good example, "Live the life of a Catholic from morning till night every day in the week," in short, be "saturated with the religion you profess. . . . A little firmness in judging between right and wrong, a little backbone in maintaining principles." To those married to Protestants he urged "morning and night prayers . . . Mass regularly on Sunday morning and communion once every month."[61] Bishop had yet to develop his commitment to direct evangelization; in 1917 he had no missiology except the traditional exhortations of moral persuasion through good example.

In a sermon of July 1916 Howard shared his ideas on the power of the priesthood. He referred to the effects of Pentecost when the Holy Spirit transformed poor illiterate men into eloquent missionaries of the gospel. He drew the analogy of Pentecost to the ordination ceremony: "The priest is an instance of the power of God to do by means of men what men could not do themselves. Before ordination he is a man without influence, unknown and unnoticed. His life is a hidden life. After the ceremony of ordination he walks forth a leader among men. . . . People who never noticed him before are now coming and asking his blessing, telling him their heart's most hidden secrets in the confessional." Aware of his own unworthiness the priest "reflects that it is God's way to choose weak human instruments to accomplish His great works." Bishop then democratizes the priesthood. "But do you think, dear brethren, that only the priest can be fisher of men? Oh no. Every man can be an apostle though he holds no commission from on high. Every man can be a preacher of the Word though he does not preach with his lips. He can be more than a *mere* preacher . . . *a good life is preaching all the time to unseen congregations,* and long after the preacher's words shall be forgotten, men will be moved by the gentle persuasiveness and irresistible power of a good example." With characteristic distrust of those who wear religion on their sleeves Bishop said that the lay person can be an apostle *"but he will not be by filling* his mouth with the catch words of religion. It will not be by boasting of his Catholicity and of his charity until his friends become weary of the word." Instead, he continued, "It will be by going out into the busy world and living the life of the Christian in a simple, humble, God-fearing way." The lay apostle, according to Bishop, must be a man of charity, one who desires the salvation of his neighbor and who "will help him secure it by showing him how much we deserve it ourselves."[62]

Howard Bishop explicitly develops his notion of lay apostles beyond the ordinary preaching through example. His portrayal of the struggle to be a good Catholic did not include an organized lay movement, nor did it entail any reference to the sacraments of baptism or confirmation as bases for apostleship. There were no allusions to anti-Catholicism or nativism, nor did he identify the good Catholic with any forms of old-world devotionalism, such as novenas and the invocation of particular saints as spiritual balm for the virtuous life. Such devotionalism was simply not a part of his experience.

A strong portion of his own self-image, those unarticulated areas of his internal life, by which he implicitly understood life, must have been dominated by individualism. Without any forms of communalism, except perhaps the family refuge from the temptations of the world, the Catholic apostle dwelled in an atomistic society that was morally neutral; one's motives determined whether one served mammon or God. The church was not portrayed as a religious sub-culture in which the faithful were nurtured by the common faith of the neighborhood but rather a place where one experienced God in mass and the sacraments and was instructed in a religious creed and moral code. Bishop presumed that this experience marked the Catholic as distinct from his fellow citizens and contributed to the betterment of the general society. The aggregate of individual Catholics made a difference in society rather than the corporate witness of a Catholic ethnic sub-culture. The Gibbons church veered away from old world ethnicity and identified the Catholic sense of peoplehood with an American Catholic behavior that was expressed in practicing one's faith in a free milieu. In the social climate of individualism, Catholic

people lived out their faith more naturally than in the socially traditional worlds of ethnic sub-cultures.

By education and family background Howard Bishop was, like
Gibbons, a southern patrician indifferent to the rationalized structure of a modern bureaucratic institution. However, Bishop was convinced that organization and standardization of procedures were necessary features of his own drive for self-improvement, as well as
symbols of a progressive society. As will be explored in the next
chapter, he founded an organization to improve rural Catholic
schools, a development that placed him in harmony with the main
trends in Archbishop Curley's administration.

CHAPTER 3

The Rural Pastor
1917–1922

The personalist character of the Gibbons church was evident in the way that the cardinal himself, rather than his chancellor, informed Howard Bishop of his appointment to succeed John Liljencrants at Clarksville. St. Louis Parish dates back to 1855 and is situated in the heart of Howard County, an area of 253 square miles of rolling hills, with the Patapsco River forming the northern boundary, and, on its southern boundary, the Patuxent River. Augustin Verot, the Sulpician who later became vicar apostolic of Florida and first bishop of St. Augustine, had been the first pastor. St. Louis was a mission in those early days; Verot lived at St. Paul's Church in Ellicott City and served St. Mary's Chapel at Doughoregan Manor, the ancestral home of Charles Carroll of Carrollton, the Catholic signer of the Declaration of Independence.[1] During the Gibbons period young priests were usually appointed to rural parishes. For example, Edward F. Ryan's first assignment as priest was as pastor of St. Louis (1911–1916). Carl J. Liljencrants was the son of a Swedish baron who emigrated to the United States in 1910 and soon converted to Catholicism. He was educated at Loyola University in Chicago and Princeton and studied for the priesthood at St. Mary's Seminary in Baltimore from 1913–15.[2] He and Howard Bishop were of the same age and ordained the same year, but since Bishop's last year as a seminarian was spent at Catholic University, he and Liljencrants were not well acquainted. While Bishop was at the Shrine of the Sacred Heart, Liljencrants was appointed pastor of St. Louis.

Howard Bishop was given only one week to prepare before he was to move from an affluent suburban parish to a small rural commu-

nity. The cardinal's short notice seems to have resulted from Liljen-
crant's sudden resignation. According to a letter from Charles
Carroll of Doughoregan Manor to James Gibbons, there had been a
"series of stories going on in the country about him [i.e. Liljen-
crants]" which Carroll said were "lies, pure and simple." He portrayed Liljencrants as an innocent victim of the polarization between
the parish and the Manor: "The chief grievance against him being
that he is most congenial to the Manor and we have been given such a
bad reputation in the county by Father Reilly [Liljencrants' prede-
cessor] that no one who is congenial here will be acceptable to
Clarksville and vice-versa." Carroll told the cardinal that he would
not "tolerate a priest here who is satisfactory to Clarksville because if
I did it would mean a repetition of the insults I had before Liljencrants came." The only solution, according to Carroll, was "to separate entirely from Clarksville and have a private chaplain whom I will
support and in return for this privilege I will allow the country side to
attend Mass here as usual."[3]

Perhaps Gibbons informed Carroll of the prospective appointment of Bishop which may have pleased the head of the manor. Four
weeks after he wrote his demands to the cardinal and three days
before Bishop was appointed pastor, Carroll expressed his appreciation to the cardinal for his "great kindness," without specifying just
what Gibbons did to warrant such an expression of gratitude.[4]

Howard Bishop's relations with John Liljencrants were not amicable. On the day of his arrival at St. Louis Parish he noted in his diary,
"A day I shall not soon forget." Liljencrants introduced him to his
rectory—"in a dreadful state of disorder" and, since there was "no
dinner prepared and no housekeeper," the retiring pastor had a parishioner bring them a meal. Bishop had immediately detected that
Liljencrants was intoxicated; "[he was] growing more unsteady every
minute." Rather than record his feelings or thoughts during the first
days at Clarksville his next diary entry is not until September 24.[5]
Liljencrants only visited Bishop twice after that first day. Since he had
left a sizable debt, of a somewhat personal nature, Bishop occasionally noted his impatience with the former pastor.[6] When Liljencrants
did not appear for an appointment with Bishop the latter remarked in
his diary, "Liljencrants did not come. I shall not fool with him any-
more. He has abused my friendship long enough."[7] About a month
later Bishop received word that "Liljencrants was sighted in Clarks-

ville this afternoon.'' By this time he was so alienated by the behavior of Liljencrants that the "thought of his brazen impertinence kept me miserable all the evening.''[8]

Howard Bishop's relationship with the Carroll family was not characterized by the friendly warmth of the sort that Charles Carroll and John Liljencrants seem to have enjoyed. Bishop was periodically invited to dine with the Carrolls after mass, but he appears to have been unrelaxed in their company and on one occasion he found himself quite bored by their conversation. As a pastor he was never in charge of things at the Manor as he was at St. Louis. Rather than attend to the maintenance of the chapel, he had to ask the family to relieve such nuisances as poor heat in the chapel. Colonial Maryland's private chapels were the only centers of liturgical and catechetical life. Doughoregan Manor was a replica of those days. The congregation was composed of the servants and those who lived nearby. In his diary Bishop occasionally noted his concern that the Carrolls provide a good example by attending mass and frequenting the sacraments. The young pastor was enough of a southern patrician to appreciate the code of *noblesse oblige*. However, he was also a modern church administrator who found himself at odds with dependency upon a wealthy family. Indeed, he investigated Charles Carroll's will in the hope of verifying rumors that the old signer had left the chapel to the archdiocese. Though a copy of the will did stipulate such a gift, later research of the original will resulted in the discovery of a codicil reversing the ownership of the chapel to the family.[9]

Throughout his twenty years in Clarksville Howard Bishop experienced only one major conflict with the Manor. It originated on April 9, 1922 when he was presiding at the Sunday liturgy. The congregation was scheduled to have its photo taken that day. According to his diary entry, after mass he met with the photographer who "informs me that his camera . . . [had been] smashed by a guest of Mr. Carroll's to keep him from photographing a half-naked woman who rode over the lawn during Mass." Howard Bishop interpreted the scene as an act of anti-Catholic hostility. "I laid down [an] ultimatum to Carroll," said Bishop. "You have given personal insult to the archdiocese of Baltimore. I refuse to enter your house or chapel until proper reparation has been made.''[10] The following day Bishop took the photographer to meet with Archbishop Michael Curley, who had succeeded to the see some few months earlier. Curley only reluctantly accepted the version of the story that Carroll "knew of the camera breaking in advance" and did not accept Bishop's "theory of a frame-up to interfere with Mass." He told Bishop to say mass at the Manor the following two Sundays "to give Carroll every opportunity to apologize."[11] The next day Charles B. Carroll visited Bishop at his rectory. He had attempted to see him the day before while Bishop was in Baltimore. Carroll was "most humbly repentant for the sacrilegious affair of Sunday but satisfied me that his own responsibility extended no farther than bringing half-drunken bums with their women companions on the place for a 'party.' [Carroll] made promises to do everything to mend matters." To symbolize his contrition Carroll said that he "will go to communion with the people Sunday week."[12] Bishop recalled that Carroll failed to be present at church that Sunday; he did see Mrs. Carroll after mass and "tactfully suggested that she take up . . . [her husband's] debt—so ungallantly evaded by him—and pay the photographer for his broken camera for honor of the family." When this had no effect, then Bishop, "showing a little anger," told her that he "would take up a collection from my people [of the parish] and pay it as an act of charity to the Carroll family. Then she began to talk Business." The photographer's bill was finally paid by the family.[13]

Curley and Bishop had discussed the possibility of building an archdiocesan mission attached to St. Louis to serve the community around the Manor in order to alleviate any dependency upon the Carroll family. However, such talk never reached the level of serious consideration as both the archbishop and the pastor were apparently appeased by the apologies and behavior of Charles Carroll. Relations between the Manor and the parish as well as between the family and the pastor returned to a condition of cordiality. The Manor chapel remains an active mission today attached to the parish of St. Louis but serviced by the Franciscan Fathers of Ellicott City.

Shortly after Bishop became a rural pastor, he began a census of the parish and the mission. In January 1918 there were 239 Catholics enrolled in St. Louis, 185 of whom were children; parishioners at St. Mary's Church at the Manor numbered 225 including 110 children. Twenty years later the figures for St. Louis were about the same but St. Mary's had fallen to 103 parishioners. Under Liljencrants there were no religious societies listed. Bishop established the Holy Name Society and the Sodality of the Blessed Virgin in each church. The latter was replaced by the League of the Sacred Heart at the parish in

1921. Later a chapter of the National Council of Catholic Men was established at St. Mary's.[14]

Life in Clarksville was filled with daily challenges, many of which had nothing to do with Bishop's pastoral ministry. He inherited the parish automobile, a broken-down Ford, that was a constant source of trouble. The county roads created havoc during wet weather and during the winter snow he occasionally took a horse and sleigh from St. Louis to the Manor chapel. It was not uncommon for him to take parishioners to the hospital in order to visit relatives and friends, to gather the children for catechism classes at the church, to run all sorts of business errands to Ellicott City or to Baltimore, and to tend to home and church chores. An elderly black woman, "Aunt" Nancy Conte, was Bishop's housekeeper and cook who lived at the rectory. She was a Catholic and attended mass at St. Louis, but according to racist customs she sat in the gallery. One former parishioner commented some time later that "Aunt Nancy" did not go to confession to Father Bishop because "he got too much on you," she explained.[15]

There were three black Catholic families in the parish. One black parishioner recalled that Bishop gave him a $5 gold piece for Christmas in gratitude for his fixing the fire for Sunday mass.[16] In late 1929 Miss Conte retired as housekeeper and cook at St. Louis rectory. In the January 1929 issue of a special archdiocesan bulletin he published an article in which he wrote on the occasion of the retirement of Miss Conte. "When a veteran warrior or statesman retires from active service the event is considered worthy of comment in the public press. House servants do not usually share this privilege. . . . [However], did not the Savior make rather pointed comment about the connection between leadership and service?" She had served for "twenty-eight years of faithful untiring service" at St. Louis Parish. At over one hundred years of age Miss Conte felt justified in retiring. With a paternalistic tone echoing his southern roots Bishop remarked that "surely there is a touch of sanctity about this dear old slave of ante-bellum days . . . yet when we speak in modern symbols, Aunt Nancy cannot be called an old-timer. In one respect at least she has been far ahead of her time, for she was a confirmed pipe-smoker fully fifty years before the modern woman took to cigarette and unlike most of her cultured white sisters of today, she handles the weed with the unconscious grace and genuine relish of a true connoisseur. May her days of retirement, unspoiled by luxury, be blessed with that peace she has so well earned as the smoke from her quiet pipe rises like incense with her prayers to God.'"⁷ Howard Bishop's article, which included a photograph of Miss Conte, was paternalistic in tone and substance, but the very fact that he wrote a tribute to his housekeeper was quite extraordinary in the 1920s, indeed even for the 1980s.

With only about seventy Catholic families in the parish, Bishop knew everyone very well. Since most of his parishioners were farmers he could not expect any attendance at daily mass and did not, therefore, keep the church heated except for Sundays and holy days. He said daily mass alone in the sacristy. On at least two occasions his mother stayed with him for a week or so. One of his nephews, who was having problems at home, stayed with him for several months. Bishop was very solicitous about the young boy's education and frequently read to him from the classics. The following selections from his diary, recorded during his first December in Clarksville, provide a glimpse of the life of a rural pastor:

December 13, 1917

Took Mother to Laurel. Called for a few moments on Father Meyer then returned home. Snow still deep but well packed on the main roadways. Felt very lonesome when I got home without Mother in the house. Called her up in afternoon to make sure of her safe arrival home. Heavy snowfall began shortly after my return and continued far into the night, when high winds arose.

December 14, 1917

Funeral of George W. Carr, who died at Mt. Hope. Hearse and one limousine came out from Baltimore in spite of heavy snow and drifts. Arrived 40 minutes before time for Mass—11 o'clock. I insisted upon mourners having a cup of coffee and waiting in rectory. Preached briefly at funeral and hastened ceremony at grave. Called at Millers in late afternoon. Mr. M let me in and I sat with him, was asked to supper by Mrs. M. The girls did not appear. Finished visit "on the other side" and left chance books for Eleanor Clark who was there.

December 15, 1917

Spent morning writing personal letters to those who had contributed to Liberty Bond purchase, asking them for an additional donation. Late in afternoon took Louis out in machine to try the roads. Got "stuck" at turning into Simpsonville Road and had to shovel our way out. Tried by phone to secure use of a horse for tomorrow, then went to Zeff's to find they had only work horses. Finally decided to wait till after Mass tomorrow and see what turned up.

December 16, 1917

Early Mass at Clarksville. Preached only briefly on John the Baptist, the Precursor. Told people not to spend their money on Christmas gifts for me. Jim Cuff took me in Isaac Smith's sleigh to the Manor. Church cold. Sleigh turned over in a drift and dumped us both going over. Came back without making short cut through Manakee's field, consequently had many exciting tilts in deep drifts on Manakee's Lane.

December 17, 1917

Finished typing and mailed letters asking contributions to Liberty Bond Purchase.

December 18, 1917

Omitted Mass and started for town immediately after breakfast about 8:15. Left machine at Taylor's to have brake lever fixed. Went to [Dr.] Riely's and had a new jacket [i.e. brace] put on. Temperature had moderated considerably but a little snow was still falling. Went to Alice's for lunch. Met Edna on way going downtown. Played with little Louise. While waiting for car at Charles and Lexington met first Mrs. Jones, then Mrs. J.P. Winand of Mt. Washington. Returned from Ellicott via Old Columbia Pike as I had gone. In evening attended Patron's Meeting at school house and spoke on Catholic education.

December 19, 1917

Slept late. Mass about 8:30. Turned off heat in all rooms except dining room, office, bath and Nancy's bedroom. Remained indoors all day, writing a few letters . . . and reading a sketch of Cardinal's career in special supplement of *Baltimore Review*. Weather much warmer and snow melting.

December 20, 1917

Gave Holy Communion, Extreme Unction and Last Blessing to Mrs. Hebb on Triadelphia Pike near Glenelg. Dropped in at Malonty's on way home. Spent most of day deciding on and ordering Christmas gifts. A magazine catalogue offered happy solution to the problem. Magazines, cigars, cash and cards will be my gifts this year. Started for Highland with Louis, but exhaust began to give trouble so we returned. After supper, finished Office, then went to examine machine. With help of Louis found exhaust disconnected and had him fix it. . . .[18]

Bishop's sermon on Sunday, December 30, 1917, was on the topic of New Year's resolutions. It was a bitterly cold day; only twenty people attended mass at the parish. At the end of 1917 he could look back at a very eventful year; he had made the transition from suburban to rural life without any major problems. Indeed he worked hard at being a dutiful and caring pastor. In his diary for January 3, 1918 he wrote a memorandum that was either a direct quote from one of his textbooks on memory or efficiency, or perhaps a reflection of his own work ethic:

Memorandum

January 3, 1918

I realize that it is largely through my success in my work that I shall obtain peace of mind here and salvation hereafter. I know that success in my work depends upon the quantity and quality of service I render. Therefore, I am daily giving better service than I ever did before. I am ambitious to excel in everything I undertake; to do better work than is expected of me. I am therefore earnestly and enthusiastically at work establishing standards, keeping records of my progress. I am planning my work more and more intelligently and carefully. I am intensely interested in preparing schedules for all of my time, materials and equipment. I am striving every day to dispatch all that I do with a higher percentage of efficiency than ever before. I am always on the alert to standardize conditions and to standardize my operations. I am thus playing the game against my past performances in finding and taking the best, easiest and quickest ways to the desirable things of life.[19]

The thoroughly individualistic character of this reflection indicates not only Bishop's penchant for continuous self-improvement but also his drive for organization, standardization, and functional efficiency. Seminary training emphasized personal holiness as the ideal so that the priest would have the interior piety in accord with the *alter Christus* notion of the priesthood; a well cultivated interiority would also be such a source of personal fortitude to weather the inherent solitude of the priestly life. Bishop's identification of sanctity with self-motivating, organized and efficient ministry presaged the new model seminary training of the second third of the twentieth century, one that emphasized professional preparation for the modern priesthood.

Howard Bishop did not articulate these ideas but he seems to have implicitly grasped their relevance to his life. For example he noted in his diary for February 8, 1919 that he had read a "very instructive article in [the] *Ecclesiastical Review* on country missions which just fit my needs."[20] Written by a Basilian priest in the Canadian rural missions, the article stressed the very qualities that Bishop had noted in his *Memorandum* of the previous January 3. After elaborating on how the rhythm of the urban parish provides almost an instant routine for the young priest, the author wrote that the country parish required a "constant foresight in organizing people, or meeting them individually so the hearing of a few confessions, the preparing fifteen or twenty children for the sacraments, is accomplished only through a succession of plans and appointments. . . . Success . . . [will] be due to a rare resourcefulness and a rare capacity for organization."[21]

Bishop's drive for efficiency manifested itself in his management of the parish finances. Early in 1918 he introduced a monthly envelope system. He maintained pew rents and regular offertory collections during that year. The latter two means of collecting money amounted to $867.20 during 1918 while the envelope system netted $398.85. In 1919 the figures were $684.85 and $461.85 respectively. In 1920 pew rents were abolished, the envelope collections totaled $1,740.75, and regular offertory collections brought in $214.70.[22] The young rural pastor had obviously educated his small family parish to adopt a modern means of budgeting their gifts, an achievement that was quite remarkable for its day. Pew rents were maintained in many parishes until the 1940s.

The parish's major fund-raising event was its annual picnic. Dating back to the nineteenth century, the Clarksville picnic, as it was and still is called, has been from its origin one of the significant social gatherings in Howard County. Bishop organized picnic workers, successfully sought donations of food and other materials for sale at the affair, arranged for promotional advertising, and managed the festivities on the day of the picnic. On August 7, 1918 Bishop presided over his first Clarksville picnic. "Heavy rain in the evening cut off the best part of day's receipts and kept many people in hall all night," lamented Bishop. However, the picnic raised $1,322 for the parish. The following year there was "a banner crowd at the grounds and everybody [was] apparently in a good humor." Profits reached over $1,500. Even during the early 1920s when there was an agricultural depression, the picnic proceeds seldom dropped below $1,500 and on one occasion earned over $2,400.[23]

Long after Howard Bishop had died a parishioner recalled that "he was a person that would innovate." At the picnic "he brought to the area a barn-storming airplane ride which was the first one in this part of the county." He also remarked on Bishop's methods of improving the economic conditions of the area. "The parishioners usually gave ten or fifteen spring chickens which were to be fried and sold at the picnic. Father Bishop devised a plan wherein he would give each household [that supplied chickens] . . . a dozen or two dozen of pure bred eggs or eggs that were a better breed than the local farmers raised and asked that they raise these chickens and in this way he endeavored to upgrade the breed of chickens in the community."[24] Another parishioner recalled the general popularity of the picnic. "We had dancing and ice cream and everything that goes along with a picnic of that kind. Then we had a tournament where the men rode horses to catch the rings. That drew a good many people. In addition, we had a ballgame between the two teams of Howard county and Montgomery county people."[25]

Mary Smith, the church organist during those days, spoke of the picnic and said that "Father Bishop worked very, very hard. . . . His whole heart and soul was in his work here at St. Louis. . . . He fitted much, much better into a rural setting than into a large parish. . . . He was very good to young people and wasn't stand-offish. He was very congenial and seemed to enjoy young people." She was one of the few people who indicated an awareness of Bishop's physical afflictions. "Well, Father Bishop wasn't at all well and suffered quite a good bit with his back. He wore an iron brace. . . . In his poor health he didn't spare himself a minute."[26]

At the end of 1918, Howard Bishop listed four "things I am to accomplish sooner or later."

1. To have a flag-pole erected on the church property and have a public flag-raising, perhaps some day in April.
2. To establish a parish school. Next fall, (1919) the most favorable time if it can be done.
3. To organize catechism classes in various parts of 2 parishes and visit them periodically. Also to have a weekly class in the Rectory.
4. Start a parish paper, to be issued monthly, and to go to every family, so that nobody be without news of church announcements, etc.[27]

He did succeed in having a flag-pole raised on the church property and in organizing catechism classes but there is no evidence of a parish paper, and the establishment of a school had to wait until he mustered the moral support of his parishioners. The need for a parochial school in such a small parish must have appeared to many as an unnecessary luxury.

A new Clarksville public school had been erected in 1914. It was the first consolidated school in the area as it replaced the county schools. According to a 1934 sociological study of Clarksville, the school, referred to as a high school, housed grades one through twelve and had a faculty of six. There were ninety-four students that year, thirty-seven in high school and fifty-seven in the elementary grades. The school was a source of pride for the residents of Clarksville, most of whom had not had the opportunity to attend a local high school. Howard's public school was a one-room school for black children in grades one through seven located two miles outside of Clarksville and had an attendance of forty-nine students under the direction of one teacher in 1933–34.[28]

Bishop's drive to establish a parish school was fueled by his frustration with organizing a catechetical program for farm children and the fear that without a strong foundation young people would gradually drift away from the faith. Even before there was a school building he had attempted to recruit sisters to staff the school. For example, in

November 1919 he visited a Sister Thomasino at Mount St. Agnes in his former parish in Mount Washington. "She phoned to Philadelphia about the case—does not think she can furnish sisters for my 'school,' "[29] recorded Bishop. About a year later he approached Cardinal Gibbons who responded with a pledge of $500 for a series of annual payments toward the building of a school for St. Louis. In December of 1920, Bishop told Gibbons how grateful he was "to learn from your own lips how thoroughly you approve of my efforts" to establish a parochial school. Of course, he was grateful for the cardinal's pledge of "material assistance" and, with characteristic candor, Bishop asked Gibbons to make the first payment next year (1921) rather than wait until the building was under construction.[30] The cardinal sent his gift of $500 in January 1921, shortly before he died.[31] There is no record of an annual gift from his successor, Michael Curley, but he eventually played a significant role in the establishment of a St. Louis school. At the end of 1921 Bishop's parish school fund totaled $5,686.[32] The parishioners donated $835, while outside donations came to $1,850. Bishop borrowed $1,800 in order to purchase thirty-three acres of land near the parish, which when cleared and divided into lots were to yield a profit for the school fund. By April of 1923 his land investment had broken even with nine more lots to be sold.[33]

The success of his building fund was due not only to Bishop's investment but also because he identified his particular case with the general need for rural education and published his views in the Baltimore *Catholic Review*. On March 24, 1922 he confided in his diary that he had "spent several hours trying to write an article for the *Review* on diocesan aid for country schools. Tore up manuscript and will try again." Later he met two people who "should be Catholic" but apparently did not receive a religious education. "There are many hereabout, *I must have a school*," he wrote in his diary.[34] The article took the form of a letter to the editor dated April 13, 1922. However, his diary dates the letter on April 12 and includes a curious reference: "Incidentally I did what I had previously refused to do—criticized the archbishop. But it is at his own request, backed up by . . . [the editor's] reassurance, so I am safe in that quarter."[35]

That Archbishop Curley courted open criticism was probably not far from the truth; Curley was a very outspoken prelate who admired the same qualities in others. However, in fact, Bishop's criticism was couched in such tactful language that it hardly appears to have been a negative commentary on the ordinary's policies. Indeed, he opened his letter with a series of positive remarks on Curley's leadership in Catholic education and his recent call for an archdiocesan scholarship fund so that children of poor families might have the opportunity to attend high school. He then pointed out that in the Baltimore archdiocese, as well as in most of the episcopal sees in the nation, there is hardly any mention of "the question of Catholic education of our country children. The very words sound strange, we have given so little thought to the subject. Here and there an enterprising country pastor has accomplished the impossible. . . . But nothing of a constructive nature has yet been done by which country parishes throughout the archdiocese may benefit. . . . The Archbishop's letter [on a scholarship fund] has opened up the subject of popular—. . . [that] is diocesan in scope—subscriptions for an educational enterprise and when such a movement is on foot the needs of the long neglected country parish which has claim, not in charity but in justice, upon the generosity of our city people must not be passed over in silence." He did not specify his plan for meeting the needs of the country parishes but initially he said, "I must beg *The Review* a little more elbow room in a future issue to put the plan before its readers." The editor responded in the affirmative: "We will give Father Bishop elbow room and more for anything he may have to say on the subject of higher education in our country parishes."[36]

In the first of two articles on "Country Parochial Schools" Howard Bishop presented a "frank discussion of the educational needs and claims of our country parishes . . . for the enlightenment of our city friends. . . ." He elaborated on the inadequacies of weekly catechetical classes. "One hour a week for religion against five five-hour days a week for secular subjects does not give a fair show to what the church considers the most important part of a well-rounded education." In a country setting it was difficult to achieve a regular class even on a one-hour basis. While city parishioners can easily get to church on Sundays, in the country "most families [do not have] enough conveyances [i.e. automobiles or buggies] to carry everybody to church every Sunday, so that the teacher is likely to look into a different set of faces each week." Hence, many pastors chose Saturday or another day, but "it seems impossible to choose an hour or day when the call of home duties does not play havoc sooner or later with

the attendance. . . . The net result of the best that the weekly class in
the country can do is a poorly instructed child who remembers the
prayers he recites each day but retains little or nothing of the great
truths of his religion." Bishop then narrates the story of the typical
young country pastor who "longs for [a] Parish School," a story that
rings with autobiographical clarity. The rural pastor dreams about
the school that "would change . . . lives of these . . . children. [It
would be] a strong hold of faith . . . in families now shy and backward
in its [religious] practice!" Bishop viewed the Catholic rural school as
a "force for good" in the community composed predominantly of
our "separated brethren." The dreams of the rural pastor are shattered on the rocks of agrarian poverty. The school becomes such an
impractical venture because, unlike the city academics, Catholic rural
education has no wealthy friends. Hence, "strong Catholics drift
townward. . . . Weak Catholics continue to lose their faith. . . . The
great hegira of the country people to the overcrowded industrial
centers goes on with our Catholics in the van of the pilgrimage."
Bishop concluded this first article with a strong admonition to the
urban church: "[Rural] people whose religion predisposes them to
lives of wholesome simplicity are being given *no* encouragement by
their church to stay where the simple life is to be found." Bishop
certainly viewed the country setting as more suitable to the life of
faith than "overcrowded industrial centers."[37]

In his second article Bishop referred to the neglect of rural parishes which he termed "the outcasts of the archdiocese, the Cinderel-
las, the beggars at the gate." So preoccupied with the problems of the
city parishes were bishops and leaders of women religious that they
seldom thought of investing money and personnel in country schools.
It would be to the self-interest of superiors of convents to consider
staffing country schools because they could provide a "productive
field" for vocations. In contrast to the "pleasure-madness" of the
cities, the recreational life of young rural people is "wholesome . . .
boys and girls alike are inured from early childhood to hard work and
self-denial. Conditions could not be more perfect for the growth of
stability of character and a deep religious sense."[38]

Until these articles Howard Bishop seems to have been merely a
dedicated rural pastor, but with his first public utterances he revealed
his vocation as a rural missionary. "The point is that the country
districts of the United States constitutes a vast field for missionary

activity. . . . The important fact is that human souls at our doors are hungering for the bread of truth and we have not been giving it to them. We are sending sisters to China; why not to the neglected districts of our own fair land? We have a Society for the Propagation of the Faith for our foreign mission. Why can we not have a diocesan Propagation of the Faith for our country missions?" Not only would an archdiocesan-wide rural missionary fund help subsidize parochial education but it would also help train "lay catechists for work in parishes when the establishment of a school is impossible, even with diocesan aid." It would also entail the establishment of a diocesan community of sisters "with the special mission of teaching in rural schools." For over twenty years the Baltimore-based Mission Helpers of the Sacred Heart, a community of sisters dedicated to catechetical work in both rural and urban areas, had been serving the archdiocese, but Bishop was advocating a teaching order of women religious for rural parish schools. He concluded the article with the plea that Catholics in the United States consider a soul in St. Mary's or Howard County "as precious as a soul in Hong Kong."[39]

From his letter to the editor to the conclusion of his second article Howard Bishop's identity moved from that of a singular rural pastor to that of the spokesman for rural home missioners throughout the church in the United States. He certainly assumed the role as the leader in the archdiocese of Baltimore. During the remainder of 1922 and most of 1923, he raised money for his school which was finally opened in the fall of 1923. Besides investing in property he sought help from the Catholic Daughters of America in Washington and Baltimore. They sponsored a rummage sale and later adopted the parish-school of St. Louis Church as one of their special projects. On Thanksgiving Day of 1922 these women organized the League of St. Louis and initiated a campaign to enlist one thousand members to raise money first for the St. Louis school, then for other rural parish-school projects.[40] Hence, seven months after his pleas for archdiocesan aid for rural schools, Bishop had achieved the goal. On December 1, 1922 Michael J. Curley congratulated Bishop "upon your splendid efforts in raising funds to build a parish-school at Clarksville." The archbishop also commended Howard Bishop on the establishment of a new organization. "I am also glad to know that some of the Catholic people of Baltimore and Washington have formed the League of St. Louis with its broad and practical aim of helping the education of our

country children. . . . The thought is a noble one and in a noble spirit
they are proceeding to carry it out. I earnestly commend this League
[to] our City Catholics who as a Catholic are far better provided with
this world's goods than their country brethren. . . ."

Howard Bishop was thoroughly immersed in parish life, but with
the foundation of the League of St. Louis, later renamed the League
of the Little Flower, he assumed archdiocesan leadership.

In his articles in the *Catholic Review* he identified himself as a rural
missionary, one who represented Catholicism to the people of
various faiths. He did not perceive his role in terms of only nurturing
the faith of his parishioners, but also of playing a vital part in the
community. As he developed into a national rural leader he refined
his vision of the missionary's role at the intersection of religion and
culture.

CHAPTER 4

The Catholic Rural Movement

The history of the Catholic rural apostolate dates back to the colonization efforts of Bishops John England of Charleston, South Carolina (1820–1844), John Ireland of St. Paul (1884–1918), and John Lancaster Spalding of Peoria (1877–1908). The Irish Catholic Colonization Society was a short-lived (1879–1891) attempt at cooperative rural settlements. Aimed at organizing the German-American Benevolent Societies, the Central Verein was founded in Baltimore in 1855 and reorganized in St. Louis in 1901. The Central Bureau of the Verein was established in that city in 1908. Under the direction of Frederick Kenkel, the Bureau was dedicated to fostering Catholic-action programs in rural and urban districts, and rapidly became well known for its social, economic and religious education among rural parishes.[1]

In 1905 Francis Clement Kelley, an Irish Canadian priest from the diocese of Detroit, founded the Catholic Church Extension Society to support the rural church in Lepeer, Michigan. Kelley's biographer, James Gaffey, points out that "his own bout with loneliness and poverty in rural Michigan was matched by priests in dioceses of the West and South."[2] Kelley became aware of the Protestant Extension Society and its 1904 assistance to 657 rural churches. The Methodists, Baptists and Congregational churches had been financing home missions for decades. After several months in Lepeer, Kelley moved his society to Chicago in 1906 because Archbishop Quigley had become supportive of the Society. In April of that year the first issue of *Extension Magazine* was published. Five years later there were 100,000 subscribers, and ten years later the Society was sponsoring the building of two memorial chapels every week. In 1916 Kelley reflected on the early days of the Society. "I really believe that the Extension Society has justified itself and proven itself and its cause. When we organized, everyone who spoke about it said that the only objection was that the Society was "fifty years too late." He recalled that the original plan was to establish "little parish bands, the same way the Society for the Propagation of the Faith is established all over the world." The plan was abandoned because of strong opposition of the proponents of the Propagation. Instead of building up an enormous central fund the Society broadcast the pleas from rural pastors in *Extension Magazine* and then immediately invested a portion of its collections in building churches and chapels as well as developing a reserve fund. "We follow the plan of not giving more than one-third of the initial cost in most cases. Very rarely have we borne the entire cost."[3]

There were no applications for aid to St. Louis Church probably because the parish under the direction of Howard Bishop, and indeed of his predecessors, was self-sufficient, with only minor capital improvements until Bishop commenced his school fund. The only application for aid from Maryland during the early 1920s came from John LaFarge, S.J. for two "non-self-supporting missions in the southern part of Maryland in the vicinity of St. Mary's City, where the founders of the Maryland colony landed." Even in St. James Chapel in that city, one of the most remote and poor missions in the archdiocese, there was a parish school. "With great expenditure and begging I have established a little parish school there, which is taught by our St. Joseph Sisters who go there every day in a Ford car," wrote LaFarge to Francis Clement Kelley in December 1922.[4] The Extension Society responded favorably to LaFarge's plea, which, like all applications, was processed through the ordinary, in this case Archbishop Curley.

In 1920, fifteen years after the establishment of the Extension Society, Edwin Vincent O'Hara was appointed the first director of the Catholic Rural Life Bureau in the Social Action Department of the National Catholic Welfare Council (in 1922 changed to Conference). Born and raised in Lanesboro, Minnesota in 1881, O'Hara trained for the priesthood at St. Paul's College and St. Paul's Seminary, where he studied under John A. Ryan, the priest-scholar of Catholic social thought. He volunteered to serve in the archdiocese of Oregon City (later Portland), Oregon, where he remained from 1905 to 1929, except for a year of graduate studies at The Catholic University of America and nearly two years as an army chaplain during the First

World War. He achieved national attention in his struggle for the passage of the first state minimum wage law. He organized a Newman Club, founded a home for working women, and immersed himself in numerous other social and educational problems.[5] In 1920 he addressed the delegates to the Convention at the National Catholic Educational Association on the topic of "The Rural Problem in Its Bearing on Education." His address was based upon his own research including the results of a survey of one thousand rural pastors. David Bovee summarized the address:

> O'Hara . . . urged the strengthening of rural Catholicism because higher rural rather than urban birth rates meant that the future of the church as a whole depended on its being strong in the country. In order to achieve this strengthening O'Hara proposed relying mainly on education. . . . O'Hara urged that Catholic rural educational forces be strengthened by increasing recognition of the rural sector, lay catechists, rural vacation schools, rural religious communities, and religion correspondence courses. Finally, he proposed a comprehensive study of Catholic rural education.[6]

Prior to his address to the N.C.E.A., O'Hara had proposed that the Education and Social Action departments of the N.C.W.C. initiate research and programs on rural life. Rather than merely incorporate the suggestions into the existing departments, the leadership of the N.C.W.C., Bishop Peter Muldoon, decided to establish a rural life bureau and asked O'Hara to become its director. Determined to remain in Oregon, O'Hara accepted the appointment on the stipulation that he remain in his archdiocese. Upon his return to the northwest he was assigned to a rural parish, and besides his maintaining the N.C.W.C. work he remained involved in several social-action projects.

Howard Bishop may not have known of O'Hara's 1920 publication of Catholic rural life issues, but he was deeply affected by O'Hara's article on "The Church and the Rural Community" that appeared in the April 1922 issue of the *Catholic Charities Review*, a publication of the Social Action department of the N.C.W.C. Edwin O'Hara's blend of sociology, economics and religion reflected his indebtedness to his seminary professor, John A. Ryan. After describing the process of urbanization, he focused on the "decay of the rural church" as sym-

bolic of the general malaise of country life. "There is a deep dissatis-
faction with country life because it has become dull and uninspir-
ing. . . . Community requires that there be thought and action in
common; that there shall be a community of interest in the important
things in life, and this requires organization. . . . The work of the
Church, as of all other agencies interested in rural life, will be to
re-create community life in the country."[7]

O'Hara's proposal for rural religious revival included the principles and practices of the cooperative movement, "not merely to make
farming a lucrative occupation, but to knit together the ravelled skein
of life into a thing of beauty as well as an instrument of utility." The
movement would restore a vital mode of life for farming families
because, as they develop such cooperative ventures as collective
credit agencies, mills and dairy interests, as well as cooperative purchasing plans, the rural communities will expand the principle to
form collective theaters, libraries and gymnasiums. The church's
role, according to O'Hara, is to promote the cooperative movement
"and thereby aid America as she has abroad." He referred to a report
on the movement in Europe that illustrated the church's contribution to agricultural cooperation and rural credit. Some graduates of
agricultural colleges were rapidly replacing those clerical leaders who
were committed to fostering new methods of farming. The church
can best be of service if it focused primarily on "stimulating the spirit
of cooperation."[8] In the tradition of John Ireland, O'Hara viewed
the church as closely allied with the positive trends in American
culture.

In a letter to O'Hara, Howard Bishop referred to his "very
thoughtful article" that he had read twice. He enclosed copies of his
April articles in the *Baltimore Catholic Review* and elaborated on his
own frustration at St. Louis Parish. However, Bishop noted that
Catholic education is "only a part of the problem. . . . The cooperative movement opens up the economic phase of the question, with
which I confess I am none too familiar but I hope to become more
so." Bishop agreed with the general direction of that movement: ". . .
it has seemed to me for some time . . . that the Catholic Church has,
in the parochial school for example, a powerful means of combating
the commercial spirit and restoring much of the simplicity . . . of
country life." In closing, Bishop acknowledged that he was "purely
an amateur in a field in which you have long experience," and asked

O'Hara to send him material on the cooperative movement and rural credit unions.[9]

Edwin O'Hara's response was delayed because of a lecture tour, and by the fact that for a period in November 1922, led by Cardinal William H. O'Connell, the opponents of the N.C.W.C. had almost succeeded in abolishing it. O'Hara has just launched a Catholic Rural Life journal, *St. Isidore's Plow,* and invited Bishop to contribute two or three articles for the fall or winter issues.[10] Bishop did not respond to this letter until August of 1923. In his response to O'Hara's invitation to submit articles on rural life, Bishop explained that the demands of developing his parish school prevented him from fulfilling his intention of contributing to the new journal. He then launched into a brief narrative of recent events related to the school. He told O'Hara of Archbishop Curley's support of the movement of rural education and that he felt "we are making headway. My own little school, now nearing completion, is the first thing to be actually accomplished, and the whole diocese is looking on to see the result of my 'experiment.' "[11]

Howard Bishop explained that prior to these positive developments he had been "at a loss to have somebody to talk to about" his views on rural education. He was, therefore, very interested in attending the Catholic Rural Life Convention organized by O'Hara and scheduled for St. Louis, Missouri in November 1923. As if to once again invoke his amateur status he informed O'Hara that at the convention he would only "look on from the sidelines." Noting the coincidence between the convention city and his League of St. Louis formed the previous November, Bishop concluded his letter to O'Hara with the quip: "Surely, St. Louis, King and Crusader, must be interested in our crusade to win the country districts for the Church."[12]

Edwin O'Hara did not wish Bishop to be on the sidelines at the convention; he asked him to contribute his views on what he would like to see included in the program.[13] Of course, Howard Bishop's response emphasized education. After reiterating news about his nearly completed parish school in Clarksville and the success of his League of St. Louis, Bishop told O'Hara that he was determined to struggle for the development of Catholic rural education in general. "To me it seems as a thing that has got to be done whether it is 'possible' or not, and we have got to find a way." However, for the first time he stated his views on the social, economic and religious impact of his scheme for parish schools.

> My thesis is this. The rural Catholic school and community centre will go a long way toward restoring peace of mind and contentment to our rural Catholic population and keeping them on the land, will provide an incentive to many city Catholics (country-fed) to return to the land and fondly; when a rural program is worked out by your bureau, what agency can carry it to the people themselves so quickly and effectively as rural Catholic schools? All of which means eventually, *winning the country districts to the faith, by solving their difficult social and economic problems through the schools.*[14]

Howard Bishop had certainly expanded his vision and refined his views of rural life during his six years in Clarksville. Moreover, he had gained self-confidence as a person and a priest. Yet, he was unaccustomed to expressing himself so openly and so strongly even when he wrote in his diary. He closed his letter to O'Hara with a blend of self-deprecation and determination. "I know you will not take the above explanation [of the thesis] too seriously as it lacks the backing of mature experience and deep study. Six years of close application to heart-breaking conditions of our little parish is all I can claim and I realize it is not enough. But, God willing, I will stick to it until something is accomplished and I thank you for letting me rave a bit."[15]

Edwin O'Hara developed a six point platform for his Rural Life Bureau. It would foster "(1) rural cooperatives; (2) better farm-home conditions; (3) rural health; (4) rural social life; (5) rural culture; and (6) rural church."[16] O'Hara established sixteen state advisory committees for his Bureau but its status within the N.C.W.C. made it the official representative of the hierarchy. Through his association with rural church people, *St. Isidore's Plow* had a subscription list of over 4,000. O'Hara, working with Frederick P. Kenkel of the Central Bureau, called the first meeting of the Catholic Rural Life Conference which, as noted above, Howard Bishop wished to attend. The selection of St. Louis as the convention city derived not only from the fact that it was the home of the Central Verein but also because it was the convention site of the American Country Life Association, an organization that evolved from a Commission on Country Life established by President Theodore Roosevelt in 1908. O'Hara was a member of the Association and was contacted by its president, Henry Isrod, who sought a Catholic representative to attend its annual meeting in 1923.

The first meeting of the National Catholic Rural Life Conference (N.C.R.L.C.) attracted about seventy-five delegates from fifteen states and Canada. There were five bishops, about forty-one priests, representatives of the N.C.W.C., the Central Bureau, the Knights of Columbus, the National Council of Catholic Women and several representatives of religious orders of men. Monsignor Francis Clement Kelley of the Church Extension Society was in attendance, and through his influence Father Thomas Carey, head of the Society's experimental parish project at Lapeer, Michigan, was elected president. Edwin O'Hara was ex-officio executive secretary and administered the conference's daily business; Howard Bishop, the only delegate from the eastern United States, was one of the seven board members elected by the convention. With ultimate responsibility invested in a democratically elected board, the N.C.R.L.C. was quite different from the Bureau, the latter being accountable only to the N.C.W.C. Besides establishing a permanent conference with an organizational structure the constitution stipulated that the purpose of the organization was to "promote the spiritual, social and economic welfare of the rural population." It also set no requirements for membership except an annual fee of one dollar.[17]

Howard Bishop was no doubt stimulated by the program, which included topics ranging from Rural Sodalities and Church Extension in Rural Parishes to the rural home and rural religious drama. He must have been a bit disappointed that there was only one speech on rural education, "Religious Correspondence Courses," by Monsignor Victor Day of Helena, Montana. Of the six resolutions passed by the first convention, two endorsed education projects: Day's correspondence courses and the Bureau's vacation-school plan, a summer catechetical program. Bishop John T. McNicholas of Duluth, Minnesota called for the establishment of a society of diocesan priests and women religious dedicated to the rural missions, but there is no evidence that Bishop and McNicholas had ever referred to this 1923 address during their discussion of the home missioners locating in the archdiocese of Cincinnati.

The N.C.R.L.C. and the American Country Life Association held a joint meeting which, because of several Protestant clergymen in attendance, was in a sense an ecumenical gathering. The Protestant rural reformers had been influenced by the Progressive movement and were "professionals who believed in progress through national study, efficient planning, and organized effort."[18] Edwin O'Hara was, in a sense, a professional while Howard Bishop certainly believed in progress with a popular, scientific method of organization. The Protestants were imbued with a blend of social-gospel, liberal theology, and social action. O'Hara and Bishop were in the stream of Catholic-Americanism that was somewhat influenced by the social gospel, that was open to the religious élan implicit in modern culture, and that was distinctively activist. While the Protestant reformers were ecumenical within their own denominations, they did not evidence any strong ecumenism toward Catholics and Jews. O'Hara, Bishop and others were not consciously ecumenical but did reveal a more open attitude toward Protestants and Jews than did mainstream Catholics. However, Bishop, unlike most rural-Catholic leaders, was certainly motivated to convert the countryside to Catholicism. Perhaps the major distinction between the Protestant and Catholic rural reformers is that the former were more attached to the Progressive movement, and were motivated to modernize the rural communities, while O'Hara and Bishop used modern methods to achieve the traditional goals of rural communalism inspired by the faith.

The historian William L. Bowers concludes that the Protestant reformers were attached to an American agrarian mythology. Recent historiography led by James A. Madison, stresses the Progressivist goals of modernizing the rural community with almost an unstated contempt for the inefficiencies of a religious rural community characterized by denominational competitiveness and an anti-modernist spirit. The reformers referred to such communities as illustrating the disadvantages of being "overchurched" and not open to the development of theology, sociology and culture.[19] Howard Bishop never used the concept of overchurched but he would consider those rural pastors who were merely caretakers rather than activists as perhaps narrowly churched and not open to the Catholic reform movements fostering education, cooperative credit and agricultural improvements.

Madison's views of the progressive character of Protestant rural reformers are substantiated by an article in the *Christian Century*, a portion of which O'Hara reprinted in *St. Isidore's Plow* in the issue immediately preceding the St. Louis convention. "At the coming meeting of the American Country Life Association [in St. Louis], the Roman Catholics will be present in force, though they are a minor factor in the rural life of America. The rural churches are predominantly Protestant and at the present time they are sick unto death." The editorial writer lamented the failures of the rural churches to follow the lead of the rural reformers. "Confronted with the stupidity of a rural ministry, which in our competitive denominationalism can never be better than it is, bright educated young farmers who head up rural organizations can no longer sit under the sermons that are heard in three-fourths of the rural churches. The Catholic hope to profit by the situation is probably futile."[20] Ironically, Howard Bishop considered the Catholics to be far behind the Protestant and Jewish communities in their development of viable rural-life organizations. However, he did not refer to the Protestant reformers but the American Country Life Association as representatives of the movement. He extolled the Jewish Agricultural Society for its colonization programs which, in twenty-five years, had "settled 15,000 families, comprising 75,000 souls, on farm land . . . in every state in the Union. And with them has gone the Rabbi, the synagogue and the religious school, besides a regular system of extension work in agricultural instruction."[21]

When Howard Bishop returned to Clarksville from the charter meeting of the N.C.R.L.C. he was immersed in his work for the League of St. Louis with little time for the new national organization. In February 1924 the League of St. Louis became the League of the Little Flower. In his circular letter to the priests of the archdiocese Bishop wrote, "I know the new name, so suggestive of childhood and the sweet freshness of the open country, and I believe that the dear child saint, so soon to be canonized, will work wonders for our country schools, our League and its members, for she had a special love for the clergy."[22] The new letterhead indicated that the director general was Archbishop Michael Curley and Howard Bishop was spiritual director.

A few years later the League initiated its quarterly bulletin entitled *The Little Flower,* "A Little Paper with a Big Message." Its logo was a white three-petaled flower encircled with "C" and "S" for country schools on each side of the top petal in a background of blue. Bishop described the obvious religious symbolism of the flower for St. Theresa, and the three petals for the Holy Trinity "whose image was so indelibly impressed upon her soul." Bishop also elaborated on how they symbolized the League's mission. "But the flower is at the same time symbolical of God's open country where plant life has its natural habitat. It is small life, the small isolated groups with which the League has to deal, like the little children of those little parishes, which are at once their greatest hope and their greatest anxiety. So small a flower is easily overlooked on the roadside. But pick it up and examine it, it becomes a thing of beauty. So too the country parish and the country child. There are to be found all of the wonderful qualities of God's own handiwork, *unblemished by urban sophistication*. But to bring out these qualities they must have the attention of leaders and *they must have a background in religious culture*. This is the object of the League."[23]

The League had adopted the two education projects fostered by the N.C.R.L.C., religious vacation schools and correspondence courses. Under the by-line of the N.C.R.L.C. News Service it was reported that the Clarksville organization noted "marked success" with the correspondence courses in preparation for first communion. "The plan is to hold a three day retreat at the close of the courses, and to discover whether the children to whom the emergency training has been applied compare favorably in their religious knowledge with those prepared at regular schools."[24] Bishop wrote to O'Hara that he was "ashamed" he had not spent more time on the N.C.R.L.C. work, but his own League had consumed such an enormous amount of time. In August of 1924 Bishop reported that "a month ago we had less than 50 paid up members [of the League]. Today we have more than 7,000. . . . The idea of diocesan aid for rural parishes and . . . schools is established for all time."[25]

In anticipation of the convention in Milwaukee (October 20–23, 1924), Bishop wrote to the president, Thomas R. Carey, informing him of the splendid work in southern Maryland of Father John La-Farge, S.J., who was then attached to Jesuit missions in St. Mary's County, and later became editor of *America* and a founder of the first Catholic Inter-racial Council in New York. "Perhaps you should encourage him to make the meeting," wrote Bishop. "I have written saying that the Jesuits of Southern Maryland should be represented."[26] LaFarge did present a paper at that meeting which also witnessed the appearance of Luigi Ligutti, then a pastor in Woodbine, Iowa, and later long-time executive secretary of the N.C.R.L.C. Bishop was reelected to the board of directors at that convention. "Depend upon me to use my small influence to address the cause in this sector in every possible way," wrote Bishop to O'Hara.[27] The rural pastor had made his mark with the success of the League, but he gained even more prestige in the history of Catholic rural life when he organized the first diocesan rural life conference in October 1925, an event he had conceived almost eighteen months earlier.

In an unsigned article published in *The Baltimore Catholic Review* Bishop noted that the conference "is unprecedented in American Church History. Never before has the diocese brought the problems of its rural missions so emphatically to the fore. . . ." He referred to the chronic rural problems derived from neglect, such as "leakage" from the faith, the proliferation of nominal Catholics and the lack of religious education. "Missionary zeal has not been wanting, but most of it has been expended in our city slums and jails and in connecting the heathen far across the seas." The rural conference was a sign that "things are changing. People are coming to see that there is a *missionary field of wonderful possibilities* just outside the city limits. At last the country pastor and the rural flock are to have their day in court."[28]

The Baltimore Catholic Review publicized the program of the conference on its front page. Monsignor Albert E. Smith, editor of this weekly, was chairman of the conference, and his paper reported fully on the three sessions, and printed excerpts from the speeches. Over 150 priests attended the morning session, restricted to the clergy, at Calvert Hall College, the high school staffed by the Christian Brothers then located diagonally to the southwest of the Baltimore Cathedral where the Catholic Center is located today. Three papers were presented with assigned discussion leaders. "The Rural Parish School" was presented by Joseph Johnson, S.J., pastor of St. Aloysius Church in Leonardtown in St. Mary's County; staffed by the Jesuits the parish had charge of four missions, two of which had schools. Felix M. Kirsch, O.F.M., Cap. of the Capuchin College at Catholic University led the discussion. Monsignor P. J. Conroy, rural dean of the archdiocese and pastor of St. Mary's Church in Bryantown, read a paper on "The Rural Parish and the Negro." John LaFarge, S.J. led the discussion. Conroy emphasized that "the time was at hand . . . when priests and laity must work together in harmony and zeal to show the colored people that the Catholic Church is their best friend." John I. Barrett, the priest superintendent of schools, spoke on "Rural Educational Activity in the Archdiocese of Baltimore."

Clergy and laity gathered for a luncheon at a local hotel; Archbishop Curley presided and the speakers were Dr. Charles J. Galpin, head of the Farm Statistics office at the United States Department of Agriculture, W. Cabell Bruce, United States senator from Maryland, and Edwin V. O'Hara. The afternoon session was entirely in the hands of laymen, both Catholic and Protestant. William Grove presented a paper on "Cooperation of the Laity in Rural Parish Activities." The *Review* reported that Grove "pictured the sad plight that ensues when Catholic laymen fail to cooperate with their pastors. Empty pews, silent church bells, lapses in religious duties . . . were . . . the consequences." D.P. Cahill, president of the Maryland Farm Bureau, spoke on the "American Farm Bureau Federation" as an illustration of agricultural volunteers and farmer advocacy. John T. Kelly, editor of the *Farmers' Magazine,* read a paper on "Cooperative Marketing: A Christian Perspective," a position advocated by O'Hara and Bishop.

The evening session, from 8:00 to 10:30, included a report on rural activities in the archdiocese of New York by Edward R. Moore, the priest head of Catholic Charities in that archdiocese, and a paper on "Music in Rural Churches" by Edward F. Reilly, a priest of Baltimore. Three prominent women representing Catholic organizations presented reports on their rural activities: Mary Mattingly of the Sodality Union of Washington, D.C., Virginia Meyer of the Catholic Daughters of America, and Mrs. J.F. Victory of the National Council of Catholic Women.

The ecumenical character of the conference was highlighted by Archbishop Curley. He said that ". . . the country pastors should cooperate in every way for the betterment of the members of their community, that they should work together for Catholic, Protestant and Jew."[29] The *Review* noted that Howard Bishop closed the day's conference with a comment on the "abundance of food for the body and the scarcity of spiritual food in the country places." It congratulated Bishop for organizing the first diocesan rural life conference, commenting that he ". . . worked day and night to make it all that he wanted it to be. That his fondest wishes were exceeded is not to be construed as luck but merit. Praise, strong and sincere, was given to him by Archbishop Curley."[30]

Bishop organized another diocesan rural life conference in October 1926, held at Catholic University, and his activity became a model for Catholic ruralists throughout the nation. Other than the above mentioned conference in Washington, D.C., there were seven such diocesan conferences in 1926. Toward the end of the 1920s there were fewer conferences, and in 1932 the N.C.R.L.C. established an organization of diocesan directors of rural life.[31] Howard Bishop's conferences were aimed at promoting urban awareness of rural problems, at encouraging local religious, economic and social leaders to foster rural programs, and at strengthening the League of the Little Flower.

Howard Bishop's League had become nearly a full-time occupation for him. Besides managing the annual collection and assembling a list of rural-parish needs for subsidies from the collection, he published an illustrated twelve-page quarterly journal. He wrote most of the substantive articles, and included reports from recipients of needs and human-interest stories that revealed a particular strand of country life. He also solicited advertising and once a year published the results of an annual collection of each parish in the archdiocese. The League had contributed greatly to Catholic rural education. Between 1922 and 1928 the parish schools in rural areas west of the Chesapeake went from 7 to 15 while schools in villages under 2,500 population (excluding suburbs) increased from 8 to 14, making a total increase of 14 schools; school population increased from 1,240 to 2,905 pupils. In 1928 the League's annual collection totaled a little over nineteen thousand dollars.[32]

St. Louis School in Clarksville, for which the League was originally established, was very small with only 57 students in grades one through ten. Since there were four Sisters of Divine Providence who lived in a partitioned area in the back of the school, the teacher-student ratio was low. One parishioner, Mr. R. Hewitt Nickols, who entered the school in the sixth grade, recalled that Howard Bishop "became intensely interested in rural education. . . . But through a determination that is hard to describe, he got the school started and the physical plant built. . . . It had no teaching nuns and he had to scurry around the countryside rather hurriedly to get us a group of teachers. . . . I was always impressed with the man's terrific drive, his determination and his singleness of purpose. He wouldn't let anything interfere with that."[33] Such determination was evident in

Bishop's pursuit of his plan to arrange for the public school buses to transport students to St. Louis. "It was quite an ordeal for parents to get their children to the Catholic school" said Joseph Thompson, a former parishioner. He continued, "After quite a number of meetings, which Father Bishop had with the School Board and the County Commissioners and influential people, he was successful in getting a law passed, with the help of a Protestant friend, Mr. Raymond Pupett, to let the Catholic school children ride in the country school buses."[34] The energetic pastor took a personal interest in the school. "He had a way of coming into the classroom and making us feel like he was one of us in this fashion, that he was an educator," said Sister Mary Bernard, C.D.P., who began teaching there in 1927. "Every so often he would call in my first and second year high school students to give them a lift and they were always edified with his industry and his clergy attitude. He had a way of dealing with children too that made them love him." She also said that "he was a determined man and what he set to do he did. We all more or less walked the chalk line but we enjoyed it because we knew it was for the best, for the good of the children, for the good of the parish; and we all did hop pretty fast under him. . . ." She said that some parishioners were not sympathetic to Bishop's attachment to the school but that they were in a small minority. "It was a kind of parish that was sleepy and it needed somebody that would give it a good push."[35]

Sister Mary of Providence, C.D.P., who arrived at St. Louis School in 1933, said it was "really a spiritual uplift for me knowing him, knowing his deep religious attitudes . . . as well as getting to know his character very well." She was particularly struck by his unassuming life style. "If one would have glanced around in the rectory one could see poverty everywhere. . . . His room was poorly furnished—the poorest mattress, quite thin—and one could know that he was practicing penance. . . . The drapes on the windows were made from feed sacks . . . put together with hairpin lace made from the core of the feed sacks. All around one could see poverty. He himself practiced it. Naturally knowing that he came from a well-to-do family one admired it all the more. While we were asked to practice poverty in the convent, we didn't mind it knowing that our pastor was doing the same thing."[36]

Sister Mary Bernard noted that "Father Bishop was a martyr with his back . . . but he kept going and many times I could see he was in pain." Both sisters commented on his "tendency to be quick-tempered." Sister Mary of Providence "admired him for keeping it completely under control," while Sister Mary Bernard said that she could tell by the "dark look on his face that he was going to explode unless you got out of his way."[37]

Thelma Gatton, a student at St. Louis School during the 1930s, had very vivid memories of Howard Bishop. She listed four ways in which he related to the school children.

1. He played baseball with all of us at least once a week in good weather despite his bad back.
2. Sometimes he ate lunch on the school grounds with us.
3. He supervised us in proper conduct at the card parties held in the school hall which we older children attended as 'Markers' and 'Turners.'
4. He allowed us to come to the little 'house-building' in back of the school to watch and 'help' Mrs. Murphy while they worked on his project, 'The League of the Little Flower.'[38]

These many recollections of Howard Bishop, though taped in the late 1960s and revealing a nostalgic longing for those supposedly uncomplicated times, are nevertheless important for discerning the personality of the man. Despite the rather formal character of his diary, in his pastoral life in Clarksville he appears "homespun" as one priest described him. His penchant for organization and efficiency was balanced by his periodic playfulness with the school children, his unassuming life style, and his general enthusiasm for his parish.

In his small parish in Clarksville, Howard Bishop developed a strong identity as a rural pastor. He expanded his sphere of influence through the diocesan press, the League of the Little Flower, and the National Catholic Rural Life Conference. In 1917 at the Shrine of the Sacred Heart in Mount Washington his pastor threatened him with scorn as if he could make no significant contribution. Six years later he was considered the spokesman for rural missionaries in the archdiocese of Baltimore and was elected to the board of directors of the N.C.R.L.C. No one ever commented on his charm, wit, or sense of humor. Instead they pointed to his administrative abilities, his single-mindedness, and above all his strong-willed determination. However, his articles in the *Review* and in the bulletin of the League of the Little

Flower reveal a writing style studded with charm, wit, and humor, and with a flare for the polemic. Through his experiences at Clarksville he came to realize directly the needs of rural communities. He articulated a very idealistic vision of rural life in contrast to his picture of the bleak industrial life of the city. His vision became more refined and more nuanced during his tenure as president of the N.C.R.L.C., 1928–1935, particularly as America experienced the severe crisis of the Great Depression.

CHAPTER 5

Leader of the Rural Church
1928–1936

Howard Bishop's drive and determination made St. Louis an "ideal rural parish." He established a 4-H Club at the school, initiated agricultural projects and egg routes for the children, and soon after enabling legislation was passed by the Maryland Assembly, he organized the first credit union in the state. He had become *the* spokesman for rural missions and schools in the archdiocese.[1] At the 1927 annual convention of the N.C.R.L.C. at Lansing, he was elected vice-president of the conference. In an address entitled, "Putting Romance into Farming," Bishop shared with the Catholic ruralists his strategies in Clarksville that aim "to inculcate an intelligent love of the land in the children of the land." He told them of his 4-H Club that is dependent upon the sisters' own self-education in agricultural subjects. St. Louis School held lectures by county agents and sponsored agricultural projects. Agrarianism is most evident in the curriculum; "nature study is cultural as well as practical" and is infused as a means of cultivating " 'an intelligent love of the land' . . . How can one appreciate art and poetry without some knowledge of nature?"

In an eloquent peroration, Howard Bishop reveals his own qualities as well as his self-image as priest:

> Next to the priesthood there is no calling in the world so full of romance—the quality that grips the imagination and fires the will as the profession of agriculture. It has furnished inspiration for the genius of poet and artist from the beginning. Our Lord drew heavily upon it for words and images with which to teach this most beautiful lesson and always in such ways as to suggest that the love

of the soil and crops and birds was strong in Him whose first human breath was drawn in a shepherd's cave.

It was the lack of enthusiasm among the farmers which pre-dated the agricultural depression of the day and exacerbated the flight to urban areas. "Even our rural schools, up to recent years, had done nothing to show their pupils that the farmer's life could be beautiful."[2] Howard Bishop was not unaware of the farmers' struggle for survival. Their lives were analogous to those of rural priests: bouts with the tedium of work, with loneliness and with disappointment at the slow pace of progress. The romantic calling of the priesthood with its imagery of the Lord's vineyard sustained him; the same image should inspire disillusioned farmers to keep faith in the nobility of their calling to their own vineyards.

Howard Bishop was the keynote speaker at the 1928 convention at St. Benedict's Abbey, Atchison, Kansas. After a long introduction justifying the church's role in the development of all facets of rural culture—"public health, hospitals, athletics, education, art, music, drama, work and recreation"—he concluded with the assertion that "The Church, I say, has a mission in the non-religious field, to study, to sympathize and, where it prudently can, to aid in the solution of the vexing problems of life by applying to them the age-old principles of the Gospel."

There are some who tend to limit the activity of the church to things spiritual on the assumption that this emphasis will lead to a religious permeation of culture. Bishop implicitly rejected the dichotomy between religion and culture as he stressed the cultural dimension of religion and the religious dimension of culture. However, his rural basis led him to identify rural culture with "nature" and to elaborate on a theology of nature as sacred space. He opened with an historical rendering of Jesus' "divine affinity for the countryside."

The environment and life of the farm furnish a *perfect* setting for an ideal Christian life. . . . I remind you how Christ Himself loved open places. Even the little town of Bethlehem, small as it was, was too large, too crowded, too busy to afford Him space to be born. The beasts of the field shared their rude shelter with Him and His first visitors were the shepherds from the hillsides led by an angel choir. Could anything be more sublimely beautiful than the opening scene in the greatest drama the world has ever witnessed? And the climax of it all, when He offered Himself to His Father on the cross, was enacted outside of city walls. Throughout His public ministry we find Him often in the fields, by streams and ravines, on the mountains much more than in the cities and towns. . . .

From this narrative of rural christology he launched into a theology of nature:

Rural life has changed since the time of Christ but the same characteristics are present now as then. The country is still the God-made habitation of man as distinguished from the man-made city habitation. All of its noble furniture, from its star studded ceilings to its undulating carpet of green, from its forests and streams to its towering mountains bears the fingerprints of the Master Craftsman, and the inhabitants know no cheap substitutes have been imposed upon them.

Bishop portrayed farm life in realistic terms of hard work that requires "self-denial, mutual consideration, charity. . . . In short we have in the country districts plenty of hard invigorating toil in which man is co-laborer with his God in the task of feeding the world."[3]

Bishop's popular theology of nature and rural life included the portrayal of the rural environment as "the simple life . . . the most congenial habitat" for the growth of Christianity. "Can there be found a people so well prepared by their environment and toil and hardship to receive with profit the Gospel of Jesus Christ? There is a striking kinship between nature at its best and the super-natural." By working with the "chosen people" of rural America, "who are at the headwaters of our native-born populations, [the church] . . . will strengthen and sustain its work in every other quarter." The emphasis upon "native-born" may have been in implicit contrast to the "foreign-born of the cities," with the latter presumably of inferior status. The vice-president of the conference then listed the ways in which the church should fulfill its particular mission to rural communities. It must above all raise "the consciousness [of Catholic rural people] of the nobility of the profession they pursue [because] few farming people are possessed of such a consciousness today." Secondly, through parish and vacation schools the church should demonstrate to the farmers of the future that they will have "improved methods of farming, readier access to markets and friends than ever before, [and] a life of useful achievement and quiet, independent contentment that is found nowhere else." Bishop's third mission activity is for the church to be actively engaged in promoting cooperative movements, credit unions, and agricultural projects such as seed-testing and pure-bred herds, in short, all "forward-looking activities [that] are helping to hold the best type of forceful imaginative men and women on the farms where they can get the most out of their religion and give the best service to their fellow men."[4]

The church's final role is to "dethrone the dollar-mark from its place of paramount importance in the people's lives." Though the church must support federal and state programs, farmers "certainly need courage and confidence to bear their trials until relief can come, and these qualities demand a strong spirituality. They must be helped to appreciate spiritual values. . . . It must open up to him the vast spiritual assets that lie hidden in his environment . . . for it is in the country a strength of faith and a depth of spirituality that will bind the farmer to the land." By developing this rural spirituality and ecclesiology the church "can do more than any other agency that exists to insure to the nation, yes, and to itself, a permanent Christian civilization on the land."[5] Howard Bishop's theology of rural-nature was a romantic vision of the idyllic life of the yeoman farmer. He was indeed preaching a crusade for the church to recover the holy land of agrarian America.

The N.C.R.L.C. was impressed with Bishop's popular theology of rural life, his enthusiasm, and his work in the annual archdiocesan programs on the local level. Bishop's League of the Little Flower also contributed to his reputation as a leader. The board of directors of the national conference nominated him as candidate for president at the annual convention held at St. Benedict's Abbey. The delegates followed suit and he was duly elected to the office on October 4, 1928. The first formal message of the new president was in the form of a Christmas greeting to the members, published in *The Catholic Rural Life*. After noting the commercial exploitation of the season, Bishop elaborated on the Bethlehem tableau as one "of serenity . . . the sweetness of perfect peace. Peasant and Prince and beast of the field . . . there is perfect fellowship, perfect harmony, perfect peace." Turning to a direct Christmas greeting to "our many friends and readers," he wrote that the Catholic rural folk "were strangely reminiscent of the group at Bethlehem. I see sturdy men of field and flock." He portrayed the wise men as having been drawn "from the distant cities [to] . . . the quiet country places where the Saviour loves to dwell." He saw priests "who, like the Blessed Mother and St. Joseph, have brought the Saviour there to be adored and loved . . . by all." Bishop extended his Christmas wish of peace, particularly "for a more happy, more contented and more permanent Catholic population on the land."[6]

Shortly after Bishop became president of the N.C.R.L.C. Herbert Hoover defeated Al Smith. Though there are historians who challenge the religious factor in the election, most Catholics attributed the Smith defeat to his religion. The so-called tribal twenties were characterized by immigrant restrictionism, and the rise of anti-Catholicism, anti-Semitism, and nativism. Wartime idealism had given way to post-war cynicism. The anti-German sentiment which had been aroused by wartime propaganda had become a general xenophobic attitude.

The anti-urban expressions of Howard Bishop were reflected in exaggerated form among fundamentalist Protestant ruralists who identified the city with foreigners, papists, and Jews. They decried the "mongrelization" of America and viewed it as symptomatic of a social malaise that required a total war to be waged by the "forces of righteousness" against the Jewish, Catholic, Negro, and foreign forces of evil. The Klan suffered a severe decline by 1928, but because Al Smith was not only a Catholic but a "wet" (i.e. anti-prohibition) Democrat as well, his candidacy fostered a revival of the three R's of the anti-Catholic animus, "Rum, Romanism and Rebellion."[7] However, anti-Smith groups had more respectable spokespersons than those of the Klan. One southern clergyman acknowledged Smith's right to run for president "even though a Catholic. And we have a right to vote against him because he is a Catholic . . . we are strongly persuaded that Catholicism is a degenerate type of Christianity. . . ." One southern official addressed a large gathering in New York: "Shall we have a man in the White House who acknowledges allegiance to the outcast on the Tiber, who hates democracy, public schools, Protestant personages, individual rights, and everything that is essential to independence?"[8]

Howard Bishop's initial reaction to the "tribal twenties" was to remain silent. Such was not the case in November 1928, when he directly responded to the "present outburst of religious hatred." In an article in *The Little Flower* Bishop said that there was a definite lesson to be learned from the climate of intolerance. "Bigotry, be it known, feeds on ignorance. . . . Hence it is that many cultured people, well informed on general topics but misinformed about the Church, fall for it and fall heavily. Hence it is also that bigotry has its greatest following in sections where [there is] . . . a comparatively low standard of education and little or no contact with Catholic life and thought."[9]

Conservative Catholics had low expectations of the Protestant majority. They did not thrive well in a condition of religious pluralism and were critical of American values. Howard Bishop and other descendants of the liberalism of John Ireland and James Gibbons urged a strategy of enlightenment, through education, to overcome the ignorance of bigotry. Bishop seized the opportunity to call for more country parochial schools as "the best antidote that has been invented for bigotry." Such a strategy for Catholic schools was considered divisive to the rural community by many Protestants of even a benign attitude toward Catholicism. It is necessary to recall, however, that Bishop viewed the parish school as a community center to reach out to all rural people. What is intriguing for those looking for signs of his later patterns of home mission activity is that Bishop issued "a call for intensified missionary activity in our rural sections." He did not specify the strategies and tactics that were to guide the activity but he inferred that it was aimed at evangelizing Catholics so that they may be prepared "to meet senseless passion with calm reason and calumny with facts."[10]

As president of the N.C.R.L.C. Howard Bishop led its executive committee to pass a measure to circulate a questionnaire among five hundred Catholic leaders, including all the bishops, on the topic of religious intolerance in rural areas of the nation. Bishop published the results of the survey in the December issue of *The American Ecclesiastical Review*. As a means "for winning a more favorable opinion of the church from non-Catholics" most of the respondents listed the promotion of Catholic literature; others were more direct-action oriented, suggesting missions, lectures, the "rural equivalent of street-preaching," and radio talks aimed at explaining the faith and perhaps making converts in the process."[11] A few respondents suggested a cen-

tral agency to deal directly with bigotry.[12] Archbishop Michael Curley
urged "a friendly, kindly attitude of the pastor towards the non-Catholics he meets."[13] Though not specified as Catholic anti-defamation
work there were proposals that referred to the Knights of Columbus
and the Laymen's League of Georgia and other groups that had
organized efforts to expose the anti-Catholic prejudices underlying
articles in newspapers and pamphlets. Almost all the respondents
called for a positive campaign of education of Catholics to improve
their knowledge of the faith. Francis Clement Kelley, founder of the
Extension Society and bishop of Oklahoma City, called for a movement to evangelize rural America and a national organization "to
bring the truth to those who know it not."[14] Howard Bishop had
clearly stated that he did not interject his own views on the proper
responses to anti-Catholic prejudice, but he revealed his support for
certain ideas by allocating a large amount of space to Kelley's proposal and those dealing with the need for a national organization to
deal with prejudice.[15]

Howard Bishop presented a digest of the questionnaire at the October 1929 meeting of the N.C.R.L.C. in Des Moines. A discussion
followed, led by John LaFarge, S.J., editor of *America,* by P.J. Boland,
general secretary of the Catholic Truth Society of England, and by
Richard Reid of the Georgia Laymen's Association. According to the
minutes "some practical steps should be taken to remove the prejudice which all agreed existed." The two suggestions which met with
unanimous approval were "to do everything possible to instruct our
Catholic laity and to urge them to take an active part in civic and
community affairs, at the same time leading exemplary Catholic
lives." A resolution was passed that called upon Bishop to appoint a
committee of three "to draw up some practical plan of action [to be]
submitted to the conference at the next meeting." Bishop appointed
Bertrand L. Conway, the priest-author of *The Question Box,* Dennis
McCarthy, former editor of the *Sacred Heart Review,* and Richard
Reid. Bishop O'Hara served as an *ex officio* member; so it was called
the committee of five.[16]

In a circular letter to board members asking for "constructive
suggestions," Bishop expressed his own ideas on the need for appropriate strategies to counter anti-Catholicism. After noting that there
are many "worth-while activities to stem the tide of bigotry and win
more converts to the Faith," he stressed the need for a national effort

to coordinate these works in the rural areas where bigotry thrives. "It is here that the need for action is felt most keenly because Protestantism with all its false teaching about life and its secret enmity to the Church of Christ is . . . most strongly established. Protestant views about marriage, childhood, civic virtue, etc., predominate and Catholicity is all but overwhelmed with the result that there are annually great losses to the Church." In the cities public opinion is "strongly leavened with Catholic thought and sentiment," but in the rural areas that leaven is non-existent. Though he stated that these were the ideas of the "leadership" of the Rural Life Conference that had engendered the concern for a plan of action, it was Bishop who articulated these notions. He called for the N.C.R.L.C. to emphasize three major points:

1. That here in the rural sections of America is at once the most important and most difficult battleground for the Church of Christ.
2. That all apologetic and missionary efforts now being put forth should be co-ordinated, adopted and applied with special emphasis to the rural sections. . . .
3. That this should be accomplished either through a central national bureau or a national organization or both. The central agency . . . should keep contact with all present local efforts . . . [and] serve as a clearing house of ideas and materials for a permanent nation wide crusade for souls that will make use of every method known to missionary science in order to achieve its end.[7]

Rarely do we have such a clear expression of Howard Bishop's perspective on the Protestant-Catholic conflict in rural America. As noted earlier, the tribal twenties had witnessed a very intensive anti-Catholic movement, one which was most extensive in the rural areas. These are the rough edges of religious pluralism that surface periodically; often they were precipitated by social and economic conditions, but usually they contained an element of historic hostility. Howard Bishop tended to accent this hostility in order to engender a crusade, but one that should be infused with the science of missiology. Such a strategy conforms with his general distrust of emotional motivation and his penchant for scientific principles of organizational efficiency.

At the 1930 meeting at Springfield, Illinois the conference formally established the Confraternity of Christian Doctrine (C.C.D.). At Edwin O'Hara's suggestion this action represented the widespread popularity of religious education, particularly the vacation-school program. Subsequent to this motion the conference decided to give the C.C.D. responsibility for the anti-bigotry campaign. In his presidential address of 1930 Howard Bishop spoke of the "inferiority complex" of rural Catholics who experience "ignorance and hostility toward the Church," especially when these Catholics are not well supported by "a live parish organization." In contrast to the triumphal tone and the call for a crusade to win converts among Protestants that was characteristic of his private circular letter, Howard Bishop's public address was respectful of religious pluralism and he encouraged enlightenment rather than militancy:

> There is a growing sentiment among Catholic leaders everywhere that ample opportunity should be afforded our non-Catholic brethren to become acquainted with Catholic belief and practice, that ignorance may be enlightened and hostility disarmed and a sentiment at least tolerant and fair developed through Catholic action among vast numbers who are now our enemies in the best of faith. It is urged that Catholic action should go even beyond this point and propose to itself the objective of greater annual harvests of converts to the Church. The Catholic rural conference . . . has thrown itself into this movement for non-Catholic enlightenment to bring its blessings to the rural communities of America. . . . If ignorance about the Church has bred hatred among so many of our departed brethren, let us see if kindly enlightenment will not lead to love.

While Catholics with a preservationist attitude viewed religious pluralism as threatening to those traditions they perceived as essential to the faith, Howard Bishop adopted a moderate transformationist position, one which saw not opposition but compatibility between Catholicism and pluralism. In his 1930 address he expressed his trust in enlightenment and the American sense of fair play. Though his private utterances on this topic were uninhibited, he never doubted the inherent values of the American ideals of religious liberty, interdenominational understanding, and civility. Rather than foster the religious separatism so dominant in Catholic culture, Howard Bishop encouraged mutual understanding between Catholics and Protestants. It would be inaccurate to characterize his attitude as ecumenical, but it was progressive.

In his 1931 address Howard Bishop implied that the ten-year depression in agriculture was partially responsible for the general depression of the era. He spoke of the role of the church and the Rural Life Conference in responding to the temporal hardships of the farmers as well as to their religious needs. However, he emphasized the ways in which the economic depression affects religious behavior rather than the means by which the church should respond to tragic dislocations endemic in the economy.[18]

In his presidential address of the following year, Howard Bishop concentrated on "six excellent reasons why the church is particularly concerned with the welfare of its rural people." The first four reasons were reiterations of his notions of agrarian society, e.g. farming has "been sanctified by religion and by God"; it nourishes family life; "childhood is the true wealth of the rural sections"; rural life is religiously, economically, and socially a "wholesome" calling. The fifth reason concerned the way the church responds to the "cruel economic injustices . . . the farming people have suffered. . . . Suffering draws the church like a lodestone." He invoked the virtues of Christian charity and saw their implementation in farm cooperatives. "The wolves of avarice will make a meal of . . . [the farmer] if he tries to go it alone. Stick together, educate the young to the value of solidarity and by your massed action, not only in buying and selling but in controlling supply and making your just demands felt, you will secure the better times we all fervently pray for." Because farmers struggled for a "home and a living . . . as part of the equipment of . . . [their] business . . . [they were] ahead of . . . [their] city brethren. And the spiritual values of family contentment, peace, religion, the things that money can't buy, you have also." The sixth reason was the church's concern for the "religious handicaps" of rural Catholic people because they have traditionally been "undervalued" and without an adequate religious education and pastoral ministry. Since 1922, when his first article in the *Catholic Review* appeared, Bishop had dedicated enormous pastoral energy toward checking the leakage from the rural Catholic Church by fostering parish schools and vacation schools, and, as president of the Catholic Rural Life Conference, by promoting C.C.D. programs.

In his address Howard Bishop urged the rural community "not to be too trustful of the nostrums of professional politicians."[9] Though raised in a Republican family his attack upon the avarice of urban industrialists and his promotion of rural cooperatives placed him in opposition to the dominant trends in the Republican party. Not until the 1932 political campaign, in which the "rugged individualism" of Hoover was pitted against the pragmatic reformism of Franklin D. Roosevelt, did Howard Bishop become very ideological as he lashed out at the structural evils of unbridled capitalism.

At the tenth annual convention of the N.C.R.L.C. in Dubuque, Iowa, on October 20, 1932, Bishop placed himself squarely behind the reformist movement.

> Let us get away from the old superstition that the country cannot be run unless the heads of government are closely allied with the big business interests of the country. . . . Why should they be chosen our guardian angels? Have recent events proved them worthy of such a trust?

Prior to 1932 Bishop and the conference had advocated rural self-help through cooperatives. Because laws favoring business, such as the tariff, were severely reducing the farmers' international market, creating a surplus in the domestic market which drove down the prices of agricultural products, Bishop advocated the legislative program of the National Farm Organization, a program that included vigorous state interference in the so-called free market. He also criticized the advances of big business into the agricultural sector (today's agribusiness) and reminded the delegates that humanity was not created for farms but farms were created for humanity. He was in accord with the conference's endorsement of the domestic allotment program that was intended to provide federal relief to farmers hurt by the tariff.

The core of Howard Bishop's 1932 address was the proposal "to lay the foundation for a Catholic Land Movement in America." Not only would the movement attract the unemployed from the cities but it would also serve "to reconstruct the social order on sound Christian principles after the minds of Leo XIII and Pius XI."[20] Because the church is the "custodian" of faith, morality, and civilization, it should foster a society that would "promote the reign of justice and charity. . . . What better time is there for us to foster the widest distribution of property ownership that is the basis of the church's economic ideal?"[21]

In the Spring issue of *The Little Flower* Bishop named the colonization movement "Landward." Prior to the depression, Catholic leaders, particularly in the rural life movement, did not advocate such measures. Howard Bishop indicated that he had studied the topic of colonization; he referred to a "well planned" movement of Catholics in Great Britain. He wrote admiringly of Chesterton's leadership in the Distributist League in England. A group disillusioned with both capitalism and socialism, the League advocated a wider distribution of productive property to assure the maximum amount of freedom.[22]

In May of 1933 Howard Bishop published the first issue of *Landward*, "A Quarterly Bulletin of the Catholic Rural Movement."[23] As president of the N.C.R.L.C. Bishop immediately proposed that his quarterly be adopted as the conference's official publication. The conference's first journal was *St. Isidore's Plow*, edited by Edwin O'Hara and published from 1922 to 1925. Father Michael Schlitz of Des Moines assumed the editorship of its successor, *Catholic Rural Life*. In 1927 the latter moved to Washington, D.C. where Frank O'Hara, professor of economics at The Catholic University of America, and the brother of Edwin, took charge of the journal until it discontinued publication in 1930 due to lack of funds.[24]

In a circular letter to the board members of the conference Bishop explained the origin of *Landward*.

> Much of the material I have published in *The Little Flower* has been of interest to our movement nationally. So the thought struck me: Why not let the forms remain after printing our diocesan quarterly, discard the local matter, put in its place more material of interest in our national organization, change the headings and let 'er go, thus producing what might be used as an organ for the . . . Conference?

Because the major portion of the printing costs for typesetting would be paid by *The Little Flower*, four issues of *Landward* (both quarterlies came to eight 8 × 11 pages) could be produced and mailed for $200 annually.[25]

Bishop Edwin O'Hara wrote a congratulatory letter to Bishop that appeared as a special feature on the front page of the first issue of

Landward. "May I compliment you on your resourcefulness and vision," wrote O'Hara. "Each year sees the movement gain momentum under your wise and energetic leadership. . . ."[26] With the appeal of low costs and with O'Hara's endorsement *Landward* was adopted as the conference's formal organ at the annual meeting in Milwaukee.[27]

The frantic pace of change during the first two years of the Roosevelt administration was reflected in Howard Bishop's diary, which had been discontinued from 1925 to 1933. He recorded the significant pieces of legislation relating to relief, recovery, and reform as if he were aware that his notes were for posterity. The pace of his own activities intensified during this same period. Besides editing the diocesan and national quarterlies he was deeply involved in all the facets of colonization, or, as he referred to them, rural rehabilitation projects. He was a very active lobbyist in Washington for the Bankhead Bill to provide the funds for rural settlement; he met with prominent spokesmen of the back-to-the-land movement ranging from Wall Street pundits to the co-founder of the Catholic Worker, Peter Maurin. He devised his own rural rehabilitation project for Clarksville and served on various relief committees in Baltimore and Howard County. He experienced severe challenges to his leadership of the N.C.R.L.C. to which he responded with characteristic single-mindedness. Woven throughout all these projects was Howard Bishop's drive to expand the Catholic presence in rural America.

In the first issue of *Landward* Bishop reiterated his views on the need for the church to harness the back-to-the-land movement with solid colonization schemes, but for the first time he stated his disillusionment with the "discredited capitalistic system built upon individual greed." He further indicated his disdain for that system that engendered a "lust of pleasure and the deification of riches" and "a dependence of the masses upon their industrial overloads." He concluded that "the unemployment epidemic seems to bring back, along with sanity, the love of home and land. It is recognized that the good sweet earth, however oversupplied and undervalued its fruits may seem for the moment to have become, is after all the real source of wealth." The return to the land symbolized "the foundation for a real civilization upon which an enduring Christian structure can be found." The church's role was twofold: each diocese should establish a rural-life bureau which would be directed by priests and which would organize and facilitate the process of movement into rural colonies; secondly, the local church would guide rural development in those areas where there are pre-existing parish structures. Because the nineteenth century church ignored the rural areas, thousands (Bishop exaggerated the figure to millions) of Catholic families gradually lost their faith. "Now while the molten metal of a new social order is again poured into rural molds, now before the landward movement cools . . . now is the time of all times for Catholic leaders to be busy influencing and directing the landward march of our Catholic people. . . ."[28]

The call for enlightened activism was based upon Bishop's own experience. In Baltimore the League of the Little Flower fostered rural settlement and became an agency to facilitate Catholic rural developments. Bishop's utopianism was balanced by his tenacious zeal. Several months before the publication of *Landward* he began consulting with individuals committed to the colonization movement. In late January 1933 he traveled to New York in order to better acquaint himself with trends during the depression.

The editor of *Commonweal*, Michael Williams, was an enthusiastic advocate of the movement. Bishop met with his assistant as well as leaders of societies organized to promote rural settlements. Through John LaFarge he met an editorial writer of the *Wall Street Journal*, who elaborated on the economic and social crisis. When Bishop asked him if the depression was cyclical, the writer responded: "It is cataclysm, i.e. catastrophic, resembling in its importance the change that came over the world with [the] fall of Rome in the 5th Century. Adjustments will be a thing of years, generations. . . . The complete breakdown of the individualistic civilization begun at [the] Reformation has taken place."[29]

At first Bishop pursued the role of broker for families wishing to settle on the land. He advertised in the League's quarterly and in secular newspapers that he would help such families find property at a reasonable rate and in vital rural parishes. He also worked with real estate agents who provided leads for property. He soon became interested in acquiring large tracts of land that could be divided for subsistence farming or rural rehabilitation projects for the urban unemployed.

Howard Bishop and other Catholic rural activists were enthusiastically in support of the Bankhead amendment of the Industrial Recovery Act which became law during the first one hundred days of the

New Deal. It provided $25,000,000 for subsistence homesteads. The terms of the Agricultural Adjustment Act that allotted funds to farmers on the basis of animal and crop restrictions were viewed as necessary stop-gap relief measures. Bishop stated that "we hail with joy the passage of the Bankhead Amendment [as] a permanent blessing of the New Deal."[30]

While Bishop was developing his own plan for a colony in Howard County, he was promoting Father Luigi Ligutti's proposal to establish a rural-industrial colony in Granger, Iowa, a center of a severely depressed mining industry. By early 1934 fifty families sought to participate in the program. Each would receive five acres that included a home and a small barn for animals and chickens. Though it was not to be an exclusively Catholic colony, the majority of the members were of Italian and Slavic origin. Federal loans to subsidize the project would be paid by the miners who worked about eighty days a year. The five-acre homesteads would provide for the economic integrity of the family and would not produce a surplus to add to the supply of farm products.[31]

Almost from this proposal's inception, Ligutti had been in consultation with Howard Bishop. The two priests had known each other at St. Mary's Seminary but their common agrarianism brought them in close contact. The proposal for the Granger settlement brought the Italian immigrant priest and the president of the N.C.R.L.C. close together. The latter relied upon Bishop as a well-known person acquainted with the various agencies in the nation's capital. As early as October of 1933 Bishop urged Ligutti to revise his proposals with greater attention to detail in order to satisfy the Homestead Bureau, housed in the Department of the Interior. In subsequent letters Bishop indicated that he intended to represent Ligutti in the negotiations with Dr. M.L. Wilson, the administrator of the homestead program.[32] Early on in the evolution of his proposal Ligutti told Bishop that "if it succeeds it will be due largely to your work."[33] After a few visits with Dr. Wilson, Bishop admitted that he could not "do justice to Fr. Ligutti's proposal. I have pushed your project with all my might."[34] But in response to particular questions on the social composition of the community Bishop was unable to provide accurate information. He therefore urged Ligutti to come to Washington, D.C. A week later Ligutti and Bishop made their rounds of government offices. At the office of an Iowa senator Bishop "dictated to his stenographer a letter to Dr. Wilson endorsing Fr. L's scheme for the senator to sign."[35] Upon Ligutti's return to Iowa, Bishop continued to "lobby" for the project. On March 8 Bishop received a letter from Ligutti that his plan had been accepted. In *Landward* Bishop wrote that "Father Ligutti's project marks the first step in the Catholic back-to-the-land movement about which we have been dreaming and praying for many years."[36]

Concurrent with his work on behalf of Ligutti's proposal Bishop was seeking support for his own rural rehabilitation project. On February 15, 1934 he presented to Dr. Wilson a "tentative preliminary draft of my plan for a subsistence Homestead Colony at Clarksville."[37] His plan was based upon the need for federal loans to cover the purchase of three farms, each of which was about 130 acres. He proposed to subdivide this acreage into 40 farms ranging from $2\frac{1}{2}$ to 15 acres. The settlers would limit their farms to "non-competitive production, such as truck gardening, fruit, poultry or rabbits." The families would engage in "the cultivation of home arts and crafts by adults and young folks of both sexes." The community's cash crops, fruit and vegetables, would be sold to a cannery, owned and operated by the settlers. A secondary outlet for their garden produce would be a roadside market. Settlers would be paid "on a relief basis" for building their homes, cannery, roads, and other community improvements. The plan was rejected by Wilson and his assistant because it did not provide for adequate cash income.[38]

In his revised plan, which was a fifteen page refinement of his original application of four pages, Bishop attempted to resolve the problem by arranging for tenants to pay off their loans on a cash or share basis. Because there would be only local industry for tenants to supplement their homestead income, they would still be dependent upon state relief funds. The plan was detailed in design. The forty to fifty settlers would be chosen from a pool of unemployed in Baltimore who had had some previous farming experience, with preference given to those individuals involved in a subsistence garden project that Bishop and others had directed in 1932–33.[39]

With experience in lecturing to graduate students of rural sociology, one of whom did a master's thesis on Clarksville, Howard Bishop composed his proposal with careful attention to specifics: "The centre of this tract is within a mile of St. Louis Catholic Church, School Hall and recreation grounds and within one and a half miles of Linthicum Methodist Protestant Church and Clarksville's large Consolidated Public School and High School with its assembly hall and recreation fields. . . ." Bishop consulted with commercial and federal land bankers as well as state agronomists. He had considered a bond issue on the "colonists' assets and prospective earnings" but was advised that farm securities were not "worth a darn." Since even his revised plan was entitled "revised tentative plan," he was circulating it through various agencies besides Wilson's homestead program.[40]

Throughout his 1934 diary there were many references to his colony plan. He subscribed to the *Catholic Worker* which, coincidentally, was first published in May of 1933, the date of the first issue of *Landward*. He referred to the *Catholic Worker* as "that vigilant champion of the rights of the downtrodden regardless of color or creed."[41] Donald Powell, who wrote for both *Landward* and the *Catholic Worker*, introduced Bishop's plan for a colony to Dorothy Day. Powell informed Bishop that she was interested in his farm project.[42] Howard was grateful but told Powell that he preferred "no publicity. I will explain why to Miss Day when I get an opportunity to see her in New York."[43]

In December Dorothy Day intended to visit the Baltimore-Washington area and see Howard Bishop. However, as she explained in a letter to Bishop, "preparations for our picket line" prevented her from making the trip, "but I am using the ten dollars you sent so generously to send Peter [Maurin] down to you as he is very anxious to meet you. . . . When Peter has thoroughly exhausted you with discussion he wishes to proceed on to Woodstock . . . and then to Washington."[44] Two days later Maurin, Bishop, and Powell shared a meal and discussion at the Clarksville rectory. "Very interesting. . . . Peter, the spokesman,"[45] recorded Bishop. Maurin and he met later that week. "[I] took him to Woodstock College after supper. . . . None of the Fathers came to [the] parlor and the expected invitation to him to stay the night and address the students never came." Maurin spent the night at the St. Louis rectory and left for New York the following day.[46] Between these visits with Maurin, Bishop wrote to Dorothy Day that he was "very much pleased with Peter Maurin's visit." He encouraged her to notify him when she planned to visit the area so he could "arrange a meeting in Clarksville. I know there are others besides myself who would be glad to be present."[47] Day never made the trip to Clarksville but the Bishop–Day association remained amicable.

In the summer of 1934 Howard Bishop visited colonization communities in Quebec and the rural cooperative program in Antigonish,
Nova Scotia. The former had its origin some fifteen years before the
Depression, but the project was reorganized during the economic
crisis. Unemployed from the cities were paid $600 a year in relief
while they cleared the land, built log houses and developed their one
hundred acre farms. Bishop visited the village of LaFerte formed in
early 1934. In *The Little Flower* he described the walk "over a rough
trail through the wilderness of this new farm city, over soggy
ground . . . littered with stumps and fallen trees." He concluded that
to achieve the goal of a viable community "is simply impossible."
Then he visited another community of "happy little villages" with
"their comfortable parish plants" that were from five to twenty-five
years old.[48] He revised his former conclusion that indeed it was not
only possible but ideal to establish rural colonies. No doubt this experience encouraged him to pursue his own Clarksville project while his
article was intended to provide historical support of the local landward movement in his parish.

Antigonish had been a Catholic model for cooperative enterprise
for several years. Composed of farmers of Scottish and Scots-Irish
extraction, the community was affected by the Catholic Action movement and the social thought of the encyclicals. M.M. Coady, a priest-
faculty member of St. Francis Xavier University and recipient of a
Ph.D. in education at The Catholic University of America, was head
of the University Extension Program with its study-club on the "new
social order" and on rural-cooperatives. "The economic doctrine of
cooperation based on the Christian virtues of justice and charity . . .
became the principal theme of the new Extension office," wrote Howard Bishop. The Clarksville pastor must have been particularly struck
by the cooperative vegetable cannery at Antigonish, for, as mentioned above, a cannery was a component of his homestead plan.[49]
Also, shortly after his return to Baltimore, Bishop proposed a study
club on the Antigonish model. He wrote to Coady that "cooperation
on the Antigonish model will form an important part of my plan . . .
and I don't mind telling you I have a great hope of success."[50]

Despite his encouraging experiences in Canada, the agricultural
conditions in the United States where there was more farm acreage in
Iowa than in all of Nova Scotia and Quebec could not sustain the type
of rehabilitation project envisioned by Howard Bishop. The federal

and state relief agencies responded with guarded optimism to the plan, but those in the Departments of Agriculture and the Interior were opposed to the absence of a viable income-producing component. On August 28, 1934 Howard Bishop interviewed Henry Wallace, secretary of agriculture. "He is opposed to [homestead colonies] without industries [that] are balanced by land taken out of production; [then] it is O.K., but at present there is difficulty in maintaining such a balance." Bishop concluded, however, that Wallace left him with the impression that his "project would not be opposed."[51]

During the remaining months of 1934 Howard Bishop lobbied for his plan in local, state and federal agencies and commissions. A deep and strong relentlessness characterized his landward efforts. But despite occasional signs of encouragement the plan failed because it lost the support of the Clarksville community.

Henry H. Ourings, whose property was adjacent to one of the prospective farms for the colony, explained why he shifted from support to opposition of Bishop's project. He told the Clarksville pastor that "this is essentially a farming community, the land is not suitable for trucking and I believe that these people will almost surely become a burden to the community. There is at present a surplus of local labor. . . ." He explained that his views represented "a consensus of opinion" among the farmers in the area, and proposed that the project would only achieve viability "in a trucking county like Anne Arundel County and be close enough to some source of outside employment." He was certainly not hostile toward Bishop. "I know you have done a great deal of work on this project. . . . I also know that practically without exception the approval you have received from the property owners is due to your personal popularity and not to the belief that the project will succeed."[52]

Howard Bishop's response to Ourings, if indeed he wrote one, is not extant. However, he apparently wrote to the County Agricultural agent for a list of complaints registered by the people of Clarksville on January 31, 1935. Eleven days after Ourings wrote his letter, John W. Magruder, the county agent, indicated that the complaints were primarily economic, i.e. non-taxpayers crowding the schools, and the removal of taxpaying property. Some people viewed the prospective colony as a potential source of "bad influence upon local farm labor." Since blacks composed a sizable element of farm labor, there may have been a racial concern implicit in this negative reaction.

There was a fear that the project would "tend to lower the value of nearby property for country homes, a demand for which is likely to develop in the future."[53] (Certainly a very prescient remark; Clarksville is a suburban or bedroom community of "country homes" today.) For this time in late January until mid-May Bishop's diary citations seldom came to more than one line with many days without any notation. This, combined with bouts of lingering illness, seems to symbolize a deep emotional malaise; down to the end he clung to the belief and hope that his idea would achieve reality. But again, with characteristic restraint, he did not express his feelings in his diary.

Howard Bishop's parish, archdiocesan, and national leadership of rural life movements reached its apogee in 1934. Besides pastoring two rural parishes, editing two quarterlies, lobbying for Ligutti's and his own plan, and visiting Quebec and Nova Scotia, he was maintaining his directorship of the League of the Little Flower and presidency of the N.C.R.L.C.

As president, Bishop experienced a severe and sustained conflict with Edgar Schmiedler, O.S.B., head of the Rural Life Bureau at the N.C.W.C. and executive secretary of the N.C.R.L.C. The Benedictine priest of St. Benedict's Abbey in Atchison, Kansas was a professor of sociology who had written extensively on rural family life. Shortly after Edwin O'Hara had been appointed bishop of Great Falls, Montana, Schmiedler assumed office in the N.C.W.C. Without the prestige of his predecessor and without a constituency within the conference, his authority was never fully accepted by Bishop and other leaders who had been duly elected by the membership.

Bishop had appointed him to the editorial board of *Landward,* but Schmiedler did not even consult with Bishop on the Rural Life Bureau's publication, *Rural Notes.* When the conference adopted a plan to establish diocesan rural-life directors throughout the nation, Schmiedler assumed authority for the program without the approval of the president of the N.C.R.L.C., Howard Bishop. By September of 1933 the Schmiedler-Bishop conflict had become quite intense. Bishop noted in his diary for September 18:

Bishop O'Hara called from Washington last night and I spent most of the morning with him. [He] sided with me in difficulty with Fr. Schmiedler on (1) impropriety of his release on homesteading without consulting me, (2) my right as president "directing the policies of the conference" to addressing bishops asking for Diocesan Directors [of Rural Life], (3) reasonableness of my request for conferences [with Schmiedler to clarify mutual responsibilities], (4) (which I did not solicit) independence of [Rural Life] Conference . . . [from the] N.C.W.C., and Rural-Life Bureau, the R.L. Director not being *ipso facto* executive Secretary, but by virtue of election solely.[54]

These points were adopted by a N.C.R.L.C. committee and approved by Bishop in October 1933; a committee was charged to revise the constitution. At that 1933 meeting of the board of directors Bishop left the chair and retired from the room "in order to facilitate free discussion of the report made by the nominations committee." Though Bishop was once again nominated president, the board discussed the need to rotate offices "in order to stimulate interest in conference activities and to make the official corps more representative both of capable leadership and of different sections of the country."[55]

The constitution-revision committee was composed of anti-Schmiedler priest-activists, e.g. Joseph Campbell of Ames, Iowa, a national figure in the credit union movement, James Byrnes, superintendent of archdiocesan schools in St. Paul, Minnesota, and Leon McNeill, superintendent of schools from the diocese of Wichita. Bishop, Campbell, and Byrnes were in close communication throughout the next year. As mentioned above they agreed with Bishop's four-point program noted in his diary on September 18; they also accepted Bishop's retirement from the office of president and Campbell as his replacement. Anticipating the constitutional amendment making the office of executive secretary elective, Campbell suggested that Bishop be nominated for that post.[56] In September of 1934, Campbell told Byrnes that "the practical thing to do would be to name Fr. Bishop to that office for one year at least. . . . It seems that Fr. Bishop, with his wide contacts, would be able in the first year to develop the membership in the conference to a point where we would be able to maintain a full-time executive secretary." In short he didn't consider Bishop to be ideal for the office, but because of his *Landward* and office experiences "he is the one man who could do this at the least possible expense to the conference during the first year."[57] Campbell told Bishop that if he accepted the office, then Campbell would accept the presidency.[58]

There is no documentation on Bishop's feelings or thoughts on the
executive secretariat except one reference in his diary (September 27,
1934). After discussing the office with Campbell he concluded,
"Looks as if I'm it."[59] However, instead of nominating Bishop the
board chose James Byrnes as the candidate for executive secretary. It
seems that the board wished to have the post situated in the midwest.
One presumes that this had Bishop's endorsement because Byrnes
and he were quite close. Indeed, Bishop addressed his letters to him
in the familiar first-name salutation, which was for him quite unusual.

The 1934 annual meeting took place in Byrnes' home town, St.
Paul, Minnesota. Prior to the board meeting, Bishop, Campbell and
O'Hara met and discussed the conference's separation from the
N.C.W.C. According to Bishop's diary, O'Hara "offered a compromise and Campbell was showing signs of weakness but I said if an
affiliation were maintained I would not return next year. . . . Bishop
[O'Hara] yielded so graciously that I suspect he wanted separation
himself."[60] Schmiedler considered separation to have been an anti-
episcopal move as the N.C.W.C. was the bishops' conference, though
the separationists were not anti-episcopal but only anti-Schmiedler,
anti-bureaucracy and anti-Washington. The constitution accepted by
the St. Paul convention stipulated that the director of the Rural Life
Bureau was only a "liaison officer" between the conference and
the N.C.W.C.

As president of the N.C.R.L.C., from 1928 to 1934 Howard Bishop
guided the young organization through severe financial crises. Under
his leadership the conference experienced a transition from religious
education priorities to promoting direct-action economic and social
programs. Not only did he provide an element of continuity but he
was able to absorb administration costs through his office at the
League of the Little Flower and by contributing his own money. The
board of directors acknowledged the conference's gratitude with a
gift of $100. Bishop continued to serve as editor of *Landward* until the
end of 1937 when James Byrnes initiated the conference's new journal, *The Catholic Rural Life*. Edgar Schmiedler returned to teaching in
1938. The breach between the conference and the N.C.W.C. was
healed with the appointment of Luigi G. Ligutti as executive secretary in 1940. He saw the conference aligned with the episcopacy in
rural Catholic action. On the other hand, Bishop and Byrnes viewed

the conference as an educational and policy-making body that would enlighten the United States hierarchy.

Howard Bishop and James Byrnes worked closely together to promote a large turnout for the 1935 convention in Rochester, New York, where Edward Mooney had recently been appointed presiding bishop. At that convention Howard Bishop delivered a nationally broadcast radio address on the "Catholic Hour"; the title of his address was "Agrarianism, The Basis of a New Order." The old order, based upon urban industrial capitalism, still prevailed in the western world.

> Individuals, groups and nations bow down to the power of greed. Unbridled capitalism, ruthless individualism holds the scepter. Money is the acknowledged ruler of the world. Now the Capitalism of which I speak, which prefers profits to persons, violates the sanctuary of human rights in a two-fold way, directly and indirectly. It makes a direct assault when it reduces the human individual to the status of a work-horse, when with a paramount concern for dividends it subjects him to all the cruel indignities and handicaps that modern industrialism knows, to the point, alas, that it is no longer easy for him, and the world about him, to remember that he is a child of God and an heir of Heaven. Indirectly, Capitalism without conscience disfranchises the individual through the wreckage it has made of that soundest of all guarantees of human liberty, the home and the family.

Howard Bishop then quoted G.K. Chesterton on how "Capitalism destroys the family and the fabric of society. But, so far as we are concerned, what has broken up households, and encouraged divorces, and treated old domestic virtues with more and more open contempt is the epoch and power of Capitalism. It is Capitalism that has forced a moral feud and a commercial competition between the sexes; that has destroyed the influence of the parent in favor of the influence of the employer; that has driven men from their homes to look for jobs; that has forced them to live near their factories or their firms instead of near their families."

The new order should be based "on the values of body, mind and soul"; the "heart" of civilization is the home while the church is "its soul." Much of factory production should be replaced by home crafts and small businesses centered around the home. "Civilization's stronghold should be . . . farms on a family basis cultivated for a living" instead of profit, "with high self-sufficiency and low dependence on cash income." Bishop advocated that the state should "facilitate the widest possible distribution of farm, home and business ownership and proprietorship. The government should monitor a thoroughly cooperationist society as agriculture, industry, business and professions would be organized on the cooperative principle."[61]

Howard Bishop's proposals for a new order were imbued with his sense of Catholic culture. Catholic principles enunciated in the social encyclicals of Leo XIII and Pius XI were in opposition to the individualist ethic of the current capitalist enterprise as well as the collectivist basis of communism. Bishop listed fascism as evil as communism, but, as noted above, capitalism was regarded as by far the worst evil because it spawned communism and fascism as well as birth control, that anti-life and anti-family menace. Individualism, which Bishop viewed as synonymous with large concentrations of wealth and power, was also inherently exploitative. Catholicism fostered moral principles of cooperation rather than capitalist competition. Howard Bishop held fast to the social-justice dimension of Catholicity. He was a Catholic distributist who believed the state should promote the "widest possible distribution" of productive property. The British Catholic historian, Hilaire Belloc, the popular essayist and novelist G.K. Chesterton, and the Dominican writer, Vincent McNabb, were distributists. Non-Catholic distributists such as Herbert Agar, Donald Powell, Ralph Borsodi and O.E. Baker appeared in Bishop's *Landward* and were guests in his home in Clarksville. The back-to-the-land movement with its anti-capitalist, anti-urban and anti-individualistic bases was vigorously promoted by the distributists.[62]

Bishop was particularly attracted to the ideas of Herbert Agar. He encouraged James Byrnes to visit Agar, who had taken a position on the staff of the Louisville *Courier Journal*. Bishop told Byrnes that Agar would "support Catholicity in sentiment if not fact. . . . But in any case here is a contact worth while and if he is anything less hostile than the head Kleaghe of the K K Klan, I think I should nab him for next year's [convention] if I were you."[63] "Catholicity in sentiment" illustrates the cultural role of Catholicism in Bishop's general perspective. Agar stated in his book, *Land of the Free,* a phrase that Howard Bishop had used on many occasions: Farming is a "way of life first of all and a business only in a secondary sense."[64] The church can more easily inform a way of life than it can inform a business. Indeed Bishop seems to have believed that with the church's influence, farming became a way of divine life. Just as the priest presides at the eucharist, a thanksgiving feast for God's entrance into humanity, so Bishop and many other social activists of his day were driven to infuse divine life into culture and mediate the religious truths in the terms of the culture. His plan for a Clarksville colony was Bishop's way of bringing Catholic communal life to the non-Catholic majority in rural America. Though that project never materialized, his plan to create a religious community of priests, brothers and sisters to engage in direct-action evangelization did become a reality.

The Cincinnati Years
1937–1953

Introduction

Alone in a tiny rural parish in southwestern Ohio Howard Bishop initiated his new missionary society with a plan and an episcopal patron but without a companion with whom to share his vision and his sense of providential direction. No other American religious community experienced such humble origins.

When Isaac Hecker founded the Society of Missionary Priests of St. Paul the Apostle in New York City in 1858 he was accompanied by three other former Redemptorist missionaries. James Anthony Walsh and Thomas F. Price founded the Catholic Foreign Mission Society in 1911, thirty miles north of New York. Hecker had received papal approval as a society of diocesan priests and his fellow priests, all converts, had seasoned experience. The Maryknoll founders received papal approval and unanimous endorsement from the American hierarchy before establishing their society. Howard was encouraged by a few bishops and several rural missionaries, but he did not even win strong approval from the Catholic Rural Life Conference. However, he still sensed the hand of Providence guiding him to begin his mission community.

In the United States the American home-mission tradition has been deeply rooted in Protestantism. During the "Second Great Awakening" there were five major groups that were identified with evangelization and with the "Rise of the Evangelical Empire": The American Education Society, 1815; The American Bible Society, 1816;

The American Sunday School Union, 1824; The American Tract Society, 1825; The American Home Mission Society in 1826. The latter group recruited graduates of Princeton and Andover seminaries and sent them to "strategic areas of 'destruction,' and supported them with quarterly stipends. . . . The establishment of the American Home Missionary Society completed a master plan of evangelist activity in the growing nation."[1]

Hecker's Paulists represent the first Catholic home mission society. Whereas the Protestants were motivated by what H. Richard Niebuhr viewed as an eschatological emphasis on the kingdom of God, the original Paulists were converts who viewed Catholicism as the living body of Christ and a symbol of the synthesis of the Holy Spirit's permeation of the individual and of humanity, the many in the one, the unifying force in the apparent diversity. Hecker and his followers preached the Catholic faith and its sacraments as encounters with Christ. Not uninfluenced by the impact of the Second Great Awakening, Hecker was inspired by the Romantic movement and the American manifestation of the Oxford movement.[2]

Primarily concerned with converting the people of the urban centers, Hecker's program of evangelization was based upon a blend of traditional Catholicism and democracy and individualism. His publication *The Catholic World* represented a synthesis of religion and American culture. From their origin the Paulists were responsible for the parish of St. Paul the Apostle in the New York archdiocese, a condition that created a conflict between pastoral concern for Catholics and the thrust for conversions among the Protestant community.

To achieve their goal of evangelization the Paulists established the Catholic Missionary Union in 1897 with the aim of sending missionaries to the south. In 1901 the Union sponsored a Conference of Missionaries to non-Catholics at Winchester, Tennessee, the Paulists' only rural outpost in the south. Among the speakers were Walter Elliot, superior of the Paulist house of studies at The Catholic University and biographer of Isaac Hecker, A.P. Doyle, the director of the Paulist Missionary Union, Bishop William Stang, bishop of Providence, Rhode Island, and Thomas F. Price, head of the Apostolate of North Carolina, and ten years later co-founder of Maryknoll. Though no one developed a detailed plan similar to that of Howard Bishop, the conference was infused with a zeal for home missions within the context of a church preoccupied with urban parish development.

It does not seem uncoincidental that Thomas Price's address parallels Howard Bishop's thoughts some thirty-five years later:

> To go out from among our people to those who know not the faith to meet in consequence rebuffs and humiliations, to work poor amidst poverty and sacrifice without hope for reward in their life— that is what our American clergy are not tending to. How many of our number do we find seeking the poor, neglected country congregations of even our own people, or so filled with zeal for the vineyards of Christ that we are burning to go to neglected places where no one else will go and to do work which no one else will do?[3]

Price's North Carolina Apostolate was based upon an offensive strategy of conversion by establishing "shack chapels" in the country and by outdoor preaching and house-to-house visitation.

Howard Bishop's vocation as a country pastor in Clarksville led him to adopt positive strategies for evangelization, particularly his scheme for colonization. The idea for his home-mission society was more influenced by Maryknoll than the Paulists because his aim, like that of the foreign missionary, was to evangelize and to establish new churches. He was not drawn to found a new Society until after Price had died. Without the strong encouragement of Price's colleague, James A. Walsh, it is doubtful that Howard would have been so determined to realize his plan for a home-mission society. One cannot underestimate the role of Walsh in McNicholas' decision to become patron of the prospective society. No doubt influenced by the American Mission Societies, including the Josephite Fathers' mission to the African-American community, Howard Bishop was the only founder to initiate his plan alone in a strange place. It is a testimony to trust in providence that this rather shy, though very experienced, country priest would at the age of fifty-two embark on such a bold venture.

CHAPTER 6

The Origins of the Home Missioners

If he were asked to comment on his identity as a priest, Howard Bishop would have underscored his role as a rural or country missionary. As early as 1922 he called for the creation of a separate diocesan Propagation of the Faith "for our country missions" on the model of the one for foreign missions. With a distinctive source of funds, rural schools could be built, a diocesan community of sisters dedicated to rural education could be established, and lay catechists could be trained to provide religious education in those mission areas with a Catholic population too small to support a school.[1]

As a rural pastor Bishop departed from the parish model that fostered Catholic separatism. Within the Americanist tradition his parish model was one that stressed the virtues of interaction between church and the larger society. The parish credit union and the school's 4H Club as well as the parish picnic were for the general public rather than for Catholics alone. Bishop viewed the parish school as a community center through which the Catholic presence in Howard County gained in stature and public impact. His notion of good citizenship entailed a kind of indirect evangelization; by breaking down anti-Catholic stereotypes he pried open the windows of toleration and acceptance, the first steps toward conversion. While he was proud to be a country missionary, most other priests assigned to rural parishes looked forward to an urban assignment. Indeed, according to the customs of most dioceses the rural parish was viewed as either a temporary training ground for young priests or the place of last resort for a problem priest.

However, the earliest document evidencing his hope to establish a society of home missioners is a notation in his diary for Pentecost Sunday, 1935:

Returning from Rochester where I went with James Byrnes to help prepare for the N.C.R.L.C. Convention in [the] fall, I stopped at Maryknoll to see Bishop [James A.] Walsh. He was deeply interested in my idea about forming a community of priests to do missionary work in rural U.S.A. [Walsh said] 'It must be done. Should have been started 50 years ago.' He gave no encouragement to my first proposal to start as a branch of Maryknoll, but cordial consent to my second, that Maryknoll train our first priests. [He] gave me a copy of Maryknoll's Constitution and pledged cooperation. . . .[2]

In the Summer 1935 issue of *Landward* the need for specialized rural missionary efforts achieved its first public expression. In an editorial entitled "Looking Landward" Bishop placed the idea within the context of his agrarian Catholicism. "The church must throw a vastly greater initiative into the country places . . . [by] bringing families from the city to the country . . . [thereby] reconstructing the social order." After calling attention to the religious, social and economic agenda of the N.C.R.L.C., Bishop urged his readers to consider the importance of evangelizing "the vast section of our own lands with their millions of unchurched families . . . just as legitimate a field of missionary enterprise as Africa and China. . . . A small but constantly increasing army of missionaries should start upon this task." Though he did not indicate that he would be involved in the organization of such a missionary endeavor he certainly gave the impression that he had considered the special character of the community. He said that it must be either "bands" of diocesan priests or "an entirely new community of priests." He deplored the notion that these missionaries would be religious-order priests who consider rural works "as a side issue" or that they could be drawn from diocesan priests "waiting for advancement to city parishes." Instead, this rural mission work "should be highly specialized and require special adaptability and special preparation. It will have to develop a distinctive technique of its own; the city methods will not do." He admitted that this work would be "drastic and perhaps expensive," and he placed strong emphasis on the "strategic importance of winning a foothold in the country." He concluded, *"Can we afford not to do it?"*[3]

Bishop sent a copy of this issue of *Landward* to James A. Walsh at Maryknoll who backed his call for a society of rural missioners. "In my own name and that of Maryknoll, I wish to express sincere gratification over the apostolic note so well struck by the excellent, editorial, Looking Landward. . . ." Walsh reminded Bishop that the Maryknoll co-founder, Thomas F. Price, "fresh from his arduous work of the North Carolina Apostolate," had informed Maryknoll of the need for home missioners. ". . . we have always strived to conceive of the home and foreign missions as the two aspects of one and the same Catholic program. Each reacts, for better or for worse, on the zeal and success of the other."[4]

Pleased with Walsh's "kind and complimentary letter" Bishop informed him that his plan had received "very favorable reactions from Father Fenlon [the Sulpician provincial and] rector of St. Mary's Seminary, and from two members of his faculty." Peter L. Ireton, the coadjutor bishop of Richmond, had also expressed positive interest in Bishop's plan. However, Archbishop Curley "reacted as I told you he would, unfavorably—but showed signs of weakening before the conversation ended. Father Fenlon said 'he can be converted' and I am confident that he can."[5]

In September of 1935 Bishop completed the first draft of a "Tentative Plan for an American Society of Catholic Rural Missions." The introductory section of the plan is almost entirely a reprint of his call for such missionary activity in *Landward*. The second part describes the decadence of urban life, "crowded and congested cities with high costs of land, housing and taxes that undermine the development of normal families and therefore . . . a Catholic program of life. For the same reason they are most favorable to birth control which is taking root even among Catholics . . . which means the growth of a type of Catholicity [that] is fast ceasing either to belief or profess." Besides destroying family life "cities are the natural habitat of Communism. In this artificial, man-made mechanistic environment, the ugly creation of misguided men came into being and in them it has found its heartiest reception. . . ." Howard Bishop had recently criticized the cult of capitalism that engenders greed and lust for riches.

Bishop's view of country life included all the virtues to oppose the vices of urban life, e.g. "large wholesome family life in a free and open setting where the stern individualism of the farmer, his love of home and family and [his] utter unadaptability to a regimented existence" stands in stark contrast to the collectivistic and regimented society endemic in communism. Catholicism needs this natural rural foundation in order to assure its "maximum effectiveness."

With the rural context established, Bishop introduced the specifics of his plan to establish a religious community of priests, similar to the Maryknoll Fathers, "with the special object of laboring for the conversion of non-Catholic people of the rural sections of the United States." He also proposed the formation of "cooperating communities" of brothers and sisters. The motherhouse of the priests and brothers would include a novitiate and a seminary and be "surrounded by a farm." The division of labor included the brothers as manual workers trained in agriculture and the building trades, such as carpentry, cabinet making, and blacksmithing. The sisters would be trained as teachers and home visitors with "the domestic arts, handicrafts and music as side lines." The priests should supplement their theological education with courses in rural sociology and agricultural economics "with special reference to small scale farming, widely distributed ownership (according to the mind of Leo XIII), cooperative organization and adult education as ideals to be striven for." Priests would also "be instructed in a special technique of spreading the gospel in rural sections, adapted from methods of present home and foreign missionaries."

Bishop was concerned that the priests also spend one hour a day at manual labor, not only as a "wholesome recreation," but also "as a means of keeping in closer touch with the lives of the people they serve and a safeguard against lonesomeness and discouragement in the missions." Each priest would also be required by the rule to return to the motherhouse once a year for a two-week visit "to refresh his spiritual and physical energies and renew contact with his Superiors and fellow members." Once again Bishop indicated his concern for the emotional stability of the home missioner, for this annual two-week visit was also viewed "as a precaution against lonesomeness, discouragement in the development of an inferiority complex as a result of long and uninterrupted life among non-Catholics where clerical contacts are few."[6]

After the society was assigned to a remote parish the superior general would appoint two resident priests, pastor and associate, to what Bishop refers to as a "base parish" of the missionary enterprise. In the optimum time of the year, two missionary priests are assigned to the base parish where, after consultation with the pastor and associate, they will decide on four or five points "well beyond the present zone of Catholic influence. Equipped with a tent, a portable altar and portable organ and accompanied by a brother or two to do the heavy work, act as ushers, etc., they will establish themselves at each of these points for two weeks, adapting the 'camp meeting' idea, so familiar in the Protestant South, to Catholic missionary needs."

Bishop envisioned the daily program to consist of morning mass and an evening service. After mass there would be a brief exhortation or instruction, while the service consisted of a "simple dogmatic instruction followed by a hymn." The priests would then respond to question-box inquiries; then after another hymn, there would be "a straight Catholic moral sermon . . . dealing with special moral problems of the times and the region." The service would normally close with benediction. Between mass and the evening service the priests would "pursue a systematic visitation of the homes in the neighborhood, omitting none, inviting all to attend the evening service. The base parish, and later the motherhouse, sends follow-up mail to all those interested in knowing more about Catholicism. The mission is repeated annually for four or five years or until there are enough conversions to establish a mission church to be serviced monthly by one of the priests of the base parish. Ideally every outpost becomes a mission, then a base parish. During this time the priests at the base parish are seeking out those who left the church and are working with non-Catholics. As soon as possible a convent would be added to the base parish where the home-missionary sisters would engage in parish visiting and do social work among the people and conduct vacation schools of religion for children." Because the ministry was in a predominantly non-Catholic area, he wanted the sisters to "wear uniforms rather than habits when on 'out duty' and [he said that they] will drive their own machines." He projected a time when the sisters would conduct a parish school, which would include handicrafts as well as the standard curriculum. Also, the sisters would conduct adult education classes in handicrafts.[7]

If there were enough brothers to do the work, then a small farm would be acquired "so as to supply as far as possible the food needs of all the persons at the Base Parish plant, and to furnish an object lesson to the inhabitants of the surrounding country in self-sufficient small scale farming." The parish is also to serve as a "model of the things it is teaching to the people. . . . No pains should be spared to help the people improve their living standards along sane and wholesome lines. . . ." Though Bishop viewed the home mission as engendering a rise in the communities' standard of living, he also was aware of the danger entailed in raising unreal expectations. It would be unwholesome to "increase the [people's] desire for expensive luxuries beyond the reach of their purses and fill them with a discontented longing to imitate their more fortunate neighbors." He did not wish in any way to foster a patronizing view of the poor. He said that "the dignity of respectable poverty should be upheld at all times." After this rather lengthy description of the typical home mission Bishop placed the social and economic aspects of the plan as subordinate to the goal of bringing the people to Christ. However, it was through "our example, our preaching, our instruction and . . . all other activities [that] . . . contribute toward that great purpose [of bringing people to the church of Christ] by showing the broad, enlightened charity of the church which seeks their allegiance and by furnishing avenues of approach to the spiritual needs of the people while ministering to their material and social needs."[8]

Howard Bishop hoped to begin implementing this plan as soon as possible and to see one base parish established in three dioceses within ten years. "It is not rapid and spectacular growth that we should want, but slow, substantial progress, building solidly as we go, never going into a new region without determination, with God's help, to conquer it for Christ if it takes a hundred years." The plan's last paragraph appears as a postscript; he said that the home mission society would be "excellently equipped" to engage in colonization efforts to develop Catholic rural farming communities. He admitted that it was not in accord with the primary missionary goals of the society but he urged its consideration as a by-product of the major enterprise of establishing rural home missions.[9]

This first draft of the plan was obviously intended to elicit a general response with particular suggestions for revisions. Yet, because it was composed without such input, it is an accurate reflection of Howard Bishop's original notions of the goals and strategies of a home-mission society. It certainly reflects his own experiences at Clarksville, particularly the emphasis upon raising the people's standard of living by featuring the handicrafts in his school and by his attempt to establish a colony. His protection of his priests' emotional stability and his concern that they may be lonesome and develop an inferiority complex in a predominantly non-Catholic environment appear to have been projections of his own experience of dependency upon the lay community for his social life. Later toward the end of his life he confided in his retreat notes that he had suffered bouts of loneliness, or, as he said, "lonesomeness," and that he had been too dependent upon the laity for friendships.[10] His seminary training had stressed the pitfalls of such dependency as if the lines between clergy and laity would blur and the commitment to celibacy would weaken proportionally.

The original plan is also devoid of the common references to the members' sanctity, as if he presumed that they would be good religious priests, brothers and sisters. Howard Bishop was not deeply religious in the "other-worldly" sense of that term. He evidenced a strong faith and placed the traditional emphasis upon the inherent grace of the sacraments but he was primarily an activist priest, one who identified Catholicity with the core of a cohesive and moral society. Though he aimed to convert the nation, it was upon the process of conversion that he fastened his zeal. However, instead of referring to "Catholicism," he commonly used the term "Catholicity." M.E. Williams notes that the term Catholicism connotes an "historical tradition of faith and practice that goes back beyond the Reformation and the East-West schism. In particular the word Catholicism is applied [with a degree of understanding] to that Christianity that owes its allegiance to the Pope."[11] Though Catholicism may be interpreted non-polemically, its usage has developed in contemporary society in juxtaposition to Judaism and Protestantism. In the original *Catholic Encyclopedia,* Herbert Thurston, S.J. wrote the article "Catholic" in which the term "Catholicism" does not appear; instead Catholicity is the proper noun.[12] "Catholicity" embraces a set of beliefs and practices; its usage connotes the universal diffusion of the faith in all of its cultural manifestation, including its moral and social expressions.[13] Howard Bishop's use of "Catholicity" appears to have been in accord with the non-polemical character of the term. There were labor priests of the 1930s such as John Cronin, S.S. of Baltimore and Charles Owen Rice of Pittsburgh who struggled against injustices in the industrial world. Howard Bishop had fought against rural injustice during the Depression by attempting to form a community of refugees from the evils of urban capitalism. Against the agrarian evils of technology and the large business farm he fought with the ideology of distributism, which he interpreted as derived from Catholic principles of social justice.

Immediately prior to his visit with James A. Walsh of Maryknoll he had experienced a severe disappointment at the failure of his colony to gain community support. Ever since he began editing *Landward* he had been zealously preaching on the moral urgency of moving back to the land. Had this colony become a reality, he probably would have postponed the realization of the home mission plan. In this context his thrust for a home mission society represents a religious back-to-the-land movement, and his base parish with its priests, sisters and brothers, its school and its farm was a religious model for colonization.

The plan appears to reflect Bishop's penchant for the practical, his concentration on very detailed ways by which his mission would be established right down to the organization of the components of the services of the "camp meetings." There is also a strongly American quality to his design for a new home mission society. It is unself-consciously experimental; a European founder of a mission society would have tended to embellish the religious heritage upon which he would build his new society and to elaborate on its specific spirituality. American founders find their spirituality in the process of doing things religious, and Howard Bishop was a true American founder. He did not attempt to root out the evils of urban and capitalistic decay but went to the rural communities where the natural and supernatural intersect and where Catholicity may be best perceived as in accord with the American ideals of yeoman farmers, the independent people of the soil. Howard Bishop submitted this plan to James A. Walsh in late September. In his cover letter of September 26, 1935, he did not mention that Archbishop Curley had refused to allow Bishop to establish his new society in the Baltimore archdiocese.[14] "Frankly, I cannot see it, for example, in the light of our needs here in the Archdiocese of Baltimore. . . . We have all the Religious Orders that the Church needs." Curley told Bishop that he was "expressing my own opinion only" and that Bishop was "perfectly free to take it up with the Apostolic Delegate or other members of the hierarchy who may see something in it."[15]

Bishop Walsh of Maryknoll responded favorably to the plan but encouraged Bishop to be specific in regard to the process in establishing the new society, such as "location, property, personnel, ecclesiastical approval" and means of financial support. Based on his experience in establishing Maryknoll he urged Bishop to develop "a careful structure of gradually obtained small objectives."[16] Because Walsh became ill, Bishop relied upon the advice of his assistant general, James A. Drought, and that of Bernard F. Meyer, an early Maryknoll priest who had prepared a privately circulated plan for a home-mission society that would send priests to poor dioceses.[17] According to Drought's suggestions Bishop's second draft of the plan eliminated "all unnecessary flourishes that might tend to irritate men of urban background."[18] Meyer was very enthusiastic about the prospective home mission society. He urged Bishop to include the statement that when a rural area has been well developed by the society the home missioners would leave. This would substantiate the notion that the new society is not in opposition to the diocesan clergy but rather it would be "supplementing their work." Meyer also advised Bishop to establish a seminary simultaneous with the establishment of the new society, but his suggestion, along with all Walsh's pleas for details on location, finances, etc., were disregarded by Bishop. However, Bishop's revised plan did include Meyer's proposal for relinquishing a well-developed area.[19]

The title of the first draft is "For The Missions of Rural America, A Tentative Plan For An American Society of Catholic Rural Missions"; that of the second draft, which was adopted for the published article, is "A Plan for an American Society of Catholic Home Missions To Operate in the Rural Sections of the United States." The second draft opened with an enumeration of the "Salient Features." Two such features were distinctive. The composition of a society was formally stated in general terms. In this draft Bishop's community is described as a group of "priests without vows, banded under a superior and a rule, in the manner of Sulpicians and Maryknollers."[20] Reflecting Meyer's proposal the revised plan also stipulated that the society would seek "limited, not perpetual tenure of mission areas." The references to Catholic urban life were free of the negative connotations so evident in the "Tentative Plan." He also excluded the romantic portrayal of rural life of the first draft. For example, he excised this statement: "It is here under God's blue dome, in His sweet fresh air, on His good productive earth . . . that the Church of God should take her stand to face the bewildering problems of the future."[21] There were subtle changes in the paragraph on the need for a new society. Rather than indicting the religious orders for sending those unfit for their regular work to the country, as he did in the original plan, he said that "there is always a danger" that this will happen. In accord with the suggestions of Meyer and Drought that Bishop must guard against alienating the secular clergy by setting the society apart from the clerical mainstream, he stated that the "Society will not take the attitude of rivals or critics of the diocesan clergy but friends and co-laborers in the Lord's vineyard." He assured secular priests and those of religious orders that each home-mission house would "extend hospitality to them at all times."[22]

The major difference between the two plans is that Howard Bishop deleted the entire section on the role of the base parish as a model for elevating the social and economic lives of the people. There were no references to adult education in handicrafts, to the farm attached to the base parish, and particularly to this social work as essential to the evangelization of rural communities. Instead, he merely stated, as almost a tertiary concern, that the society will try to do "all that it can to help the people improve their temporal welfare in order to win their confidence for the sake of the higher service it hopes to render them."

The published plan was almost verbatim a copy of the second draft except that Bishop deleted the reference to the society's colonization "work for the establishment of Catholic rural farming communities." Hence, most of those features of the first plan that were particularly derived from his Clarksville experiences and that bore the imprint of Howard Bishop's religious agrarianism never achieved public identification with the foundation of Glenmary. However, Bishop did reveal his singular dedication to respond to the need for a specially trained home mission society that would mount an offensive effort to win rural America for the Catholic Church, one that will act as "the advance guard, the shock troops, to open up new and even hostile territory."[23]

On December 6, 1935 Bishop met with Archbishop Amleto G. Cicognani at the Apostolic Delegation in Washington, D.C. In arranging the meeting he explained to the delegate that he would be addressing Paul Hanley Furfey's seminar in sociology at The Catholic University of America on that day and could meet with him at the delegate's convenience.[24] Though there are no extant diary notations for that meeting, on the day following the meeting Bishop wrote a letter to Cicognani in order to "explain more fully my object in submitting my plan to you." He told him that Archbishop Murray of St.

Paul had prompted him to consult with the delegate on the "canonical procedure in the matter of establishing communities . . . and if
you think there is sufficient merit in it you may advise me on the best
procedure . . . to get it established." Of course Bishop understood
that he would need the endorsement of a bishop and informed Cicognani of the likelihood of Murray's endorsement, "but perhaps
there is more need in the southeastern or southwestern states." He
explained his hope to begin "without the formality of canonical procedures." He would establish a "small band" of home missioners in a
base parish "with plenty of non-Catholic territory around it"; with
adequate sources of funding and a bishop's consent the mission
would develop and later apply for formal canonical approval.[25]

Cicognani responded to the plan "with keen interest" and assured
Bishop, "There is no doubt about the existence of a great field of
work of that kind." He gave no encouragement to a non-canonical ad
hoc band of missioners but rather underscored the need for a local
bishop to whom canon law "has reserved the right to establish diocesan institutions and societies of the common life" after the appropriate Sacred Congregation of the Vatican had given its nihil obstat.
He also told Bishop to stipulate the sources of financial sustenance
and advised him to consult with Curley not only because he was
Bishop's ordinary but also because of Curley's experience as a priest
and bishop in the rural south.[26]

After the publication of the plan in the March 1936 issue of the
American Ecclesiastical Review, Bishop enclosed a reprint of the article
in a letter to Cicognani dated April 8, 1936. He told the delegate of
Curley's non-committal response to the prospective society but indicated that he was "far more receptive" than when he was first introduced to the idea. He informed Cicognani that Curley not only consented to the plan's publication but "even allowed me to go so far as
to state in the article that the suggestion [to publish it] was his own."[27]
Bishop's next step was to circulate a reprint of the article among the
U.S. hierarchy and asked Cicognani if he could quote his positive
response to the plan in an introductory letter to the bishops. Cicognani could not allow his name to be associated with the plan because
it would be viewed as an improper imposition upon the authority of
the ordinary and because in the event the society sought Vatican
approval he would be expected to provide an unbiased opinion of the
merits of the ordinary's application for a nihil obstat.[28]

Archbishop Curley's immediate response to the publication of Bishop's plan was to remark that "maybe something will come out of it."[29] However, he consistently encouraged him to seek support from other bishops and, when Howard Bishop circulated his plan among the hierarchy, Curley wrote a cover letter identifying the Clarksville pastor as a "priest in splendid standing," as the founder of the League of the Little Flower, and as a leader of the N.C.R.L.C. "Father Bishop is now turning his attention to the establishment of a missionary enterprise to do for the vast non-Catholic sections of Rural America what the Maryknoll fathers have been doing so admirably for China and Japan. . . . While I feel that there is no field for this project in my own Archdiocese, I give him the fullest permission to interest and secure the cooperation of other Bishops in his plan."[30]

Even before his plan was published (March 27, 1936) Bishop visited William J. Hafey, ordinary of the diocese of Raleigh, who responded very positively to the home mission idea. Hafey and Bishop traveled to New Bern, North Carolina where they visited with a seasoned rural missionary, Father Michael Irwin.[31] Howard Bishop was drawn to the home state of his parents and to the diocese where Thomas F. Price, the co-founder of Maryknoll, established a home mission society called the Apostolate of Secular Priests of North Carolina, whose ultimate goal was the conversion of the south. A few years before his death Howard Bishop recalled that Thomas Price had attended primary school with his mother in Wilmington, North Carolina and that he had been a guest in the Bishop home in Washington, D.C. There is no doubt that Bishop was aware of his place in the rural missionary path first charted by Price.[32] Though the Apostolate did not extend beyond North Carolina, it attracted such men as Irwin, who remained in rural mission work long after Price left for Maryknoll.

Bishop noted that Irwin received his plan "with glowing enthusiasm."[33] Shortly after this meeting Irwin elaborated on the plan in a letter to Bishop. He told him that it was "a wonderful and zealous plan" and that he believed Bishop "to be a chosen instrument" for its successful implementation. Irwin said, "You have the health, the strength and the maturity of judgment that comes with fifty years. You have an open mind which at once inspired confidence in me, and I feel sure that others will receive the same impression."[34]

The seasoned missionary urged Bishop to study the lives of the early Jesuits, who "almost set the world on fire with their enthusiasm and zeal." The pioneer home missionaries should adopt "the Ignatian spirit . . . because it has produced men that could stand alone. . . ." Irwin related that Thomas Price had made "a profound study of the spirit of the Jesuits. . . . He was a servant of God himself, a model of personal holiness, but he was weighed down by lack of means, by too much time spent in gathering [recruits], by caution and hesitation in the support and approval of his Bishop [Leo M. Haid, O.S.B.], and by taking in beginners—who would never be big subjects—for an active, outside apostolate, but who might have fitted in a monastery society so called looking after their personal sanctification in community life." Hence, he urged Bishop to proceed slowly and to "storm heaven with prayer for light, wisdom and the proper men . . . and for ways and means to support the beginnings of the work."[35] Father Irwin and Bishop Hafey thought that the home missioners should be confined to the south but "I think otherwise," wrote Howard Bishop.[36]

The week-long visit to Raleigh included accompanying Hafey on confirmations at black parishes, one of which was an "improvised store church." Some three months later, Bishop Hafey dined with Bishop in Clarksville. He invited Bishop to settle in Raleigh and "start at once or sooner with a group of 'seasoned' priests." However, Howard Bishop was opposed to starting in the field; he wished to establish a seminary before embarking on evangelization.[37]

On his return trip from Raleigh to Clarksville, Bishop stopped at Richmond where he met with Peter L. Ireton, the Baltimore-born ordinary of the diocese. He too was very interested in the plan and suggested to Bishop that he locate his headquarters in the Richmond area. Influenced by Bernard Meyer, Bishop wished to settle in a large diocese and establish a seminary rather than form his community from ordained priests and locate in a small rural diocese where the community would be rather remote and obscure.

A diary notation for April 15 indicated that the plan was mailed to the bishops; one presumes that this meant all the ordinaries in the United States. Some six weeks later Howard Bishop embarked on a tour of the northeast to what he referred to as "my first missionary 'shopping' journey to interest bishops in my plan and secure a location."[38] On this and another tour in the same area in late June he received encouragement from the bishops of Harrisburg, Pennsylvania, and Brooklyn, but Bishop Maurice F. McAuliffe of Hartford was enthusiastic. Bishop James A. Ryan of Omaha, whom Bishop had known when he was rector of The Catholic University and who supported the plan, had written to McAuliffe.[39] The latter was so supportive that he presented Bishop with a check for $1,000 to help him establish his community. The prospective founder was so encouraged by the gift that he told McAuliffe that he "had laid the cornerstone of the project."[40] Bishop had hoped Cardinal Hayes of New York would at least provide an endorsement but was told that by policy he did not give such an endorsement "for fear of seeming to dictate to other Ordinaries." Bishop Joseph Schrembs of Cleveland was supportive, Cardinal Mundelein of Chicago was non-committal, while Archbishop Murray of St. Paul remained very supportive. Murray advised Bishop to establish his community in either Hartford or Philadelphia, as he "eliminated others I mentioned. . . . I think too many of our bishops lack *Catholicity,* hence, their failure to see my plan," remarked Murray.[41] Despite Murray's and McAuliffe's strong endorsements, neither invited Bishop to establish his community in his diocese, and later Cardinal Dougherty, though sympathetic, followed suit. They seem to have echoed Michael Curley's opinion to the effect that there was no need for a new religious community that would only compete for funds and personnel for a task that was simply diocesan. Hence, opposition to the plan focused on problems of overlapping with diocesan rural missionary efforts that called into question the need for a separate religious community. Such criticism was obviated by Howard Bishop's emphasis upon the need for a broad "offensive" movement aimed at convert-making, an emphasis that had never animated diocesan mission efforts except that short-lived effort by Price in North Carolina. It was not coincidental that it was one of Price's own missionaries, Michael Irwin, who strongly endorsed the plan. Perhaps most bishops were not opposed to the plan, but they simply did not wish to take the ecclesiastical or financial risk of opening their dioceses to a new community.

John B. Morris, bishop of Little Rock (1907–1946), was the only episcopal critic who published his opposition in the Catholic press. As the editor of *Extension,* Bishop W.D. O'Brien explained that Morris had originally intended to write directly to Bishop but at O'Brien's suggestion it was published in *Extension* as "an open letter."[42] Morris had founded Little Rock College in 1908 and St. John's Seminary in 1911, both of which were established as home mission seminaries in

Top left: William Howard Bishop as a young man, around the time he attended Harvard. *Top right:* Cardinal James Gibbons in his later years (Bachrach photo). *Bottom:* The Bishop family at their summer home in Clifton, Virginia, in 1906. Dr. Francis Besant Bishop sits in the rocking chair by the front door. Theresa Bishop is sitting next to him. William Howard Bishop is leaning against the pillar, front center.

Top: St. Louis Church in Clarksville, Maryland, where Bishop began to formulate his ministry to rural America. *Bottom left:* Michael J. Curley, Gibbons' successor as archbishop of Baltimore. (Photo courtesy Sulpician Archives, Baltimore.) *Bottom right:* St. Louis School in Clarksville, opened in 1923 when Bishop was pastor there.

Top left: Bishop in his Clarksville garden. Although raised in the city, Bishop was attracted to rural living. Top right: Bishop around the end of his Clarksville years. (Photo courtesy Marquette University Archives.) Bottom left: James A. Byrnes, a priest of the St. Paul diocese, was first executive director of the National Catholic Rural Life Conference. Bottom right: Msgr. Luigi Ligutti, successor to Byrnes, and long-time NCRLC executive director. (Photo courtesy Marquette University Archives.)

Top: Archbishop John T. McNicholas of Cincinnati following the blessing of the Glenmary motherhouse in 1941. He is flanked by Bishop, on the left, and Raphael Sourd. *Bottom left:* John T. McGinn, C.S.P., who encouraged Bishop's methods of rural evangelization. (Photo courtesy Paulist Archives.) *Bottom right:* James E. Walsh, M.M. with Bishop, left, and Sourd in 1942. Walsh later became a missionary bishop in China.

Top: Raphael Sourd preaching in the open air in 1941. The location is not identified. Street preaching had a large place in Glenmary's early apostolate. *Bottom:* "No Priest Land" in 1938. This Glenmary map showed the U.S. counties without a resident priest.

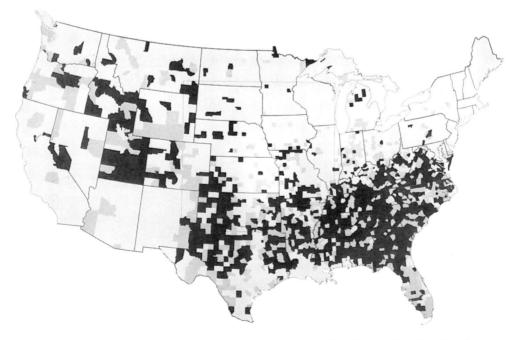

Top: The first motherhouse of the Glenmary Home Missioners in Glendale, Ohio, around 1939. *Right:* The first issue of *The Challenge,* published in 1938. The four-page periodical announced plans for "the conversion of rural America with the same earnestness and determination ... as our foreign missionary societies are laboring for the conversion of people of foreign lands."

VOL. I

The Challenge

NO. 1

VAST AREAS OF NATION PRIESTLESS

Almost 1,000 counties in the United States lack the advantages of resident Catholic guidance —this is the No-Priest-Land of America.

A MISSIONARY MAP OF THE UNITED STATES

SHADED SECTIONS REPRESENT COUNTIES WITH NO RESIDENT PRIEST

HERE IS THE CHALLENGE — We are not the givers but the receivers—A CHALLENGE FROM NO PRIEST LAND TO THE MISSIONARY ZEAL OF CATHOLICS

AND one very striking fact: these counties include most of the areas of the United States where the birth rate is highest. Their young people settle down for life in cities, towns and open country in every section of the United States. This means that our No-Priest-Land is exercising a stronger influence upon the future destinies of America than any other section. The populations of our cities are being kept up by the inflow from these and other rural sections in which Catholic influence is weak. They are the reservoirs of the population supply.

Within these scattered areas are to be found many highly respectable and influential families, people of refinement, culture and high ideals of civic righteousness, people whose ancestors have contributed to our Nation's noblest traditions, and whose sons, no doubt, will continue to do so. But even among these favored classes religion is counting less and less. Each succeeding generation yields a weakened allegiance to the faith of its more pious Protestant ancestry.

But within these regions are also millions of people of a more backward type — the backwoodsmen, the mountaineers, the farm tenants, share-croppers, and day laborers. They are the under-privileged people. Their schools are poor. Illiteracy is widespread. Ignorance, prejudice and superstition hold a powerful grip upon their minds. Their religion is fed to them by uneducated or poorly educated leaders who are rapidly losing their confidence and support. A very large percentage of them ranging in different sections from 30% to 90%, are unaffiliated with any church.

It is in such sections as these that lynchings, feuds, moonshining and prohibition movements have been in greatest respect. It is in such sections that the Ku Klux Klan boasts its largest membership and most enthusiastic support.

Suppose our No-Priest-Land were some great island out in the Atlantic or Pacific. Suppose we knew that along with their many fine natural traits there was deep social degradation and spiritual starvation among millions of its inhabitants. Suppose we could mark from year to year the drift of its younger population into our own borders to become our fellow citizens in city, town and country and could note their neutralizing effect upon religious life and practice in the places where the Church is strongest today. What would be our attitude toward that island and its people? Is there any question but that we should long ago have sent a missionary society among its millions to teach them better ways of living, and most of all, to teach them the way of eternal salvation? Would they not have become by this time the

most favored of all our foreign mission fields? Not only because of the great need of Christianizing influences among them, but also because the destinies of their offspring were so closely tied in with the welfare of our own present and future generations.

Yet as a matter of cold fact these millions among whom there is so much need of missionary laborers and no priests to break the bread of truth to them are even closer to us. They are our brethren and fellow citizens, shar-

(Continued on Page Four)

O, PRAY TO-NIGHT!

O, pray to-night,
So many souls are groping in the dark,
So many stars are waiting for a spark
To give them light.
O, pray to-night!

O, pray to-night,
Dawn is so far away
For those whose ray
Of hope is lost from sight—
O, pray to-night!

—Margery Murphy

65 MILLION UNBELIEVERS IN THE U. S.

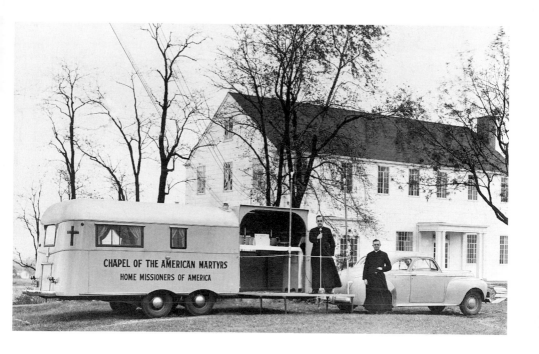

Top: A trailer chapel in Glendale, Ohio in 1941, outside Glenmary building known as the "barracks." Raphael Sourd is speaking at the microphone while Bishop waits nearby. *Bottom left:* Clement Borchers, second superior general of Glenmary (Carl Carlson photo). *Bottom right:* St. Anthony Church in Norton, Virginia.

Top: The first Glenmary Sisters. From left to right: Eloise Woodward, Joan Wade, Opal Simon, Gertrude Kimmick and Dorothy Hendershot. *Bottom left:* Mother Mary Catherine, first mother general of the Glenmary Sisters. The picture was taken in 1955 (Carl Carlson photo). *Bottom right:* Brother Vincent Wilmes teaching children in 1954 near Otway, Ohio.

response to the needs so well publicized by the founder of the Extension Society, Francis Clement Kelley. Hence, he considered Howard Bishop's plan to be an unnecessary duplication of efforts that had been underway for over twenty-five years.

Morris appears to have interpreted Bishop's plan as a personal affront to him and to the many diocesan rural missionaries who had experienced such severe hardships and deprivations. "For thirty-five years as a priest and thirty as a bishop next month, I have labored in this southland confronted constantly with the situation you [Father Bishop] describe. . . . My first thought on meditating on your proposed method of solution is prompted by my reflection upon the wonderful work of the many diocesan missionary priests which it has been my inspiration to have witnessed throughout my career."[43]

After a lengthy discussion of his seminary, Morris embarked on the main problem that confronted the rural missionaries, "a monetary one. . . . The question, then, is how should this necessary money be obtained and through what agency collected and dispensed." There is no need to establish a new agency, continued Morris, for "we have one . . . already perfected . . . The Catholic Church Extension Society." He then quoted a previous statement he had made on the Extension Society, one in which he said, "What a triumph Church Extension has helped us glory in; it has changed our dirge of sadness into a hymn of praise." The bishop of Little Rock concluded his reflection on Howard Bishop's plan: "it is not . . . the increase of the number of organizations that is needed to solve our problem, but a multiplicity of effort, concentrated to give greater strength to this one organization [i.e. The Extension Society] and greater means with which to do this work."[44] As noted earlier, Kelley's Extension Society antedates the foundation of the N.C.R.L.C. By 1936 it was a well endowed organization that limited its home mission efforts to funds rather than personnel. In this sense, it was similar to the diocesan offices of the Propagation of the Faith. Though the criticism was unfounded, Howard Bishop was still disturbed by Morris' opposition to the plan. When he visited Extension headquarters in Chicago he discovered that Kelley's successor, Bishop W.D. O'Brien, was responsible for publishing Morris' piece but he was told that the article's publication was "not meant as opposition, only to provoke discussion *which did not result.*"[45]

Howard Bishop responded to Morris in a letter dated September

8, 1936. He extended to the missionary bishop his "hearty congratulations for the successful establishment . . . of a Home Missions Seminary . . . under your able and zealous direction. . . . [It] is certainly a Godsend. . . . I cannot see how such an enterprise [i.e. Morris' Seminary] need conflict in the least with the plan that God, through no merit on my part, has put into my mind and heart to develop. . . ." He then expressed his conviction that his plan, "even if it should achieve a success far beyond my dreams, need not conflict" with the home mission seminary in Little Rock. He anticipated that his new society would "open up new sources of generosity" in the east where the people had never been "thoroughly warmed up on the subject of Home Missions." Bishop closed this letter to Morris with an expression of "good will and . . . prayers for an abundant harvest."[46]

Another source of potential opposition to the plan was the Missionary Servants of the Most Holy Trinity, a community of priests and brothers founded by Father Thomas Augustine Judge (a Vincentian) and canonically approved in 1929. A community of sisters, the Missionary Servants of the Blessed Trinity, was approved in 1932. Both the men and the women religious worked in the rural south. Shortly after the publication of the plan, Bishop noted in his diary that a Brother Benson had visited him in Clarksville. He was undoubtedly Jochim V. Benson listed as a Trinitarian priest in 1937. Bishop remarks that Benson was "Surprised about my plan—had comment ready to send to Msgr. Kerby [i.e. editor of the *American Ecclesiastical Review*] for publication. [Benson] agreed to alter it so as not to draw attention of clergy to similarity of our objectives." Bishop was able to persuade Benson to change his article because he pointed out that the Trinitarians had "never published their objectives either as *exclusively rural* or to *make conversions*" (his italics).[47]

Benson's six-page letter to the editor of the *American Ecclesiastical Review* opened with a lengthy treatment of the similarities between Bishop's prospective community and those founded by Father Judge: "they work in base parishes, do parish visiting, home care, and are trained in a specialized seminary with a farm where the students work and which produce the food for their community table."[48] Just as in Bishop's plan, the Missionary Servants' sisters did not wear habits and they drove automobiles. In his plan, Bishop wrote that "the laity must be pressed into service"; the lay community founded by Judge, the outer Missionary Cenacle "numbers hundreds of lay people." According to Benson the Trinitarians were not engaged in a "defensive" strategy, but he did distinguish between the goals of Bishop's mission idea and their own objectives. Bishop's society would be more dedicated to convert-making and would work "exclusively" in missionary districts, while Judge's communities were more explicitly aimed at retrieving former Catholics in both urban and rural areas. Also, the home missioners would be secular priests without vows; the Missionary Servants took simple vows.

After he had established the distinguishing characteristics of his community, Benson concluded his letter with expressions of enthusiasm for Bishop's plan and an emphasis on the need for a home mission society. "Father Bishop's plan could and should be adopted. There is *room* for a dozen more native religious organizations." As if he were anticipating Morris' open letter, Benson said that "objections, obstacles, fears will be hurled against it. . . . Financial concern will cause anxiety and a certain amount of hesitation. . . ." To allay some doubts, Benson admonished all to perceive the plan within the context of Divine Providence. "If Bishop's society is established as a gift of the Holy Spirit, if it is begun on this unpractical and unmodern Faith and trust in Providence, [then] . . . the conversion of America will one day be an accomplished fact."[49] When Bishop moved to Cincinnati to initiate the society he received strong encouragement from the superior (custodian general) of the Missionary Servants.[50] Many years later, a few months before he died, Bishop confided in the superior of the Missionary Servants that he had known Thomas Judge, "but not well. I remember as a high school boy, attending a mission he gave at St. Matthew's Church, Washington, and going to the rectory to discuss with him the vocation that was sneaking up on me in spite of my efforts to get away from it. So far as I can recall, he had not yet founded the Missionary Servants."[51]

During March 1936, the month the plan was published in the *American Ecclesiastical Review,* Howard Bishop suffered severe back pains. His doctor admitted him to Mercy Hospital in downtown Baltimore. After four days of heat therapy he left the hospital.[52] Periodic flareups of his sacrum problem combined with his long-standing curvature of his back and with the use of special shoes to compensate for the irregular length of his legs compelled him to purchase an infrared lamp. "Between my backache and my sacrum trouble I'm between the devil and the deep blue sea," he wrote in his diary. "When I get going on my back exercises, that starts my sacrum pain again. When I rest from these and only take the heat, my back begins to ache again! Is this part of my preparation for Founder of a Community?"[53] His physical problems remained a constant factor throughout his life, and to compensate for the discomfort of bending over a desk he had constructed a stand-up desk at which he would spend several hours a day in correspondence. In 1936 Bishop was also subjected to severe headaches as well as pains in the lower gastrointestinal tract. During one of his visits to St. Paul, Minnesota, he stayed at the Mayo Clinic in Rochester. After three days of tests there was no seriously negative diagnosis. The headaches were attributed to nervousness; the recommended treatment was primarily hot baths.[54]

Among the priests of the archdiocese of Baltimore Edward P. McAdams was the most enthusiastic in support of the plan. Ordained in December 1901, McAdams had served a rural mission church for three years before his appointment as a pastor in Glyndon, Maryland. By 1936 Howard Bishop and McAdams were good friends; they discussed a suitable name for the home mission society and Bishop decided on the title: The Society of the Nativity, or the Nativitarians, commemorating the Bethlehem scene that Bishop had frequently invoked as the fusion of the divine and the human within a rustic setting. McAdams seems to have supported the name and told Bishop that he had been "talking to a number of priests about your whole plan and I have found them favorably inclined but wondering how you will be able to inaugurate and maintain it."[55] Bishop had also encountered favorable opinion among the Baltimore clergy, but they too posed questions about ways and means. "[It] is only natural," wrote Bishop to McAdams, "for it is no easy problem."[56]

In an article in *Landward* Bishop took his plan before the members of the Catholic Rural Life Conference. He explained that the conference had been primarily concerned with social justice issues, while its attention to spiritual needs had been limited to rural Catholics. "Some of us have begun to think that the Catholic Rural Movement is incomplete, while this is the case." The movement's general message that shed the "light of Catholic social teaching upon rural problems . . ." was, said Bishop, "a patriotic and Christian thing" to do. He urged Catholic ruralists to go beyond the social teaching by shedding "the pure light of Catholic Faith" upon those spiritual problems "that underlie our temporal disorders." If the movement fails to extend itself to "the other sheep," then "we shall be stopping short of doing an apostolic thing." Bishop then informed the readers of the plan's publication, and in another section of that issue of *Landward* (Summer 1936) he presented the introductory summary of his plan.[57]

Bishop was very active in the conference. He edited its official organ, *Landward;* he was a member of the board of directors and a confidant of James Byrnes, its executive secretary. During the summer of 1936 he and Father J.M. Campbell, former president of the N.C.R.L.C. and executive secretary of the National Cooperative Service Bureau, went to Antigonish, Nova Scotia, the foremost Catholic cooperative venture in North America. As noted in a previous chapter Bishop had visited the area and was well acquainted with the work of Father Coady at St. Xavier's. Coady had visited Clarksville the previous March and stayed at the St. Louis rectory for a few days. During the latter half of August, Bishop and Campbell attended a conference at Antigonish. Bishop's diary includes frequent superlatives regarding his experiences of the trip. He was particularly struck by the warm welcome from so many social and religious activists in the area.[58]

Upon his return to Baltimore on September 2, Howard Bishop began preparations for attending the annual convention of the N.C.R.L.C. to be held October 14 in Fargo, North Dakota. Aloisius J. Muench, bishop of Fargo, and James A. Byrnes had articles on the conference in that Summer 1936 issue of *Landward* in which Bishop's summary of the plan had appeared.

In late September Byrnes notified Bishop that he had recently discussed the plan as well as Bishop Morris' criticism with Archbishop Murray. Byrnes thought that the latter was motivated by the need to broadcast "to the world . . . what a splendid institution he had developed in Little Rock" and by the *need* to "pay a debt of gratitude to Church Extension for service in the past with the hope, possibly, that they might be of service in the future."[59]

Bishop submitted his plan to the board of directors for its endorsement, and it was the subject of discussion at a luncheon meeting. Father John T. McGinn, C.S.P., located at the Paulist House in Winchester, Tennessee, a rural mission established in the late 1890s, was to speak on behalf of the plan. McGinn responded enthusiastically to the plan's publication. "There is not a word in your summary that has not been verified by my own experience," wrote McGinn to Bishop.

He was particularly appreciative of Bishop's detailed descriptions of his missions to non-Catholics. "Time and again I have been mortified at the greater success of revivalists and just as often was I confirmed in the opinion that we were making obvious blunders. How they might be obliterated you have outlined with the greatest accuracy."[60]

Father Leon A. McNeill, secretary of the N.C.R.L.C., had sent a written request to Bishop that he present an outline of his plan at the convention. He wired his acceptance and asked McNeill of Wichita, Kansas to include McGinn on the program.[61] Bishop also asked the president of the conference, Father William Malloy of Grafton, South Dakota, to have a secular priest, preferably from the west, "who is sufficiently favorable to the plan and sufficiently rural," to share the program with Bishop and McGinn. He informed Malloy that there was "opposition in the West which centers in a certain office [i.e. Extension Society] in Chicago." He noted, however, that this opposition "ought not be too difficult to overcome." To McNeill he was not so explicit about the opposition but he did specifically state that his purpose for inviting commentators favorable to the plan was "not to close out the possibility of hostile discussion but solely because my presentation of the plan is entirely non-controversial and for the simple purpose of getting a clear statement of the plan to the people. Contrary arguments have had abundant opportunities for expression in the printed periodicals."[62] Also sharing the luncheon podium was Dom Virgil Michel, the liturgist from St. John's Abbey, who was to speak on a topic unrelated to Bishop's plan.

Morris' criticism had so affected Howard Bishop that he became very apprehensive of the plan's reception at the convention. Just two weeks before the Fargo meeting Bishop wrote to McGinn that "it would be an excellent idea for us to scrupulously avoid a controversial tone as if we were meeting arguments or attacks from opponents of the plan." Rather than manifest any sense of diffidence "it will be better to give the impression of perfect confidence and unhurried zeal for a cause which it will take years to develop." He urged McGinn to assume a "generous and encouraging attitude toward all missionary projects" for rural areas and to dispel "any fear that success of our venture will become a threat" to any other missionary efforts. He restated his commitment not to pose any interference with or allow any overlap to the activities of other agencies in the field. He asked McGinn to "develop your own arguments based upon your experience."[63] Since McGinn's support at Fargo was solicited by Bishop he offered to pay his living expenses while at the convention.

John T. McGinn's speech on behalf of the plan was replete with references to his own experience. As a Paulist committed to home missions within a rural setting he shared his frustration with the fragmentation of his ministry. "For the vast majority of us who work in the country districts it is a practical impossibility to devote all our time to the task of making converts. Our Catholic congregation must be served, and these demands are numerous and exacting." Such would not be the case with a society driven by a "singleness of purpose."

McGinn compared the home to the foreign missionary; each must be motivated by a zeal that identifies the "making of converts as the ruling passion of his life. All thoughts, plans, reading, and prayers center around this one ambition." The home missionary has certain obvious advantages over his counterparts in other parts of the world. "But anyone who has endeavored to make converts in these United States knows that bigotry, prejudice, and ignorance can constitute a barrier that calls for a quality of determination not inferior to those who go to the heathen."

The Paulist of Winchester struck "a personal note" by referring to his own missions to non-Catholics. "I have conducted missions of this kind from the Motor chapel car in Oregon, on the street corners in Oklahoma, and in public halls throughout the South. These missions lasted for a duration of a week or two." Though these efforts were effective, they represented only a temporary and preliminary means of evangelization. Howard Bishop's prospective society would be "a devoted band . . . who lived the daily life of the farming community, sharing their success and their poverty, their joy and sorrow [and] would force themselves upon the attention of the people. They would become the object of discussion, debate, and study. They could not be ignored."

McGinn said that "one of the most desirable features of Father Bishop's plan" was that his missionaries would be committed to living the gospel of good works and practical charity. They would feed the hungry, nurse the sick, shelter the homeless. They would also be well trained in "mission science and technique." The Paulist concluded with a strong endorsement of the plan because "it meets the needs of our non-Catholic rural districts. . . . My own enthusiasm is shared by

many of my confreres and others who have studied his purposes. I
trust that . . . [the plan] will receive the study, discussion and
prayer . . . [it] so richly deserve[s]; and that his plan may soon become a reality."[64]

McGinn's speech was non-defensive in every way. Derived from his
mission experiences it did not touch upon the evils of birth control or
the virtues of the agrarian way of life or in any way condemn urban
depravity.

William T. Malloy had arranged for Father Frank J. Nester of
Cando, North Dakota to speak on behalf of the plan. We have no
record of his speech but Bishop was very pleased with the responses
to his, McGinn's, and Nestor's speeches. "Many questions were asked
of priests, including Archbishop Murray. . . . An air of good will and
approval pervaded the session," noted Bishop in his diary. He also
wrote that two Jesuits from the Queen's Work in St. Louis "definitely
approved of [the] plan in conversation with me, and Fr. LaFarge, S.J.
gave evidence of pleasure and approval."[65]

On October 13, two days before the luncheon address, the board of
directors considered the plan. "The chair advised that the members
of the executive committee [i.e. the officers], with the exception of
one [perhaps Bishop O'Hara, for diplomatic reasons, did not explicitly support the plan], had given individual endorsement to the plan,"
but that the committee as such had not officially acted on the question. "The board assigned John LaFarge to formulate a resolution on
the plan" according to his best judgment.[66]

LaFarge's resolution was as positive as a non-committal statement
could be:

> Organized effort of priests and religious is necessary in order to
> bring the truths of religion to the sixty per cent of the American
> people who are not affiliated with any Church group. The pro-
> posed establishment of an American Society of Home Missions to
> operate in the rural sections of the United States, which hold a
> strategic position with regard to the growth of Catholicism
> throughout our nation, is worthy of our serious consideration.[67]

Bishop commented in his diary that LaFarge "went the limit on
making the paragraph [resolution] on my plan as near approval as
possible." He thought the Jesuit editor of *America* "would have gone

all the way if I had permitted because there was not a murmur of opposition at the luncheon discussion." Howard Bishop exclaimed that it was "a wonderful conference, the best in many ways that we have yet held." He was particularly impressed with Dom Virgil Michel's address on "cooperation and the liturgical movement." He found Archbishop Murray to be at his best when he spoke on "the development of the family in . . . solidarity, in community and nation . . . [within the context of the] . . . Mystical Body of Christ." Because Bishop O'Hara was called away from the conference, Howard Bishop was asked to go on the radio in his place. We have no extant record of this radio speech, but one assumes that he emphasized the work of the conference rather than his own plan.[68]

After the meeting in Fargo Bishop returned home via St. Paul and Fort Wayne where he met with Archbishop Murray and a representative of Bishop John Noll. Later in the year and early in 1937 he visited Cardinal Dougherty twice, Bishop McAuliffe in Hartford, Bishop Ireton in Richmond, and Bishop O'Hara in Savannah. Each of them was supportive and would welcome the home missioners in the diocese but would do so only on the condition that the society be formed from veteran priests already in the field rather than from a new community.

With the assistance of his close friend, Monsignor Edward McAdams, Bishop established a group of "sympathetic priests" who would provide support for the plan. An organizational dinner meeting of nine priests (ten were invited) was held at Clarksville on January 4, 1937. "Society of Nativity gets first boost in Diocese of Baltimore" exclaimed Bishop in his diary. "They responded wonderfully to my plea for cooperation and suggestions about getting my plan on foot. Formed themselves into a nucleus of a Society to sponsor the cause and pray for realization."[69]

On March 9, 1937, sixteen priests out of the twenty invited, met at McAdams' rectory at St. Joseph's Parish in Washington, D.C. "to advance [the] cause of rural community." The major question centered on fund-raising to enable the nascent society to be born. Some encouraged an immediate establishment and then funds would follow; others encouraged the formation of a delegation to meet with Archbishop Curley, but this met with a negative response.[70] McAdams strongly favored Richmond but after a meeting with Ireton on March 27, Bishop was not encouraged. He paraphrased Ireton's thoughts: "For us to headquarter in a diocese less important than Baltimore after being refused Baltimore would put venture under dishonesty [sic] with Bishops. . . . Nevertheless he [i.e. Ireton] would discuss possibility with Curley as a matter of courtesy before deciding if I wished." Ireton and Bishop decided that the archdiocese of Cincinnati under John T. McNicholas, O.P. would be a good prospect for establishing the new society. Ireton even promised to write to McNicholas on behalf of the plan.[71]

Howard Bishop was not very optimistic that he would be welcomed in Cincinnati. On April 13 he arrived in St. Louis, Missouri where he attended a session of a committee to draw up a Manifesto of Catholic Agrarianism, and the next day, speaking before a group concerned with "Expansion of Catholicity on the Land," he focused on his two principal interests: "Colonization on a simplified basis and my religious community plan as the offensive measure [i.e. convert making] to be pursued." He was pleased with the "lively discussion" of his address. While in St. Louis he visited with Luigi Ligutti, who was then vice-president of the N.C.R.L.C., with J.M. Campbell, his priest friend active in cooperative work, and with Father Lester J. Fallon, C.M. of Kenrick Seminary. The latter invited him to talk to the seminarians on the plan for a society of home missioners. Fallon, who like John T. McGinn led many missions in rural areas, was vitally interested in Bishop's prospective community. Indeed Fallon was so encouraging that it strengthened his "conviction [that] there will be a ready and hearty reception for us in rural areas."[72]

He and Bishop Muench traveled to Chicago on April 15 to attend a conference on Integrated Society. With Ralph Borsodi and Herbert Agar, major spokesmen for distributism on the program, the conference was aimed at the twin evils of industrialism and finance-capitalism. Dr. O.E. Baker of the U.S. Agricultural Department, and an ally of Borsodi, was also on the program. Bishop had been in correspondence with both men and had entertained Baker and Borsodi at his rectory in Clarksville. Baker at one point considered Bishop to be too radical in his critique of capitalism. Other Catholic ruralists were in attendance as well: James Byrnes, William Malloy, Luigi Ligutti and Virgil Michel. Later that day Bishop visited with Monsignor McGuinness of the Extension Society who urged him to consider Erie, Pennsylvania as a receptive diocese for his society.[73]

Bishop arrived in Cincinnati on April 17. His diary notation for that day is of obvious historical significance:

April 17, 1937

Archbishop of Cincinnati agrees to headquarters me. Cincinnati 7:30 AM Mass at *St. Louis Church*. Bishop [Joseph H.] Albers and Msgr. [Frank A.] Thill (I had called up latter from Chicago yesterday) both definitely interested in my plan. Msgr. Riker [Matthias F. Heyker] . . . very courteous, later took me to Archbishop after Thill secured interview for me. Archbishop made no effort to conceal his very deep interest. He asked many questions and proposed many difficulties. Kept me to dinner. Fr. Snyder [i.e. Joseph J. Schneider], Dr. Sperti, Arch., his brother (a Dominican), and I. After dinner, told me:

1) Find out if Arch. Curley will release you.
2) Write out chronological steps of organization and send them to him. "Will you sponsor me?" "Yes, provided canonical questions can be solved O.K."[74]

After a brief stopover in Kentucky, Howard Bishop returned to Baltimore elated with the Cincinnati experience and eager to fulfill McNicholas' request to compile a chronology of events and comply with canonical guidelines. With characteristic drive and determination, two days after his return to Baltimore he drove to The Catholic University to consult with a specialist in canon law, Father H. Louis Motry, who responded: "I will give my blood for it."[75] The consultation produced immediate results; the next day Bishop sent to McNicholas "Practical Preliminary Steps." He specified his intention to enlist a small band of priests and seminarians to establish a "headquarters" with a small farm and with a temporary novitiate to develop a rural-mission training course at a house near St. Mary's Seminary, to secure a temporary novice master from an established community, and as soon as feasible to initiate a fund-raising campaign and a publication for publicity and promotion. The second part, "Steps for Canonical Erection," included four stages in the process of church approval of a new religious foundation.[76]

Rather than request in person a release from Archbishop Curley, he was advised to place the request in writing "so as to get a *reply in writing from him.*"[77] On April 27 he wrote to Curley to inform him of McNicholas' tentative acceptance of the proposal to establish a rural mission society in his archdiocese. He told him of the conditions, the first of which was that he would be available to begin work. Bishop then asked Curley to give him a leave of absence and to provide him "reasonable assurance of reinstatement if for any reason (not affecting my standing as a priest) I shall have to abandon the undertaking and seek employment again in this Archdiocese."[78]

"Put in a great deal of time praying for a favorable answer from Archbishop or rather such an answer as God knows best," wrote Bishop in his diary on the day following his letter.[79] After a week of what must have been some anxiety he met with Curley. "After twitting me about 'flying in the face of angels and saints' by asking to have my reinstatement incurred in case of failure . . . he said he would grant me a leave of absence but *I would be at his mercy* as to the kind of reinstatement." Bishop continued to quote or paraphrase Curley in his diary: ". . . in strictest confidence . . . [Curley said that McNicholas was] a man of great ambition—anxious for a red hat—doesn't know a thousand dollars from a dollar—insincere in his sponsorship only to further his ambitions. But he is a good man, nothing against his character."[80]

When Bishop asked Curley how McNicholas' attitude would "affect me [or] the establishment of a community in this diocese," Curley failed to show how it would, but restated his opinion that the plan was "unpractical."[81] The following day, May 4, Curley wrote Bishop a letter releasing him from the archdiocese in order to "found a new congregation . . . for work in [home] mission field," and in the event that Bishop wished, he could return to the archdiocese and "we shall do what we can for you."[82] On May 5 he had a five minute interview with Curley. He recalled in his diary: "Would you say A of C is unsuitable to sponsor a religious community? A. [answer] Not exactly that. He is not the kind of man I would like for such an undertaking. Need a straight-forward, outspoken, fearless [person as a sponsor]," said Curley. To which Bishop responded, "That is why I prefer you. . . ." Curley then said "out of the question." He then notified Bishop that he could leave with a thirty day notice. The Clarksville pastor asked that he be relieved of his duties "when the regular clergy changes are made," i.e. around the end of June.[83]

It was not until one month after this meeting that Bishop received a telegram from McNicholas in which he stated that Curley had given "the necessary permission to begin your work here" and that Bishop could issue a statement on the establishment of the headquarters of his new community in the archdiocese of Cincinnati. The telegram concluded with the remark, "I would think it well to say as little at first until we can work out together a carefully planned statement."[84]

Prior to this telegram McNicholas wrote to Curley asking him to release Father Bishop. He said that he had "heard a great deal about Father Bishop during the past twenty years," but still needed a letter from the archbishop of Baltimore. "I told Father Bishop very frankly that I am too old to encourage new works but that I was afraid not to encourage his society. I have for twenty-five years been considering with the late Bishop [James A.] Walsh of Maryknoll the necessity of a society of Diocesan priests for Home Mission."[85]

Curley's response indicated that his permission for a leave of absence had been granted in a letter to Howard Bishop and that he would remain incardinated in the archdiocese of Baltimore. Curley then gave him a qualified recommendation:

Father Bishop, as a Priest, is an excellent one—none better in fact, but he is not a hundred percent when it comes to executive ability. He has done splendid work in a little rural parish here and he has also carried on, with real zeal, the work of the League of the Little Flower. There is no need to recommend him to your kindness. I know that you will be kind to him.[86]

Curley concluded with a lengthy argument against Bishop's plan but his references to existing home mission efforts by ordinaries in the east indicates that he identified a "mission" as a small country parish rather than as a source of evangelizing the countryside with the intention of making converts. Though Curley believed that home mission work is the responsibility of the ordinary rather than a specially trained community, he nevertheless gave Howard Bishop his permission. "Father Bishop has been so prayerful about it and so intent upon it, that I am going to let him try it."[87]

Archbishop Curley's letter did not include a reference to Bishop's national leadership in the N.C.R.L.C., a role that was perhaps more related to the success of his plan than his role in the archdiocese.

Upon receiving word from McNicholas, Howard Bishop began to circulate the news of his imminent departure for Cincinnati; the plan was soon to become a reality. On June 6 he spoke to the seminarians at St. Mary's and had supper with the faculty. He was quite sanguine about gaining recruits for his nascent society: "No Seminarians have volunteered yet," he wrote in his diary.[88] However, Bishop informed McNicholas that "Two of the finest young priests in the Archdiocese are deliberating and praying on the question of entering our community." Because these priests needed "plenty of time to make up their minds and [because] it is not wise to push them too hard for a decision," he expected to arrive in Cincinnati alone. "I firmly believe that by early fall there will be others with me," wrote Bishop to McNicholas.[89] On June 16 Howard Bishop visited with the archbishop of Cincinnati. He was told by his new ordinary that he would be assigned as administrator of St. Martin's Church in Brown County, an assignment that included responsibility for a rural mission and chaplaincy of a convent of Ursuline Sisters. McNicholas told him he could move to Cincinnati "as soon as I like."[90]

The following Sunday Bishop explained to the parishioners at St. Louis and at the Manor "the meaning of my change." He informed them of the "history of my rural missionary project" and displayed a missionary map that he had prepared, one that later became famous as the "no priest land" map. The parishioners of St. Louis presented him with a gift of $50.[91]

A week later he introduced Father Joseph J. Leary to the St. Louis parishioners. Leary, who had some rural experience in southern Maryland, was his replacement not only as pastor but also as director of the League of the Little Flower. The congregation "dropped into the sacristy—at my suggestion—to greet Fr. Leary and bid me goodbye after Mass." The people presented Bishop with a purse of $130. At Clarksville there was a reception after mass. "I did not dream the people felt my going so deeply."[92]

After a few days of farewells in Baltimore and Washington, Bishop took the train for New York where he visited with Bishop James E. Walsh, superior general of Maryknoll, the successor of James A. Walsh, the co-founder, who had had such influence upon Archbishop McNicholas. After reading the plan Walsh said that it is "unanswerable. There is nothing left to do but carry it out." Together they discussed the "missionary spirit, rule, etc. Our ideas are practically the same. He seems delighted with the whole prospect." As if alerted to Bishop's visit with Maryknoll as the source of a new missionary work, six seminarians visited him after night prayers and sang for him.[93] Before departing on July 7 he met with a group of Maryknoll Sisters who evidenced a deep interest in his project.[94]

With a consciousness that he was beginning an effort that could be called a "domestic Maryknoll," Howard Bishop returned to Washington, D.C. On July 10 he met with John Spence and Austin Healy, the two young priests who were undecided about joining the new home mission society. However, Bishop considered them to have been "75% mine, but demand more time."[95] The next day Edward McAdams and Howard Bishop departed by car for Ohio arriving on July 12. The first line of his diary notation reads:

LANDED AT ST. MARTIN TO BEGIN WORK OF FOUNDING HOME MISSION SOCIETY.[96]

CHAPTER 7

The Foundation Years
1937–1939

When Howard Bishop arrived in Cincinnati he found an archdiocese roughly two-thirds the size of the archdiocese at Baltimore. Long considered a point in the German triangle, composed of Milwaukee, St. Louis, and Cincinnati, Howard Bishop's new diocese was administered by an Irish-born archbishop well known for his commitment to developing a well organized church structure, particularly in education. The Cincinnati prelate established the Athenaeum of Ohio (1928) that was originally authorized to administer seminaries, colleges and universities and later supervised secondary schools as well. In 1935 he opened the Institutum Divi Thomae, a graduate school of science that was dedicated to a Thomistic synthesis of faith and reason. Under the direction of Dr. George Speri Sperti, scientist and inventor (viz. "Sperti Cream"), the Institutum represented McNicholas' commitment to what Professor Steven Avella refers to as "Practical Thomism."[1]

McNicholas and Curley may be viewed as paradigmatic of modern Catholic separatism, that is, they built institutions parallel to those of the secular society, a separation often identified with the Catholic ghetto. However, Curley was more given to a bombastic and triumphalist defense of the church while McNicholas, the Roman trained Dominican, was more subtle and diplomatic in his defense of the faith against the secularism of society. It appears that the two prelates not only had opposing styles of leadership but also clashed in personality. On one occasion McNicholas invoked Curley's wrath. The Cincinnati prelate headed an investigating committee that had effected the removal of Reverend James H. Ryan as rector of The Catholic University of America in 1935. When Curley, who had admired Ryan, heard of the "calamity" he referred to McNicholas as "the juvenile Savon-arola of Cincinnati."[2] The historical analogy was inappropriate. The acerbic and cynical Florentine reactionary actually was more repre-sented by Curley than by McNicholas, the then canon law theologian and ecclesiastical diplomat. As noted in the previous chapter, Arch-bishop Curley's refusal to allow Howard Bishop to establish his home-mission society in Baltimore was symbolic of his departure from the expansive policy of his predecessor, Cardinal Gibbons. Whereas the latter allowed all religious communities, even small ad hoc diocesan groups, to establish houses in the archdiocese of Balti-more, Curley was determined to hold the line on new communities and even to limit the number of solicitations and recruitment drives of the established religious orders. On the other hand, McNicholas, a Dominican, was in the tradition of Gibbons; he tended to view re-ligious communities as potential channels for the movement of the Holy Spirit. Bishop George J. Rehring recalled some years after How-ard Bishop's death that Archbishop McNicholas was not immediately impressed with the founder of Glenmary but "He felt that the Holy Spirit was not restricted to any particular instrument" and that "he did not want to stand in the way of . . . [divine] inspiration. . . ."[3] McNicholas was distinctively mission-minded, including rural mis-sions. While bishop of Duluth, Minnesota he established a special mission house for young clerics who on the weekends would serve at mission stations.[4]

In 1933 the archbishop and his suffragan bishops of the province, with the exception of Bishop John Floersch of Louisville, issued a pastoral letter on the "Problems of Agriculture from the Standpoint of Catholic Principles."[5]

It opened with the principle that the "first duty of the farmer is not to produce but to live." It emphasized the contemporary condition of alienation brought on by industrial capitalism. In the Thomistic tra-dition of natural law ethics, the bishops' letter stated: "It is the artist's function to dignify and ennoble material things: it is the reverse of the rational order when the production of material goods is the means of brutalizing and degrading those who produce them. . . . There should be in the occupation of the farmer a dignity and inde-pendence that are not possible in . . . modern industry."

The pastoral advocated specific reforms in the agricultural life of the nation. It opposed "the industrialization of American agriculture and a system of corporate farming," and favored rural corporations based upon principles of social justice and the condition of "neighborliness." Just as local markets are dominated by the farmer rather than the blind forces of supply and demand, so international markets should be dominated by voluntary cooperation among the nation states. The letter implied an endorsement of the notion of rural colonization of the unemployed. It extolled the family farm, rural Catholic education and the social encyclicals of Leo XIII and Pius XI.[6] The dispassionate rhetoric, the syllogistic reasoning, and the clear enunciation of principles were characteristics of the practical Thomism of the era. Indeed, the letter was more philosophical than pastoral and was certainly contrary to the style of Howard Bishop's speeches and writings that were emotive exhortations. As president of the N.C.R.L.C. Bishop wrote a circular letter to each of the bishops conveying the executive committee's "whole hearted appreciation of the Pastoral Letter . . . deploring certain unchristian and self-destructive tendencies in modern farm life and favoring . . . 'cooperation among farmers.' " After further congratulatory remarks the president invited the bishops to the next convention of the N.C.R.L.C. in Milwaukee where their "presence . . . would give great encouragement to the meeting."[7]

In 1944, five years after Howard had successfully established the Home Missioners of America, McNicholas expressed these written remarks on the founder. In a letter to a Roman episcopal member of the curia (an anonymous bishop—the salutation "Your Excellency") he admitted that he was "reluctant to have Father Bishop undertake the work in Cincinnati." He mentioned Curley's endorsement of Howard as a priest. "I am under the impression that the Archbishop has changed his mind," wrote McNicholas. He said that Bishop Ireton of Richmond would have sponsored the society but could not act contrary to Curley's views. He also mentioned a remark of Bishop Corrigan, rector of The Catholic University. "He used to say jokingly: I am sure Father Bishop is a divine agent, because he has no human qualifications." McNicholas then gave his own opinion of the founder. "I should also say that when Father Bishop came here, I gave him very little encouragement at first. I assigned him to a rural parish and told him to pray. He prayed for two years before the priests of the diocese took any notice of him. . . . Gradually all the

priests have recognized him as a sincere saintly man. . . . Father
Bishop has many qualities that are not revealed at first interviews. He
is a very prayerful man; he loves the Church with every fiber of his
being. He seems cold and devoid of emotions but that is not the fact.
Interiorly he can be disturbed and experience great emotion. He
thinks clearly and wishes to be guided by the Church."[8]

When Bishop arrived at his new rural parish, docility and spirituality were not his major attributes. Almost immediately he arranged for
an office in the Fenwick Club. He commuted from rural Brown
County to Cincinnati during the week and served St. Martin's Church
and its mission church, Holy Name, in Blanchester, Clinton County,
Ohio. He had a chapel constructed in the rectory at St. Martin's so he
could say daily mass without heating and lighting the church. Located
near St. Martin's was the convent of the Ursuline Sisters who taught
in the public school at St. Martin's, Ohio, after the Catholic school
had closed. After his first interview with McNicholas, Bishop noted
that "My attitude about St. Martin—as a cradle, but not as a headquarters [of the new society]—is opposed by the archbishop."[9]

In a letter to Archbishop Curley, Howard described his "pretty
little parish" in Brown County. "Our people are nearly all farmers
and nearly everybody within a radius of three or four miles is Catholic." The mission in Blanchester, eight miles from St. Martin's, was
located in a Protestant area with a small minority of Catholics. He
explained to Curley that there were three small towns in the parish
boundaries which had neither a mission nor a resident priest. "The
set-up is so ideal for use as a training field for priests newly arrived or
newly ordained for our society that I am holding it for that purpose.
Here they can work according to a definite, approved program under
observation of an older, experienced man as Pastor, before being
sent out to the mission field."[10]

Howard reminded his former archbishop that it was "an influential friend of mine in the East," i.e. James A. Walsh of Maryknoll, who
asked McNicholas to "be kind to Fr. Bishop." He referred to the
Cincinnati prelate "as the soul of kindness" who had taken "deep,
constructive interest in my plans."[11]

Though he did not mention that he hoped to recruit priests from
the archdiocese of Baltimore, Bishop did refer to the hand of providence in the design for the home mission society.

According to Sister Aloysius, one of the Ursuline Sisters in St.

Martin's, Fr. Bishop imposed his ideas upon St. Martin's Parish without first attempting to know the people: ". . . when he came to St. Martin's he immediately thought that we needed to raise money for the parish by [placing the annual picnic] on a two day basis and the people were stunned." Because the parishioners were very fond of his predecessor they did not readily accept Howard Bishop. The fact that he viewed his pastorate at St. Martin's as secondary to his prospective home mission society exacerbated the problem. Eventually the pastor and the people developed an amicable relationship. Sister Aloysius recalled that Howard Bishop tended to favor the Holy Name mission-parish in Blanchester.[12]

In the summer of 1938 Father Bishop founded the first summer vacation school at Blanchester. Staffed by two Ursuline Sisters who lived in the home of a parishioner, the school was also the center of a Catholic-information class three evenings a week. Howard was very sanguine about the immediate prospects of attracting priests to join his home mission society. The two young Baltimore priests, Austin Healy and John Spence, who had expressed interest before he departed for Cincinnati, were at the top of his list of potential recruits. On July 27, 1937 he received a "wonderful letter from Father Spence. He and Austin Healy have definitely decided to join our community. All now depends on Archbishop Curley's answer when he returns" to Baltimore, Bishop wrote in his diary.[13] The Spence letter is not extant but a recorded interview some sixteen years after Bishop's death indicates that Spence had viewed Bishop's invitation to join the society with the understanding that the two would be co-founders.[14] Such a misapprehension may have originated with John Fenlon, S.S., the provincial of the Sulpicians. A few days before he left for Cincinnati Bishop noted in his diary that Fenlon told him how "shocked he was at my [Bishop] saying the other day [that] I would not be satisfied with anybody as superior but myself. . . . I told him I was only thinking aloud when I said that, not expressing a seasoned judgment. I then drew out of him that I am not a suitable person for superior as I do not attract men to me. I admitted it and expressed willingness to have a better man lead our group if he can be found with the same knowledge and interest in the project."[15] The next day Spence informed Bishop that "he and Austin Healy had consulted with Fenlon and had been advised not to change for a while. Also, not to sign up until I have six men."[16]

In his 1969 interview Spence stated that Anthony Vieban, rector of the Sulpician Seminary in Washington, D.C., had urged him to be very cautious before making his decision to join Bishop's society. Educated at the North American College and ordained in Rome in 1933, Spence stated that Bishop "asked me to be co-founder of the Society." The prelate recalled a luncheon meeting with Bishop and McNicholas during which the archbishop told the founder that a new religious community could not develop if it did not have "a viable source of revenue" and that St. Martin's Parish was not "a viable root" for the new society. McNicholas offered Bishop an affluent parish which both he and Spence visited later that day. While the latter was very impressed with the financial aspects of the offer, "Father Bishop indicated to me that definitely he did not want that place as a starting point of his Society. He felt that it was too worldly . . . [and devoid] of any concept of the missionary spirit that would be needed by the candidate for the Society." Spence urged him to consider the suburban parish as a challenge to his ability to nurture a missionary spirit and to use its financial resources and the land for building a novitiate for the society. As a result of this disagreement Spence "began to form a deep impression that there would be between us a negative relationship." Vieban had warned him that he should not give up his status in the archdiocese of Baltimore "unless you are positive that you can get along with your co-founder."[7] After notifying Bishop that he could not work with him, Spence departed for Washington, D.C. Bishop recorded in his diary that he had received a letter from Spence in which he "vehemently and finally . . . [rejected] the proposal that he himself had made to come with me."[8] Hence it appears that Fenlon and, more particularly, Vieban had planted the co-founder notion in Spence's mind and that he went to Cincinnati with high expectations that he would share equally in the authority of the nascent community. From Bishop's point of view this must have appeared quite unreasonable; Spence was four years out of the seminary with no rural mission experience, in contrast to Bishop's twenty years in Clarksville and fourteen years as an activist in the national Catholic rural movement.

Austin Healy, assistant pastor of Nativity Parish in a suburb of Washington, D.C., spent two weeks with Bishop in September of 1937. Had Archbishop Curley given his consent, Healy would have been one of the original band of rural missioners. Instead Curley told him,

"There can be no question at this time of your leaving the Archdiocese to associate yourself with the community which Father Bishop
intends to establish." He reminded Healy of the shortage of priests
and informed him that if rural work is your particular bent "I can give
you a few years taste of that in the near future. . . . For the present
stay where you are. Souls are just as precious in the great parish of
Nativity in Takoma Park as they are on the hillsides."[19] In a letter to
this biographer Austin Healy remarked that "perhaps you can tell the
temperature of that year by the tone of . . . [this] letter."[20] Despite
Curley's unwillingness to release Healy he was personally supportive
of Howard Bishop's home mission efforts; in October of 1937 Curley
sent $500 to him as "seed money" for the foundation of the
community.[21]

Howard Bishop had never perceived his prospective community as
a local organization; his was a national vision. Through contacts with
ecclesiastical leaders and personal visits to seminaries, and, in mid
1938, through the publication of *The Challenge,* he attempted to develop interest in his plan, to attract candidates and to raise funds.
Simultaneously he built a network among the clergy of Cincinnati,
but his relatively reserved personality prevented him from making a
strong impression in large gatherings of priests. He was much more
effective in an informal setting, as a correspondent, and as an associate editor and writer for a publication.

In September of 1937 Agnes Mahon, a young woman from Baltimore, who was a leader in the Student Mission Crusade, arrived in
Cincinnati as Bishop's temporary secretary. McNicholas approved
the arrangement with Mahon and she was assigned to live in the
chaplain's house at the Ursuline convent. Though Bishop relied upon
Mahon to help organize his office, to type letters and to be a companion in the struggle to establish a new community, they both shared a
dream that Agnes would become a home-mission sister.[22]

Twenty-five years old when she joined Bishop in Cincinnati, Agnes
had been an active member of the Catholic Evidence Guild, had conducted street-corner preaching in Baltimore, and on one occasion
had worked with Frank Sheed and Maisie Ward. In a sense Agnes had
almost as much direct experience in preaching to non-Catholics as
Bishop, but hers was in an urban rather than rural setting influenced
by the Catholic Evidence Guild, Bishop had developed his own strategies and tactics suitable to the hinterlands of America.[23]

At an early age Agnes had embarked on her religious journey that included daily mass, frequent communion, and eventually spiritual direction. Though an athlete of no small talent, Agnes was dedicated to strengthening her spirituality as a student mission-activist and social volunteer. By the time she met Howard Bishop shortly before he left for Cincinnati, she had blended her activism within a contemplative style of spirituality. A few months after she arrived there Agnes experienced a severe interior struggle, a periodic manifestation that is characteristic of highly emotive, affective prayer life.

During the crisis Howard Bishop became quite concerned with Agnes' stability. It appears that he did not know her well enough to appreciate this condition with the context of her spiritual journey. Instead Howard seems to have overreacted. After he consulted with his own spiritual director, Howard decided that Agnes should return to Baltimore.[24]

Agnes attended Mt. St. Joseph's College in Emmitsburg in the fall of 1938. After graduation in 1942 she entered the teaching profession in a Catholic school in Baltimore. Eventually she received an M.A. in education at the University of Notre Dame. Agnes has remained under spiritual directions over the years and has also been a spiritual guide to others. She is a member of the Third Order of the Carmelites and in retirement is a part-time hospital chaplain. In her own way she has maintained a home-mission style. That brief interlude in Cincinnati was a critical period in her life as well as a crucial time in the life of Howard Bishop groping for signs that his dream of a home-mission society was indeed viable.[25]

Howard Bishop considered Agnes as his spiritual daughter. He was fifty-two and she was twenty-five years old when they were together in Cincinnati. There was never a hint of scandal associated with this relationship. However, in one of his prayerful reflections Howard did resolve to avoid situations in which "looks, touches and conversations . . . could easily become a temptation to carnal indulgence."[26] Hence this relationship tested his resolve and there is no doubt that he passed the test.

Father Bishop attempted to nurture another vocation from Baltimore. Paul Thompson and several members of his Clarksville family arrived in Cincinnati on February 1, 1938. Though in his late teens, Paul had only one year of high school. Howard was unsure of the young man's ability to pursue the priesthood, but he proceeded along those lines. At first the Ursuline Sisters tutored him; then he was sent to a high school seminary in Louisville and later to St. Gregory's minor seminary in Cincinnati. He was a candidate for the home mission society for less than two years, but remains grateful for having had many enriching experiences, particularly the opportunity to complete high school.[27]

Howard Bishop's major concern during the early days in Cincinnati was obviously to found the home mission society. The National Catholic Rural Life Conference provided a context for him to broadcast the need for such a society. He still edited *Landward* and was on the program of the 1937 Convention in Richmond. In an editorial in the Summer-Autumn 1937 issue of *Landward* he placed his plan for a new society within a movement among "Catholic leaders." He succinctly summarized the purpose of the society: "to make substantial progress in spreading the gospel to the vast unchurched in America . . . to overcome the prejudice among the many sincere people of the non-Catholic sects and start them toward the reunion of Christendom . . . to hold gains in these days of many temptations and defections from the Church of Christ . . . [by working] for conversions in our rural areas." He told his readers of the "wide acceptance . . . [of the need for a home mission society] among Church leaders; the ground for the establishment of such a Society is now being laid in the Archdiocese of Cincinnati." He concluded with a reiteration of the need in rural areas "because it is there that the Church is weakest . . . because the cities are dependent upon immigration from the rural sections for their survival to say nothing of the increase of their present number of native born."[28]

In his address at the Richmond Convention of the N.C.R.L.C. Howard seems to have been publicly responding to Bishop Morris' opposition to the plan published in *Extension* the previous year. When the isolated diocesan home missioner struggles against loneliness, the home mission society would not permit their missionaries "to feel that they are alone and forgotten."[29] In order to achieve a strong Catholic mission in rural America "something more is necessary than the haphazard, sporadic, scattered and intermittent efforts that have characterized the past . . . rural missionary work."[30] Building upon the model of the Catholic foreign mission societies, Bishop emphasized the need for an offensive missionary strategy with well trained priests, volunteers and sisters operating out of a base parish and responding to the "varying needs of different communities. Medical missions, the visiting of families by trained workers, the holding of vacation schools for children and various forms of study clubs for adults . . . are several ways to meet these varying needs." Bishop referred to his mission map with the one thousand priestless counties, a project that became identified with the home mission cause throughout the Catholic community. In his conclusion the founder gave credit to the bands of diocesan missionaries for making some converts and breaking down anti-Catholic prejudice. "This in itself is highly worthwhile and can be done on a somewhat extensive scale. But the high *intensive* work of invading and permanently occupying new territory with all the personnel and equipment of a campaign to be pursued in terms of decades . . . is the task of an organized society. The task is great but the millions of unreached souls in our beloved America are worth the expense of effort and funds."[31]

In his diary Howard merely recorded the fact that he presented a "talk of my missionary project." He did note that John LaFarge read the resolutions passed by the board of directors "in which my work was given unsolicited though brief notice."[32] During this visit he addressed "colored students at Richmond Union, a Protestant College for colored people sustained partly by city funds. A fine response. . . ."[33] With only this brief notation in his diary there is no indication of the nature of his address nor of how or why he was invited to speak at a black Protestant institution. However, the fact that he did illustrates a relatively open spirit. Of course his missionary efforts were aimed at "farmers and farm tenants, colored and white."[34]

In February Bishop attended a N.C.R.L.C. board of directors meeting in St. Paul. Ligutti was president and James Byrnes was executive secretary. Howard had hoped to speak with Archbishop Murray and Byrnes but was unable to arrange a meeting. At Byrnes' rectory he expressed his frustration with the conference's lack of support for his missionary society. "I let loose on James and Luigi." Bishop wrote in his diary "(1) Lack of cooperation on *Landward*. I would like to be relieved. (2) The conference should give strong support to my Society, not bury me like it did last year. The reaction was not wholehearted but better from J [Byrnes] than L [Ligutti]."[35] At the board meeting the following day he proposed that at the next convention a sectional meeting [should be] given me for my own and other missionary intentions." Because this proposal elicited "hesitation" among the board members Ligutti asked Bishop to submit a written "scheme" of the proposal. Bishop Muench suggested that priests would be most interested in his Society. Hence Howard Bishop proposed a luncheon meeting for priests and another session open to all. There was no immediate decision on this latter proposal, but a month later when he was visiting the local chairman of the next convention Bishop was convinced that "Byrnes and Ligutti [were determined] to block me."[36] At the Vincennes Convention Howard shared a session with another rural missionary, Steven Leven, of the Oklahoma diocese.

By this time *Landward* had ceased to exist; its successor *The Catholic Rural Life Bulletin*, edited by James Byrnes, became the official publication of the N.C.R.L.C. The new journal was a quarterly but nearly three times the size of *Landward* and much more diversified in content and contexts. The new publication symbolized the shift from the personalist pioneering leadership of Howard Bishop to the more professional and modern leadership of Luigi Ligutti, soon to be named a monsignor.

Some nineteen years after Howard's death Ligutti recalled his association with the founder of Glenmary. He and Bishop had been merely acquaintances at St. Mary's Seminary in Baltimore, but, as mentioned earlier, Howard had lobbied for Ligutti's homestead colony in Iowa and the two worked closely together on the N.C.R.L.C. ". . . to me he [Bishop] was a very fine, good friend," said Ligutti. "We were very candid to each other though at times we disagreed on certain things."[37] The major disagreement centered on the fact that Howard Bishop "just absolutely insisted that his program would be the . . . leading program and nothing else. . . . I said no, we must have balance. He was very bitter at times. I think he was especially bitter, trying to scare me. . . ." Ligutti considered him to be an "absolutely superior" priest, and when asked about whether Howard was "a man of principles," Ligutti replied, "Oh, yes he was. He had stubbornness . . . a terrific temper." However, he also recalled Bishop's "good sense of humor. We would laugh together so very often." Ligutti emphasized a facet of the founder's personality—tenaciousness. "He was like a wild dog. He'd dig into a thing . . . regardless. . . ."[38] Despite their disagreements, Ligutti promoted the new society of home missioners. However, from Bishop's point of view, the leadership of the N.C.R.L.C. showed an unenthusiastic attitude to his plan. On the other hand, the N.C.R.L.C. invited the founder to speak on a number of occasions, and published several of his addresses. Despite a few misunderstandings, Howard Bishop, James Byrnes and Luigi Ligutti remained good friends.

The first issue of *The Catholic Rural Life Bulletin* (May 1938) published a short letter from Howard Bishop. James Byrnes, the editor of the new publication, had asked Bishop for a five hundred word piece "on the nature of a swan-song,"[39] but he decided to contribute a short summary on the "genesis" of his society. "As to my present task, it's new to me only in name. The thought had been with me for many years. . . . A few years' experience [as a rural pastor in Clarksville] was sufficient to convince me of the importance of a vast missionary field that was being overlooked by the Church in America." He then developed his strategy for offensive missionary measures. "By this I mean measures that will on the one hand invade the cities for new rural dwellers, and invade purely non-Catholic rural territory for new converts to the church on the other. . . ."[40] By the time this letter was printed Bishop had published the first issue of *The Challenge,* the official publication of the Home Missioners of America.

The headline of the first issue reads "Vast Areas of Nation Priestless," below which was Bishop's missionary map of the United States. In the lead column Howard Bishop presented the basis for the challenge to "the missionary zeal of Catholics."[41] The fastest growing portion of the population were residing in the country areas and were increasingly counted among the unchurched. If the church did not assert itself in rural America, then these religiously unaffiliated, who were dominating the migration to the cities, would adversely affect the church's strong urban presence, particularly because these unchurched tended to be dominated by a strident anti-Catholicism. "Ignorance, prejudice and superstition hold a powerful grip upon their minds. Their religion is fed to them by uneducated or poorly educated leaders who are rapidly losing their confidence and support. It is in these settings that lynchings, feuds, moonshining and prohibition movements have been in greatest respect. It is in such sections that the Ku Klux Klan boasts its largest membership and vast enthusiastic support." The priest-editor was aware of the "many highly respectable and influential families" in these particular areas. These were the people "of refinement, culture and high ideals of civic righ-

teousness. . . . But even among these favored classes religion is
counting less and less. Each succeeding generation yields a weakening influence to the faith of its most pious Protestant ancestry."[42]
Hence, Bishop's missionary thrust was aimed at converting not the
pious Protestants but rather those who were unchurched or at best
lukewarm in their religious affiliation. Long overdue was the new
home mission society that would "teach better ways of living and,
most of all, teach them the way of eternal salvation." He only revealed a society of a patronizing spirit as he considered these rural
peoples "as our brethren and fellow citizens sharing our own United
States with us from birth to burial. They are as much American as we.
Priests should be motivated to break the bread of truth" with these
millions of unchurched.[43]

The small periodical was entirely the work of Howard Bishop. He
visited the farming areas and Appalachia to take photos of those
people who represented the needs for home missionaries. "The
Sharecroppers—Neglected, Exploited, and Desperate. The Mountain Fold—A wide stock going to seed; The Negroes—Ignored and
Exploited but Unconcerned." He explained that the sharecroppers
were virtually serfs or slaves. The southern mountaineer was "a bit
quick on trigger and predisposed to moonshine and brawls and
feuds." However, his were not the sins of "our refined society—he
does not massacre the unborn." Bishop praised the Josephites who
"have been doing magnificent work" in their missions to the Negro
community. However, "the Church of Christ must increase its effort
in their behalf."[44] Bishop warned his readers that communism and
socialism were making progress among sharecroppers and Negroes;
this was an additional challenge to Catholics' missionary zeal.

The Challenge was an instrument for winning vocations, for raising
rural mission consciousness, and for broadcasting the need for
friends and funds. In the first issue it published letters of endorsement from bishops along with their photographs. Bishop James E.
Walsh, the successor of the co-founder superior general of Maryknoll, James A. Walsh, wrote a very warm letter in which he placed the
home missioners within the movement initiated by Thomas F. Price.
Also included in several issues were: a one-page plea for membership
in the Friends of the Rural Mission, who would contribute money and
prayers for the movement; coupons for subscriptions to *The Challenge,* and pages to promote vocations to the home missioners. There

were regular Catholic patriotism articles linked to mission-minded-ness; there were feature articles on the desperate need for social justice. The second issue, as well as subsequent issues for the next few years, was eight pages in length.[45]

On July 23, 1938 Howard Bishop recorded in his diary that he had "meditated long on my first year in Ohio . . ." He listed the year's accomplishments:

> Arrival of Agnes Mahon to take up work on September 1, 1937.
>
> Arrival of Paul Thompson about February 1, 1938.
>
> Decision of Earl McGrath [a seminarian from Cincinnati] to come to us. July 5, 1938.
>
> Publication of two numbers of *Challenge*. Numerous endorsements from Bishops and other church leaders and some cash.[46]

Eight days later he traveled to Gethsemane, Kentucky, where he made an eight-day retreat at the Trappist monastery. The day after he began his retreat Archbishop McNicholas, his invalid brother, also a Dominican, and Dr. Sperti visited the monastery. The abbot invited Bishop to dine with the guests that evening. After dinner McNicholas addressed the gathering and "took particular pains to mention each member of the party, beginning with me, and making very helpful reference to our new Society and No Priest Land and asking their prayers for us."[47] On the last day he recorded in his diary that he had "a fine talk with the Abbot of this place. We see eye to eye in the Agrarian question. This is the only community in America which has kept up true agricultural traditions and is really an agricultural order. Their roots are in Heaven and in the soil. There are no halfway houses."[48]

As a home missioner Howard Bishop had been drawn to the Cath-olic Evidence Guild founded by Maisie Ward and Frank Sheed. These two street preachers would set up a "pulpit" in Hyde Park and other public places in London and embark on a popular catechesis fol-lowed by a question-answer period.[49] Bishop met them in Washing-ton, D.C. and was impressed by their dedication. Perhaps the most effective American member of the Guild was Stephen A. Leven, a priest of the diocese of Oklahoma City. While Leven was a seminarian at the American College in Louvain he spent a summer in London preaching with the Guild. After he returned to his diocese in 1928 Leven occasionally spoke spontaneously to people gathered at the courthouse in the state capital. Then in 1932 he gave the first Catholic Evidence lecture and for twenty-seven years was a street preacher in the summers; in the late 1930s he established a street preaching institute that attracted priests, religious, and lay people, including a contingent of young women from Rosary College in River Forest, Illinois.[50]

In preparation for the N.C.R.L.C. meeting in Vincennes (October 1938) Howard Bishop asked Leven to share the program with him. "As you are the originator and best known exponent of motor mission work, your appearance is both inspirational and informational for all of us."[51] Leven, who was completing a doctoral program at Louvain during this period, wrote Bishop that he "will do all in my power" to attend the October meeting of the N.C.R.L.C. He also stated, "I have been following your work in organizing the Home Missionary Society ever since it was first spoken of by a mutual friend, Father Leon McNeill of Wichita, and I planned to make contact with you on my return to the States." Leven mentioned that the two had met at the Wichita Rural Life Convention but that he doubted Bishop would remember him.[52]

With characteristic candor Bishop informed Leven of his correspondence with his bishop, Francis Clement Kelly, telling him "I would love to have you [Leven] with us and to quote my own words 'I have been so daring as to hope that when your Excellency realizes the broad, national scope of the work we aspire to do, your generous missionary heart will be as I hope and that he [Leven] should come to us and help us succeed for the greater good of all missionary effort in America. I do not know how either of you will receive this suggestion, but I assure you it comes from the heart.' "[53]

In his response to Bishop's invitation, Stephen Leven said that it "touched me very deeply." He even indicated that he had himself considered joining the society because Bishop's work "comes very near my own heart." However, he did not think it was "God's will for me. . . . Since you were so frank in your invitation, I feel that I must be equally frank in my reply."[54] At the convention in Vincennes Bishop met with Leven and "tried to interest him in our work, but in vain."[55] This was confirmed by Leven in his autobiography but with a significant variation. Leven reported that Kelly had given permission to ask him "to become a co-founder with him of the 'Home Missioners.' "[56]

In a 1972 letter to the Glenmary Home Missioners, Leven, then bishop of San Angelo, Texas, reiterated the invitation to become a co-founder of the society. "He [Howard Bishop] spoke very warmly about his plan which I had come to know quite well from previous reading and discussion with some of my priest friends. He told me how he had prayed not to be led astray by vain visions, and had asked repeatedly to remove him from the scene if such a society was not his will."[57] Bishop and Leven remained good friends; after the home missioners were established the founder sent young priests to Leven's street preaching institute.

Shortly after Leven said he could not join the nascent society, Bishop noted in his diary that he couldn't sleep because he was "worrying over slow development of our plan and continued lack of another priest."[58] He had received a few inquiries from priests and seminarians, but at the time he penned this note of frustration in his diary he had only one seminarian committed to the society. He was also encouraged by several bishops, and seminary rectors provided him with a forum to explain his mission society to their students. For example, Albert Meyer, later cardinal archbishop of Chicago, welcomed him to St. Francis Seminary in Milwaukee. Bishop noted that he had "a good talk" with Meyer. "He is heartily sympathetic with my plan."[59] Father Raphael Sourd, spiritual director at St. Gregory's minor seminary in Cincinnati, had indicated moderate interest in the society. A native of Fayetteville, Ohio, a small rural town not far from St. Martin's, Sourd had met Bishop on his arrival in the archdiocese. In late October Sourd decided to join Bishop in a street preaching campaign the following summer but he delayed a decision to join him on a permanent basis.[60]

Howard suspected that McNicholas may have lost some confidence in his plan. However, when he visited the archbishop on December 10, 1938, he was reassured that if there were such lack of confidence "it was gone." Motivated to initiate a home mission campaign, he successfully sought approval from the archbishop "to give a series of lectures to non-Catholics after Christmas." During the first week of January, Howard Bishop secured a theatre in Lynchburg for his series of public lectures. He had cards printed which he distributed personally in the stores of the town; he also composed an an-

nouncement for the weekly papers at Blanchester and Lynchburg.[61]
In his preparations he converted scripture references from the Catholic Douai to the Protestant King James version, began to rehearse a
small choir from St. Martin's, and coached a few Catholics on questions to be asked during the discussion period following the lecture.[62]

On January 16 Howard Bishop began his first home mission campaign; the lecture was on "God and Mass." Though Lynchburg was a
"priestless town" not far from Blanchester it was reported to be very
bigoted. "I have seen no evidence of it," wrote Father Bishop. About
fifty people attended the first of a six-part series of lectures. According to Bishop, "the audience [was] exceedingly quiet and attentive."
Other than the question from the Catholic "planted" in the audience, there was only one other. "Everybody [was] being respectful," Howard concluded. The following topics rounded out the lectures: Christ and the Church; The Church and the Bible; Forgiveness
of Sin; The Eucharist and the Mass; Mary the Mother of Christ.[63] By
the third lecture questions were being asked spontaneously.[64] Beginning with lecture four, a question box circulated which elicited eleven
questions. When he talked on the eucharist and the mass there were
many questions: "Four persons from some queer sect like Pentecostal brethren came to heckle me privately. . . ." His Marian lecture was
"longer than usual. There is no doubt of the strong human appeal of
the Blessed Mother when she is properly presented to a non-Catholic
audience." Bishop concluded the lecture series with a blessing for
which the audience stood and Howard shook hands with everyone as
the people departed, a custom he had started at the first lecture.[65]

A second lecture series was presented in Batavia, Ohio and featured Raphael Sourd and Howard Bishop. Unlike at Lynchburg, this
one was held in a Catholic church, obviously an inhibiting factor for
non-Catholic attendance. Though relatively well received the lectures
were not as lively as the previous ones nor did they merit any positive
comment in Bishop's diary. He didn't record the third lecture series
that he alone presented in Blanchester, where he preached at a mission church. The public lecture series was well covered in the Spring
issue of *The Challenge*. In this article entitled "Skirmishing on the
Mission Front," Bishop stated that these "preaching campaigns were
not intended as a test of the effectiveness of missionary preaching in
such places, nor were they in any sense a sample of the type of offensive effort that our methods call for." Instead they were simply lec-

tures with little preparatory "spade work" and no base parish from which to organize a sustained effort. However, Bishop and Sourd intended to go to the same places the following summer "with an open-air program."[66]

Throughout the winter and spring of 1939 Howard Bishop was in frequent contact with James J. Navagh, a priest of the diocese of Buffalo who had indicated an interest in joining the society. In early March he traveled to Brant, New York to visit him, and in mid-April Navagh visited Cincinnati. Howard noted in his diary that the young thirty-five year old priest is a "very quiet man, not given to glib talk and wisecracks. Seldom laughs, very serious but in an unassuming way. There is a suggestion that the human side in him is insufficiently developed. Says he plays no golf, cards, or baseball—all take too much time—but instead he works."[67] However, a sense of trust and good will developed between the founder and the potential candidate. Navagh deferred the decision to join the society to his bishop, John A. Duffy. In early May Howard met with Duffy, only to discover that the bishop would not release Navagh, at least not for a year or two.[68] Though as late as the following October he told Navagh and Bishop not to worry, he never gave him permission to join the home missioners. Later Duffy appointed Navagh director of the Missionary Apostolate of the diocese. In 1952 he was auxiliary bishop of Raleigh and in 1965 he became ordinary of the diocese of Paterson.

While Navagh's bishop was reluctant to lose him to a society yet to be born, Howard Bishop's ordinary was very supportive of the home mission plan. At an archdiocesan clergy retreat in June of 1938 McNicholas gave "a fine tribute" to Howard Bishop. He said that he had known of Bishop's "work for a quarter of a century." He discussed the plan and presented "his own conviction that a religious society is necessary instead of just diocesan work, basing this on an opinion of Bishop Walsh, founder of Maryknoll," Howard noted in his diary. McNicholas concluded by saying that his priests were free to join Bishop "with his full permission and encouragement." At this retreat Howard felt "totally inadequate" in making friends and companions among the Cincinnati clergy, feelings that appeared to him to have increased by "His Grace's wonderful boost last night." He admitted that this may have been the product of his imagination. He also confided in his diary that "My shyness is nothing new but doubly painful in a place where I am not known."[69]

Bishop and Sourd preached at open-air meetings in southern Ohio during June 1939 reported on by Bishop in *The Challenge*. To those accustomed to the "dignified services" in the church he explained that the home missioners were following the example of Jesus and the primitive church. "Yes, gypsy-preaching you may call it," but how else will the unchurched and non-Catholics in general receive "our invitation to Christian unity." The preachers used loudspeakers, played records of popular hymns, and presented a slide show of "pictures of the life of Christ and other sacred subjects on the screen."[70]

In this same issue of *The Challenge* under the headline "Announcement Extraordinary" was the news that Raphael Sourd had joined the Home Missioners of America. The spiritual director at St. Gregory's Seminary had for some time demonstrated an interest in "convert making." When Bishop arrived at St. Martin's Parish in July of 1937, Sourd was there to meet him. The major factor in his decision was the street preaching experience.[71] Some nineteen years after the death of Howard Bishop, Sourd recalled reading the plan in *The American Ecclesiastical Review*. He said that he was "not personally attracted to Father Bishop." Their personalities were quite different. When he mentioned this to McNicholas, the archbishop considered it to be an advantage as if the two would establish a balanced beginning. Neither Bishop nor Sourd ever considered the latter to be a co-founder of the society. Sourd confirmed Bishop's reference to his strong interest in convert-making and that their time together convinced him that, despite their difference, he could live and work with Bishop. Unlike Spence, who considered Bishop to be impractical in turning down wealthy parishes for the poor ones, Sourd admired the founder's priorities.[72]

Raphael Sourd's entrance into the society added to the permanence of the pioneer home missioners. With seven seminarians enrolled by the summer of 1939 Howard Bishop announced "The First Roll Call" in *The Challenge*. Five of the seven student members were from the archdiocese of Cincinnati. Paul Thompson, the young parishioner of St. Louis Parish in Clarksville, was the first to join in February 1938, while Alphonsus Atkinson of Inwood, West Virginia did not arrive in Cincinnati until the fall of 1939. Both Thompson and Atkinson chose to remain laymen and returned to their homes in the early 1940s. The Cincinnati students were ordained priests for the home missioners: Clement Borchers, Earl McGrath, Francis Massarella, Edward Smith and Benedict Wolf. With the exception of Edward Smith, who had been a seminarian at Maryknoll, all were attracted to the society during one of Howard Bishop's talks at the seminaries. Smith was introduced to Bishop by priests who were on the watch for promising prospects for the society.[73]

In an article in that Summer issue of *The Challenge* Francis Masserella clearly conveyed the pioneer spirit that prevailed at the first official gathering of the Home Missioners of America. "He [Father Bishop] gave us a very pleasant welcome and by his kind and cheerful ways won the affection of all of us. We assembled in his room and thus began in so humble and simple a way our little community."[74] According to Howard's diary the date of the meeting was June 29, 1939. "Our first meeting as a Society occurs at St. Gregory's Seminary where we began a summer course in conjunction with theologians from St. Mary's." The theologians met for a preaching class while Bishop taught the philosophers a reading course in rural sociology. They gathered together for night and morning prayers, and for spiritual conferences.[75]

The first weekend (July 1–3) was spent in St. Martin's Parish when Bishop rented a "little farm house . . . where I provided seven beds, seven wash basins and a bucket to haul water, 3 coal oil lamps, some window shades and rugs. All of us but Sourd spent the night there. We gathered in the yard after inspecting our quarters and sang Holy God We Praise Thy Name, then recited the beads. . . . Thence back to the church of St. [Martin's, a mile walk] where we sang the 'Te Deum.' "[76] At Sunday mass the next day Bishop "announced to [the] congregation our Society was beginning in their midst."[77] Many years later Benedict Wolf recalled the time at the old house in St. Martin's. "We had to carry water from an old pump, about one hundred yards away from the house. He [Bishop] really liked to rough it. Each night that we were there, he would gather us around and we'd have our night prayers together. . . . After our prayers we would have a songfest and a gabfest, and talk over things. He'd tell us all kinds of stories about his mission experiences, and some of his dreams."[78]

At the end of July the home missioners gave their "first course of sermons" in the town of West Union located in Adams County, designated by Archbishop McNicholas as a mission area for Bishop's pioneer society. On July 30, 1939 the founder gave his first formal talk "to our Boys":

Under the inspiration of Christ's love for mankind and the guidance of the Holy Spirit we are privileged to begin a great work.

Missionary need on all sides overwhelming as represented by 20+
millions or about $\frac{1}{6}$ of 130 millions. Very special need in rural sections largest proportion non-Catholic, largest influence on future
of America.

We shall pursue our work by:
(1) establishing bases among them.
(2) spreading our influence all about these bases.
(3) spreading the contagion of missionary effort among diocesan
    priests.

Preparation necessary:
(1) We must sanctify ourselves.
(2) Steer free from sophisticated spirit and professional spirit.
(3) Study our mission needs.[79]

Two years is not a long time to establish a new community, but to
Howard Bishop, driven and determined to achieve his goal with characteristic impatience, the time seemed quite long indeed. Throughout this period he gave many speeches to students and made several
appeals for funds in parishes. He corresponded with bishops and
with potential candidates. He edited one issue of *Landward* and four
issues of *The Challenge,* ran a parish and a mission, and maintained an
active spiritual life by frequent conferences with his Jesuit spiritual
director and by annual retreats. However, throughout this time he
only recorded one day of deep worry about the slow pace of his
progress. The strong Cincinnati representation in the society indicates the deeply significant role of place in the foundation of the
Home Missioners. Not only did McNicholas welcome him and provide him with a rural parish but he publicly encouraged his own
priests to consider joining the new society.

Howard Bishop's shyness and diffidence would have been inhibiting factors for progress had he not been encouraged by his archbishop. However, the person and the plan were more important to
him than the place. His opening remark to his "boys" on July 30, 1939

reveals his deeply religious commitment to fulfill the need for rural evangelization: "Under the inspiration of Christ's love for mankind and the guidance of the Holy Spirit we are privileged to begin a great work."

CHAPTER 8

The Men Missioners
1939–1946

The Home Missioners of America was not a canonical religious community in 1939. There was no rule to provide for spiritual, ministerial and material needs of the group and for the governance of the community. It was an ad hoc gathering of two diocesan priests and five seminarians. Had McNicholas succeeded to the archdiocese of New York (as would have been the case had Pius XII fulfilled the wishes of his predecessor) then the future of the society would have been in jeopardy. As founder Howard was considered the superior, but according to canon law Bishop's superior was McNicholas. Hence, all substantive questions were brought to him for his decision and approval.

In a letter of "cordial approval of the Catholic Home Missioners of America," McNicholas assured the founder that "you have the confidence of the priests of Cincinnati." The archbishop added, "You came to us a stranger. Your brother priests for nearly two years have observed you and weighed very carefully the work that you hope, in God's Providence, to do. The corporate judgment of our priests now is one of cordial approval." McNicholas noted the "diocesan" character of the society, but indicated that "in due time" the society may "merit the approval of the Holy See." In the meantime he authorized the society to accept invitations from other dioceses to take charge of regions that were priestless. He closed with a reiteration of his commitment to release those seminarians who wish to join the missioners but would only do so if they are "thoroughly zealous men . . . who have given evidence . . . of real self sacrifice." The letter, antedated August 15, 1939, but composed in 1944, marks the official beginning of the Home Missioners of America.[1]

Until the home mission seminary was established, students attended the Cincinnati seminaries: St. Gregory's and the major seminary, Mount St. Mary's, with fees paid by the archdiocese. However, if a student for the home missioners was from another diocese, then the community was charged $200, about 80% of the cost. As was the custom in many dioceses McNicholas cautioned each seminarian that once he decided to join the home missioners or any other society he would not be allowed to return as a candidate for his archdiocese. Because Raphael Sourd had been spiritual director at St. Gregory's and therefore knew many students quite well, McNicholas told Howard Bishop that he must refrain from private recruiting and limit his contact at the seminaries to his own students and relate to the others only in the public forum unless they sought a private meeting. Though McNicholas publicly supported Bishop's society, rumors circulated that he would never permit seminarians to enter any society until some time after they were ordained for the archdiocese. Though Howard Bishop was short-tempered and was determined to control the flow of events, he was still very deferential toward his episcopal sponsor. On a practical level, the disagreements between the archbishop and the founder were very few; indeed there was a general agreement on all major questions. McNicholas even contributed funds to the society. On one occasion he presented an anonymous gift to the Extension Society with the stipulation that it be given to the Home Missioners of America.[2]

During the society's first eight months Howard Bishop and Raphael Sourd lived at St. Martin's. Since there was an assistant pastor also in residence, the two priests could travel for fund-raising appeals and vocation talks at seminaries and high schools. Because of his familiarity with the area Bishop covered the northeastern and middle Atlantic states while Sourd focused on the midwest. As will be discussed later, the two men were able to work well together because they were such opposites. Sourd tended to be intuitive and impulsive whereas Bishop was analytical and controlled. With family nearby, Sourd easily found some relief from the routine. Howard Bishop became quite friendly with his adopted family, the Santens. Margaret Mary Santen founded the guild in support of the home missions, and Harry Santen gradually became Bishop's confidant and financial and legal advisor.

Sourd made his first appearance in *The Challenge*'s Christmas issue of 1939. Sourd focused on mission efforts at St. Mary of the Assumption Church in Manchester, which the community had renovated after the past summer's "open-air preaching campaign." Sunday mass was offered there every two weeks. In Buena Vista, twenty miles away, the church was ruined by a flood in the mid 1930s. Subsequently, the home missioners offered mass in a private home. Sourd described the missionary strategy: "our base town of two thousand inhabitants boasts a daily newspaper and a weekly. Both editors have been helpful and cooperative though neither is a Catholic. At our request these newspapers are now publishing weekly releases on Catholic life and doctrine that we supply to them . . . thus helping us spread Catholic truth. These releases will serve to clear the atmosphere of lingering prejudices and stimulate interest in the Church of Jesus Christ. It is one of the follow-up activities carried on between our preaching campaigns." The other was an inquiry class for non-Catholics and Catholics. A priest from Fayetteville, Sourd's hometown, and the Catholic people "of our tiny mission" sponsored card parties and bingo games to raise funds for the home missionary efforts.[3]

In the same Christmas issue that Raphael Sourd was identified as the priest-missioner, Howard Bishop identified himself as the founder and vocation director. In an article on "The Conquest of No-Priestland" he once again revealed his broad vision. He related the social encyclical of Pius XI, *Quadrigesimo Anno,* to the need for restoring the social order in the United States through developing the nation's spiritual roots in the rural area by bringing Catholicity to the "65,000,000 people who are not affiliated with any church." He noted the restoration of a "ghost parish" in southern Ohio. He referred to the home mission work as a Catholic "revival service" in this area. He placed this effort as a minuscule part of what is needed, but nevertheless it marked significant "headway . . . in a region formally given over to the Ku Klux Klan."[4]

In an article entitled "Home Mission Vocation" the founder attempted to appeal to those young men who would be attracted to the rugged life of working with mountain people, with sharecroppers of both races, and with the generally alienated people of the rural areas. Indeed he portrayed the rural missionary in the imagery of the lone frontiersman of the faith.

The young man who prepares for the Home Missions will not have to learn to speak Chinese, but he will have to study the environment, the work and the ways of many different kinds of rural people from the swamp people of the Swanee River region who are neighbors to the alligator and the crocodile to the lumbermen and fishermen of the Columbia River, the habitat of the salmon and the tuna. He will know the prejudices and superstitions, the loves and the hatreds, the virtues and vices of the backwoods sections, from the mountains of Pennsylvania to the plains of Texas. He will know climates and crops and seasons and the economic and social conditions among landowners, tenants and farm laborers from the great wheat ranches of the Northwest to the plantations and the little mountain "clearings" of the Southeast. He will know how to defend himself not only against hecklers who may try to break up his meetings but against snakes and mosquitoes and the germs of disease that threaten his life or health. He will know how to apply first-aid and simple remedies to himself and others in case of injury or sickness where doctors cannot be reached. He will know how to help the poor and ignorant to have better crops and healthier surroundings. He will know how to cook a meal that will be fit to eat. He will know how to mend his own clothes when he has to. He will be equally at home driving a motor chapel over the smooth state roads or riding a horse through rough mountain trails.

But most of all and best of all, he will know how to touch the hearts of simple people with the glorious and saving truths of the Gospel of Jesus Christ. He will know how to make them take home his words from sermons and inquiry classes to their quiet firesides where they will repeat them to their children and ponder them in their hearts—and then come back for more and more again.[5]

Howard Bishop may have been more analytical than Sourd but as a writer Bishop blended analysis with his romantic attachment to the land and the home mission cause. He became almost triumphal in his depiction of that life. ". . . THERE IS NO OCCUPATION IN AMERICA THAT DEMANDS MORE IN BRAINS, SANCTITY, JUDGEMENT, AND PHYSICAL AND SPIRITUAL ENDURANCE THAN THE HOME MISSION-FIELD, NOR IS THERE AN OCCUPATION THAT OFFERS A RICHER, MORE VARIED, OR

MORE SOUL-SATISFYING CAREER TO THOSE WHO STUDY
FOR THE CHURCH."[6]

Howard encouraged his seminarians to write for *The Challenge*.
Edward Smith contributed a brief didactic story of a poverty stricken
young boy yearning for the spirit of Christmas but frustrated by parents who were ignorant and prejudiced against all religion.[7] In the
Spring issue of 1940 Francis A. Wuest, a recent candidate and a second year theologian at St. Mary's Seminary in Cincinnati, contributed
an article on the "Rural Family and Family Life." The unity of the
farm family and the family's "constant contact with nature" were
sketched in idyllic terms. "The genial sunshine, the blossoming trees,
the golden grain, the welcome rains and murmuring brooks—all
these have a deep meaning and a soul-stirring effect on rural dwell-
ings. In the country God's works on creation are still undis-
turbed. . . . The farmer is more interested in being good than in
making good."[8] The triumphalist character of Wuest's portrayal of
the role of the church in country life represented a trend among the
pioneer home missioners, one which derived from the romantic character of the founder's perspective on the rural urban dichotomy.

In the second meeting of the society of five seminarians and Raphael Sourd, Bishop opened his talk with the simple message that the
church in America increases by births, immigration and conversion
and that because of low birth rate and immigrant restrictionism conversions represent the "only great promise." He listed three advantages of a "convert program."

1. Salvation open to converts.
2. Helps toward the Christian social order.
3. Brings back fallen-aways.

He then spoke on the methods of the home missionary: preaching in
churches, in halls and in open-air meetings. One may appeal to the
"stray non-Catholics in church; few people attend lectures in halls."
His experience was that these open-air meetings "require no effort
from the people" and allow for "maximum accessibility." He also
noted the use of open-air evangelization by Jesus and the apostles and
by contemporary Protestant preachers and its neglect by Catholics.
He told the community of the need to study the methodology of such
preaching. Besides preaching, the home missioners should be cate-

chists through individual contact both casual and methodical, such as follow-through letters and calls.[9]

Howard Bishop favored specific programs to foster the establishment of "a new social order." At that second meeting he spoke on the need for medical missions (clinics and hospitals), for credit unions, and for 4H clubs. He reiterated his commitment to the colonization efforts of the landward movement and to the general "social uplift" of the community through adult education in domestic crafts and new farming methods. He also informed his pioneer community of the need for publishing printed propaganda along the lines established by *Our Sunday Visitor*. The outlines for his talks were positive in content without any references to urban decay, except for criticism of the evils of birth control in the cities.[10]

Of course he continued to draw parallels between the foreign and the home missions and proudly referred to his society as "Maryknoll's sister movement."[11] On one occasion his portrayal of the need for home mission efforts received national attention. At the seventh national congress of the Confraternity of Christian Doctrine (C.C.D.), held in Philadelphia, November 15–18, 1941, Howard Bishop spoke on the Home Mission Society.[12]

In an article in the *New York Times* (November 18, 1941) there were several excerpts from Bishop's talk.

The Rev. W. Howard Bishop of Glendale, Ohio, addressing a session on rural confraternity work, said that it was time "that we stopped high-hatting and snubbing and overlooking our home missions in favor of the foreign missions.

"I am a firm believer in the foreign missions, as every true Catholic should be, and I think one of the finest achievements of the Catholic Church in America is the establishment of the American Foreign Mission Society of Maryknoll.

"But it is high time that our home mission job ceases to be the Cinderella or red-headed stepchild of the Church. Our Lord said, 'Go and teach all nations,' and He made no exception of our own America.

"No, Our Lord wants us to go into our own country and convert our own people. The almond-eyed children of the Orient and the black-faced children of Africa are no dearer to Him than the spiritually starving children, white and colored, of our beloved United States. Nor have we the right, as church leaders, to be concerned for the one while we ignore the very existence of the other," Father Bishop said.[13]

Three days after this article appeared Monsignor Thomas J. McDonnell, the national director of the Society for the Propagation of the Faith, an organization responsible for expanding the awareness of missions and for fund raising, wrote an irate letter to Howard Bishop. After quoting the *Times* excerpts he said that "This statement will do serious harm to the mission cause in the United States. We feel that you are creating division and misunderstanding among our Catholic faithful." He then reminded Bishop of the Society's contribution to home missions and told him that such statements as he expressed "must be stopped" or American Catholics may not continue to meet the financial needs of missions throughout the world. He also told Bishop that he had informed the episcopal committee of the national council of his divisive statement.[14]

Howard was deeply distressed with McDonnell's reprimand. "Not once but three times," wrote Bishop, "I have read [your letter] and I cannot detect one friendly or even tolerant expression in its two pages of accusation and rebuke." He reminded McDonnell of their friendly correspondence "that so recently preceded . . . such a reprimand," as well as the fact that he had no "authority to administer it [i.e. the reprimand] to one who is in no sense under your jurisdiction." He then proceeded to inform McDonnell that the *Times* reporter relied upon an advanced copy of the address and that the article represents portions of the manuscript lifted out of context. "Had our situations been reversed and had I found you guilty of an indiscretion according to press reports, I should have given you a chance to explain before taking such a drastic action as you report has been taken against me. That, it seems to me, would have been the part of justice."[15]

Bishop explained his address in terms of the need for an offensive missionary effort at home similar to the strategy of the foreign missions. His speech was not intended to be divisive but rather creative, that is, to place home and foreign missions within one great effort rather than to discriminate against evangelizing the "pagans and the separated Christians of the United States, black and white, who are our own kith and kin.'"[16] Bishop enclosed a Maryknoll publication and a copy of *The Challenge* to verify the mutual respect and affection between the foreign and home missionary societies. In his diary Bishop remarked on the "presumptuous tone" of McDonnell's letter. "What right does he have to reprimand me?" He then noted that he left the letter with McNicholas "to read and advise me.'"[17] There is no evidence of the archbishop's views on the conflict. But since that diary citation was November 25 and the letter was dated two days later it is nearly certain that it was mailed. In Cincinnati the Home Missioners of America were rapidly becoming an integral part of the diocesan life. In May of 1940 Archbishop McNicholas allowed the society to live in the old Greene mansion. Monsignor Mathias F. Heyker, chancellor of the archdiocese, stipulated that the society could occupy the house for one year without paying rent, but it was required to pay taxes, to refrain from making any changes or partitions, and to make sure "that the students be careful not to deface the house during the summer months.'"[18] Located on 1840 Madison Road in a very wealthy area of town, it was viewed as a temporary residence until Bishop found a suitable rural location.

In the meantime McNicholas accepted Bishop's resignation from St. Martin's. On July 1, 1940 the founder explained that his "responsibilities as head of the Home Missioners of America have so increased that it has become impossible for me to do justice to both positions.'"[19] Bishop was reluctant to accept the offer of the mansion. As he noted in his diary, "There seems to be no backing out of the Madison Road proposition. Let us go through with it and make every effort to find property.'"[20] Concerned about "war talk" and its consequences on a building program, he was determined to at least secure a piece of property with a modest house.

In June 1940 the society's subdeacons, Borchers, Massarella and Wolf, began mission classes in preparation for the July open-air evangelization campaign in Brown County. Bishop explained their role: "Their part this summer is to explain to our wayside audiences the [slide] views from the Acts of the Apostles that are thrown upon a screen before and after the principal address of the evening which is given by one of the Fathers [i.e. Sourd or Bishop].'"[21] During the six-week campaign the Home Missioners purchased an eighty-seven acre farm with a thirteen-room house located in Glendale, Ohio, thirteen miles north of Cincinnati. Bishop described it as "a very

respectable old farm residence with a delayed vocation to sanctity."
He understood the fact that it was "not a pretentious place but . . .
within our small financial reach without the necessity of a great debt
to hamper our progress."[22] The center hallway of the house was partitioned to form a chapel; St. Gregory's Seminary donated an altar,
and on the feast of All Saints the five seminarians and the two priests
celebrated the first community mass at the first motherhouse of the
Home Missioners. Howard Bishop spoke in characteristic language:

> We look at our beautiful little altar and its fresh, white coat, decked
> with chrysanthemums of the dying season. We think of the genera-
> tions of priests for whom it has been the center of worship in the
> past and of future generations for whom it will yet be the altar of
> Divine Sacrifice long after we have been gathered to our fathers.
> The symbol on the front of the altar—the entwined Greek letters
> Alpha and Omega—give point to our meditation. He who is the
> Beginning and the End, ever old ever new, will keep our infant
> Society, made of the raveled ends of many parts, and weave it into a
> fabric of a future which none of us can foresee.[23]

The community at the motherhouse, referred to by the name of
the town, Glendale, numbered five: Bishop, Sourd, and the three
recently ordained deacons, Borchers, Massarella and Wolf. On December 1, 1940, Vincent Wilmes, a brother candidate, arrived at Glendale. Born on a farm near O'Fallon, Missouri, Brother Vincent's
spiritual director was the famous liturgist, Father Martin Hellriegel,
then chaplain at the Precious Blood Convent in O'Fallon. Vincent
recalled that he gave Hellriegel as a personal reference in his application to the society. It is not unlikely that Bishop met Hellriegel at a
convention of the N.C.R.L.C., for the latter thought Bishop was a
good judge of character. Vincent was a "bit startled" when he first
met Howard Bishop. "I think [the] *Challenge* had pictured him with a
young picture, and he seemed much older." His first impression was,
however, quite positive. "Well, coming there as a stranger, I felt like I
was being well treated. Although I was a newcomer, they just accepted me as a gift."[24] With much work to be done at the new motherhouse, Brother Vincent settled into several jobs. It was not until the
1960s that brothers were allowed to pursue academic studies. Bishop
was a traditionalist on the division of labor among priests and

brothers but he was never known to manifest a social clericalism nor to "talk down" to the brothers.

The first Christmas at Glendale was a festive time, but war in Europe and the Far East cast a cloud over the event. Howard Bishop recorded his brief Christmas sermon in his diary. He referred to the prince of peace and commented on how the "world's leaders have spurned His generous gift." In these days of darkness America is "blessed beyond all others with the things that give security and hope. . . . [But] even here we feel the tremors that are shaking Europe to ruins. Only in God is there real security and real hope. And of all institutions on earth only his Church can be sure of lasting through." The founder then declared, "At such a time and in such a nation as America we dare with His help to begin our new Society."[25]

Howard Bishop predicted the rise of the "new world . . . from the ruins of the old," a condition that would require "new institutions with a new outlook and new methods, for this will be a new period in the life of a very old Church. . . . In a land where all human hope is not yet gone, in a land which may be destined to become the almshouse and the hospital of an impoverished and wounded world— here, in this land of hope, under God, to begin an institute that can bring the only wealth that is lasting and the only remedy that can heal . . . our mission of war-weary, heart-sick disillusioned separated brethren—when peace may finally come upon the world." The founder concluded with a challenge to the members of his newly formed society: "These are for us not days of despair but days of dedication. Let each man take his vocation as a message straight from God. Let each man resolve to give himself to the limit of his power. Let us resolve here on this Christmas morning, with the example of Christ's self-giving for mankind before us, to give ourselves for the extension of Christ's Kingdom on the earth."[26]

During that year he made a thirty day Ignatian retreat at the Jesuit novitiate in Milford, Ohio, a suburb of Cincinnati. He was allowed four days of recreation rather than the usual one day break in the middle of the retreat. Those days were spent in rides in the country; home mission business was prohibited. Howard Bishop first noted the desire to make such a retreat in early 1940. He noted in his diary for January 22 that "the life of St. Ignatius has impressed me so profoundly and made me so sensible of my insufficiency for the work to which I have dedicated myself that I have been considering making a 30 day retreat at some Jesuit House."[27] He consulted with his Jesuit confessor, Francis Haggeney, but he hesitated to recommend an Ignatian retreat because Archbishop McNicholas was a Dominican and because of the "wide divergence" between Ignatian and Dominican retreats. Obviously Bishop sensed that there was no such episcopal objection.[28]

On June 7, 1941 Archbishop McNicholas ordained thirteen young men to the priesthood; three were committed to the home missions: Francis Massarella, Clement Borchers, and Benedict Wolf. The following day Raphael Sourd preached during Massarella's first mass at St. Francis de Sales Church in Cincinnati. Sourd had known the newly ordained priest for many years, was well acquainted with the family, and had served as an assistant pastor at St. Francis Parish. That same day Howard Bishop preached at Clement Borchers' first mass held at St. Michael's Church in Fort Loramie, Ohio. He noted in his diary that he chose the sermon topic from the prayers at the foot of the altar: "I will go up into the altar of God, of God who gives joy to my youth." Howard was "deeply impressed by the deep, quiet faith of the solidly Catholic neighborhood and by the Borchers family."[29] A week later Bishop preached at Benedict Wolf's first mass in LaRue, Ohio. He recorded the contrasts between the two experiences: "The situation was the reverse of Ft. Loramie. The Wolf family are poor—the Borchers well to do. Ft. Loramie is all Catholic, LaRue practically all Protestant—we have only a mission church [the mass took place in a school auditorium]—pastor lives in a distant town. . . ." It was a very festive occasion. ". . . everybody was happy. A lovely dinner served in school. . . . Numbers of Protestants at both Mass and dinner."[30] Of Father Wolf's nine brothers and sisters eight were in the service of the church; his five sisters were nuns, one brother was a priest, one was a Benedictine brother and one was a seminarian.

The founder had decided to send his young priests to the Preachers' Institute at The Catholic University of America under the direction of Ignatius Smith, O.P. Bishop told Smith that "our three young shepherds" will be "entrusted . . . to your tender care." He was concerned that the three priests "live together so as to keep up their community spirit as far as possible."[31] Bishop suggested boarding them at the O'Hara home but Smith replied that he had arranged with Louis Arand, the Sulpician president of Divinity College at Caldwell Hall, to have them live on campus. Bishop had asked him about discipline, to which Smith responded with his assurance that the men at the Preachers' Institute "have to work hard in the hot weather that they have neither time nor energy for play. We have had not a single case of disciplinary trouble in ten years."[32] Louis Arand did arrange for them to stay at the university and must have been impressed by Howard Bishop's recommendation.[33] He told Arand, "You may feel perfect confidence that their clerical standing is excellent and their conduct, judging from all past experience in their regard, should be of the best."[34]

Fathers Borchers, Massarella and Wolf were "greatly refreshed and enthused from their six weeks of study and travel."[35] They returned from Washington, D.C. via Maryknoll, one of the streams at the delta of the home missioners. Besides his enormous debt of gratitude to James A. Walsh of Maryknoll, the Glenmary founder had consistently referred to the Home Missioners as descendants of the other co-founder, Thomas F. Price, originally of the Mission Apostolate of North Carolina. He also noted the influence of the Paulist Fathers' evangelization in the urban areas, Stephen Leven's "street preaching activities," and his own experiences as rural pastor and long-time participant in The Catholic Rural Life Conference. One day after their return from the east each of the three young priests departed for a street preaching assignment. Borchers was sent to the Paulists in Winchester, Tennessee where they had a summer trailer mission; Massarella went to the Vincentian summer preaching campaign in rural Missouri; Wolf went to work with Stephen Leven in Ponca City, Oklahoma.[35]

The Winchester Paulists had begun the trailer-chapel campaign in September of 1937; two Paulists, James Cunningham and Thomas Halloran, led the mission on "St. Lucy's Motor Chapel." Actually the trailer was twenty-three feet long, and besides the chapel and living accommodations for the missionaries it had a confessional, a pamphlet rack, a balcony and a sound system.[36] In an interview Benedict Wolf said that whereas the Preachers' Institute at Catholic University centered on the techniques of homiletics, Stephen Leven's focus was a blend of scripture and apologetics within the context of the street-preaching mission.[37] The Vincentians had embarked on their first motor-mission campaign in Missouri as early as 1934. According to an N.C.W.C. news release (July 9, 1937), the Vincentians at Kenrick Seminary trained seminarians in street-preaching to non-Catholics during the summers. One group was under the direction of L.J. Fallon, C.M.,[38] a Vincentian founder of the Catholic information agency adopted as a state program by the Missouri Knights of Columbus; in 1948 the agency came under the direction of the Supreme Council in New Haven.

Howard Bishop established a small Catholic Information Center in Adams County, Ohio. Though it was short-lived, it illustrates the broad-based character of his evangelistic efforts in rural America.

While the three young priests were engaged in post-ordination studies, Howard Bishop was preparing for their next experience, a blend of a novitiate and mission school at Glendale. Because the Home Missioners had not received canonical status, the "novitiate" was an unofficial year of formation that emphasized spirituality and missionary training. It was referred to as a probandate or probationary year as well as a novitiate. However, the term "mission school" describes the year's major function in the light of Howard Bishop's diary and correspondence. Howard Bishop had renovated an old farm shed to house his office, but the farm house was too small for the community of five priests, one brother and the four prospective priests then in their third and fourth year of theology. As Bishop noted in his diary some seven months before the invasion of Pearl Harbor, "with rising prices and war we may not get a chance to build so cheaply for 4 or 5 years. Meantime, our numbers increase and our old house becomes uninhabitable."[39] Within a span of only four months a rectangular two-story frame building that Bishop termed "modern colonial" was ready. On October 26, 1941 the founder celebrated a solemn mass in the new chapel (24' by 30') and Clement Borchers preached. Besides the chapel, the first floor included a community room and conference hall, while the second floor had twelve sleeping rooms and a bath. The attic was unfinished but it was constructed with a dormitory in mind. With its elongated structure and its simple wood materials the building earned the nickname "the barracks." Even before it was built, the old farmhouse was used for an office, dining room and kitchen. For someone to direct the mission course for his young priests the founder turned to Maryknoll. In a letter to Bishop James E. Walsh, Howard requested a Maryknoll priest who would teach a course in homiletics, in scripture with an emphasis on mission preaching, in apologetics, and in rural sociology. He would act as a consultant on spiritual and practical formation.[40] Walsh recommended Francis MacRae, a forty-five year old priest who had spent almost ten years as a missionary in South China. Because of ill health he had returned to assist in the society's novitiate. At that time he was engaged in promotional work in Cleveland. Bishop was very pleased after MacRae visited Glenmary a week later, and it was decided that he would teach homiletics and scripture and help in spiritual formation.[41]

A major misunderstanding occurred when Raphael Sourd overheard MacRae say that Bishop Walsh had told him that he was expected to do Maryknoll promotional work while he was in Cincinnati. Bishop noted in his diary that "our house must not be made a spring board for Maryknoll propaganda activity."[42] He wrote to Bishop Walsh about the matter which he said was "of some delicacy . . . and I pray that . . . [it] may not endanger the very friendly and cordial relations that exist between us personally and between our Societies. . . ."[43] Walsh replied with assurances that MacRae would not engage in promotional activities; he displayed "some irritation that we 'even thought of such a thing,' " Bishop recorded in his diary.[44] Not long after MacRae arrived to begin his year with the Home Missioners of America, Bishop noted that "he is a jewel. He takes the boys out for softball after dinner. It brings life into our group—a thing we sorely needed."[45] Relations between the two societies were not damaged by Howard's rather impulsive letter to Walsh. The Maryknoll periodical *Field Afar* included an article entitled "At Home" which featured Howard Bishop's adoption of the "foreign-mission technique of settling permanently on non-Catholic territory and laboring among non-Catholics on a full-time, year-round basis."[46] To further illustrate the continuation of cordial relations, Howard wrote to James E. Walsh: "Good Father MacRae is a wonder of patience, tact, industry, piety and zeal."[47] In the Christmas edition of *The Challenge* an article on MacRae included a reference to how his presence among the home missioners tended to "cement closer than ever the bond of friendship" between Glenmary and Maryknoll."[48]

In the first mission school Bishop taught rural sociology. He introduced the students to the distributist agrarianism that he had absorbed from Belloc, Chesterton, and Agar and to the programs of the National Catholic Rural Life Conference. Raphael Sourd, who was frequently out of town on fund-raising appeals, had little experience in organized rural life activities. In October of 1941 he and Bishop sponsored a Home Missioners exhibit at the N.C.R.L.C. Convention in Jefferson City, Missouri. The booth was quite elaborate with "automatically waving flags and our automatic stereo-opticon with screen."[49]

The entrance of the United States into World War II affected the Home Missioners less than more established religious communities. Their vocations remained slow but steady, and they had no institutional development to maintain during a period of privation and rationing. In his first mid-winter newsletter that he referred to as "a casual letter sheet of timely gossip," Howard Bishop published his first exhortation in the context of the war. "In all the stress of war and war-like preparations in which we heartily cooperate with all other good citizens in striving for a victorious and a just peace—we must *not* forget that other victories must be won. . . . There must be a spiritual victory. . . . Let us pray for peace with justice and let us meanwhile redouble our efforts to PRODUCE . . . that spiritual awakening that will ensure a just peace." Employing the rhetoric of war, he referred to the home front, "Christianizing America from the roots up," as a significant process of "spiritual regeneration" within the general campaign for a spiritual awakening. He made a plea for vocations "to wage the warfare of the spirit against unbelief and sin [and] to make peaceful conquest"[50] of those priestless counties.

In the subsequent issues of *The Challenge* the founder continued to explore the home mission themes in terms of "A Call to Battle" and "On the Firing Line." The latter was an article on the society's open-air missions. In 1941 the Kuntz family of Dayton, Ohio contributed funds for a trailer chapel modeled on those used by the Paulists of Winchester, Tennessee and the Vincentians in Perryville, Missouri. Named the "Chapel of the American Martyrs," the patron saints of the Home Missioners of America, the trailer was first used in the spring campaign of 1942. In *The Challenge* Bishop explained that "The missioners have found the trailer set-up an excellent means of introducing the Catholic Church to the people. Large numbers have been enabled to see at close range and to have explained to them the altar, vestments, candles, crucifix, chalice, missal, stations of the cross and confessional."[51] Occasionally one of the missioners, either Raphael Sourd or one of the young priests, would say mass in the trailer. In the evening after prayers, hymns, and talks on Catholic topics, the people could inspect the trailer. There would also be "distribution of

literature, medals and holy pictures as well as enrollment of interested people in the monthly edition of *Our Sunday Visitor*."[52] Sourd
wrote to Bishop about one of the first trailer-chapel experiences.
"Last night was glorious. Tried on the vestments on the platform . . .
asked the crowd to be reverent and no untoward incidents occurred.
Many stood in awe and rapt attention. I believe it is a good piece of
technique."[53]

From Brownsville, Kentucky, Sourd reported that the groups
averaged 75 to 110 people. "Very interested and very attentive. Holy
pictures, medals and statues in great demand. The boys and girls are
asking for the '*little dolls*,' meaning statues." Occasionally, the missioners were "tantalized 'by anti-Catholic remarks.' " On one campaign, he said, a Jehovah's witness "tantalized us by numerous incon-
gruous questions for several evenings."[54]

An incident on July 18, 1942 entailed rumors that the two missioners were arrested as spies because they revealed blueprints and
were taking pictures of the people. The following day Bishop noted in
his diary: "More rumors. Priests had said all non C's would go to hell;
priests had not paid their bills at store. Enemies have been very busy.
The few Catholics are upset, the non C's in an ugly mood."[55]

During his many years on the missions, Sourd experienced only
two violent situations. On a follow-up visit to an elderly man interested in learning about the Catholic faith, the man's son fired a shot-
gun above Sourd's head.[56] About a year later Sourd was preaching in
Kentucky. During a question–answer period "a stone was thrown
into the [trailer] chapel, one struck the opposite side, and then a third
found lodgement about the left temple of the speaker—drawing
blood and narrowly missing his spectacles. . . . So Howard old Boy,"
continued Sourd, "the first blood has been shed by HMA, for Christ
in America (even though only 50 drops oozed from over the left
temple)." Sourd concluded on a positive note: "Our meeting was a
huge success! Placed many truths before their minds, corrected false
notions, answered several questions that showed deep interest."[57]

Brother Charles Reedy, the second Home Missioner brother, accompanied Sourd on his 1943 campaigns. Besides his general responsibilities for the trailer he assisted him in the movie presentation and
in the informal discussions after the question–answer period. From
one of these missions he wrote to the Glendale community that "Due
to God's grace, to Father Sourd's being known and loved and to the

monies, we have been favorably received, corporally at least in all towns." Brother Vincent, who was Howard Bishop's man of all trades, remained at Glendale. In his letter Brother Charles implied that he knew the burdens of Vincent's job: "To Brother Vincent, until the travellers return may you be empowered with special energy to do the many jobs there. . . ."[58]

When Sourd was not preaching he was normally touring the midwest engaging in fund-raising appeals and in vocation talks at high schools and seminaries. Bishop toured the east coast once or twice a year. He became particularly close to Bishop Richard Cushing, the auxiliary bishop of Boston. He also visited Baltimore/Washington on these tours. However, his primary concern was to administer the society's work that entailed an enormous amount of correspondence.

Because of his rather abrupt manner and his demanding work schedule, secretarial help was a continuous problem. As mentioned earlier, Agnes Mahon was a part-time secretary in 1937–1938. The following year Gertrude Kinnick, also a candidate for the Home Mission Sisters, did some secretarial work until 1942 when the sisters' program became organized. On June 11, 1943 Loretta Ernst, a professional secretary from Cincinnati, became his secretary. She also organized a bookkeeping system; she remained in the latter position long after Bishop died. Appropriately her last post was as archivist. Though Mrs. Ernst was frequently subjected to Bishop's short-temper, she developed a loyalty to Glenmary, the origin of which she attributes to the sensitive concern of Raphael Sourd.

Bishop and Sourd were very proud of their three young confreres. After completing the course at the mission school Borchers, Wolf and Massarella received assignments in No Priestland. After a week-long retreat at St. Meinrad's Abbey, Howard visited with Francis R. Cotton, the bishop of Owensboro, Kentucky to discuss the prospect of mission work in his diocese. Together they visited several missions. A few weeks later he visited Appalachia, Virginia. Though this mining area posed a strong mission challenge, it struck him to be almost prohibitively strong "with probability of long period before converts come in. Perhaps not the best place to start in."[59] The diocese of Owensboro offered "wonderful opportunities."[60] Bishop Cotton offered St. John the Evangelist in Sunfish, Kentucky as a base parish for the society or a church in Clarkston. At first Sunfish appeared too primitive, particularly the parish rectory. Bishop wrote to Cotton,

"The whole situation seems to demand from the start a house where our men can live with simple comfort together. This house should be in a parish they can call their own . . . otherwise the temptation to spend their leisure in the home of some one congenial family or on unnecessary calls on the convent, to the detriment of the Sisters' work, is very strong. Such, I fear, might be the case if they should try to headquarter at first at Sunfish with inadequate living quarters." He was concerned that besides Sunfish the missioners would be responsible for another parish with a school. "Too much care and worry about schools will divert their attention from the non-Catholic mission field, the purpose for which they will be sent." He told Cotton that he was not "trying to dodge responsibilities for these young men." He wished "to proceed with caution in assuming for them such responsibilities as might slow down or hinder their work for non-Catholics." By way of a postscript Bishop told Cotton, "We definitely accept Edmonson County as a mission field, subject to satisfactory arrangement for a base parish with a residence."[61]

Two days later the Glenmary founder informed Bishop Cotton that he had made "the mistake of playing safe by counting on only the average zeal in our young Fathers, not that I did not know that they had more, but just for safety sake. Now that I have gone to the root of things with them, I find I am safe in counting upon them to be real missionaries from the start. So we accept Sunfish and Edmonson County as soon as you can say 'OK, go ahead!' " The two-school issue was settled because the missions where school plans were initiated remained under other priests. Bishop concluded with the news that he would send "a seasoned man along to help the young man get adjusted."[62]

Bishop Cotton was pleased with the founder's decision to settle the first mission in Sunfish. "I have spoken to a number, including some bishops, of your wonderful attitude towards taking territory in the Owensboro Diocese," wrote Francis Cotton to Howard Bishop.[63] Father Clement Borchers was appointed pastor at Sunfish, and Howard explained to Cotton that "the old man" who will accompany Borchers to help him adjust to the mission was himself.[64]

Sunfish is located in Edmonson County, one hundred miles southwest of Louisville. The church of St. John the Evangelist had been a mission of St. Joseph's Church in Leitchfield, some eighteen miles from Sunfish. It had a small school when the Sisters of St. Francis of

St. Francis, Wisconsin taught about eighty students. They lived on the second floor of the school, while a small two-room shack had been built to accommodate the occasional overnight stay of Father Louis Beruatto of Leitchfield. Howard Bishop referred to it as "a frame shack of about the type used as camp shacks and hunting lodges." It was a spartan rectory heated by a wood-burning stove; a hundred yards away was the water cistern and the outdoor toilet facility was about the same distance from the house. Such living conditions caused Bishop some serious doubts: "a caller who has business with one of . . . [the priests] should not have to feel that he is holding up the house." Borchers did not complain of the primitive rectory: "Hardships? Where are they? I left all of that in the city." There were plans to build a three-room addition to the shack but wartime restrictions for material prevented any substantial building. Borchers and a carpenter planned "the very simplest possible addition that will come within the maximum limit of $500.00 placed by the Government on unauthorized building during the War."[65] Despite the primitive rectory Howard Bishop was very pleased to see his plan for a base parish finally implemented, some six years after it had been sketched in the *American Ecclesiastical Review*. He wrote in his diary on June 17, 1942.

Today Edmonson County ceased to be priestless. Fr. Borchers, 1st Pastor of Sunfish, said Mass and reposed the Blessed Sacrament in the tabernacle. I have not left the place today but I go to bed supremely happy. We spent the day arranging the furnishings and our personal effects brought from Glendale, in our two-room mansion. I put up curtains and drapes. I took a bath cottage style. What a luxury!!! God Bless the place. What a sweet, peaceful serenity always.[66]

Though he was fifty-six years old at this time, Howard Bishop enkindled the idealism manifested at St. Louis, in Clarksville, in the League of the Little Flower and in the National Catholic Rural Conference. In early September the Home Missioners took charge of their second parish in the Owensboro diocese, Sacred Heart Church in Russellville. Father Benedict Wolf, who grew up on a farm in Agosta, Ohio, was appointed pastor by Bishop Cotton. According to the tentative rule, based on the published plan, each mission should have two priests in order to protect the individual from the loneliness of rural life. Because the counties served by Sacred Heart were adjacent to Borchers' parish in Sunfish each could drive the sixty-five mile distance between the two parishes "to visit frequently and spend one night a week in each other's house," wrote Howard Bishop in *The Challenge*.[67]

The Russellville parish had only 100 Catholics; the two mission counties attached to the parish, Franklin and Logan, included only a handful of Catholics. In an interview, Benedict Wolf explained that the day he arrived the previous pastor left and he therefore had to fend for himself. He knew absolutely no one. He was told that the hotel in the town of 4,000 people would provide him with meals.[68] Because Wolf was a very good student Bishop had decided that he would eventually be sent to graduate school in preparation for teaching at the Home Missioners' seminary. Indeed, prior to being assigned to Russellville, Wolf taught the four Home Missioners' seminarians at the summer school in Glendale.

Nearly concurrent with Wolf's appointment was the assignment of Francis Massarella to be pastor of Our Lady of Lourdes Parish in Otway, Ohio. Located in the archdiocese of Cincinnati, the Otway parish reached out to Holy Trinity mission in Pond Creek which actually had more Catholics than Otway. Massarella, later assisted by the recently ordained Francis Wuest of Cincinnati (ordained in 1942), was also responsible for the two original missions of the society located in Manchester and Bueno Vista, Adams County. Hence, by mid-September of 1942 the little Society of Home Missioners was settled in three base parishes with their several missions located in previously priestless counties.[69]

This was the first year of United States involvement in World War II. It was also the first year that the home missioners took root in the soil of rural America. Writing in *The Challenge*, Howard Bishop took note of this parallel.

This has been a momentous year for the United States. History has been made faster, perhaps, than any previous year. Our American boys have been sent away to save America from godless enemies abroad, and the account they have been giving of themselves fills our hearts with rejoicing. It is one of the truly heartening touches on a sad, sad picture. May we not hope that the sending of four young priests as soldiers of Christ into our home field to save

America's soul from sin and error may be the beginning of victory just as momentous in a different way. We pray that our brave fighting men abroad will soon win their fight and come home. . . . But the fight of the spirit that our missioners are waging will last for generations. It will last until America is Christianized.[70]

In 1942 only one priest, Francis Wuest, was ordained. In July of 1943, after a year of mission school, he was assigned to Otway. Massarella who had poor health was transferred to Sunfish to assist Borchers. Edward W. Smith, Francis E. McGrath, the first seminarian to commit himself to Glenmary in 1938, and Herman J. Foken were ordained on April 17, 1943. All were from the archdiocese of Cincinnati; McGrath was the best student and destined for graduate study; Smith who was active in youth work had organized a Junior American Missioners in Glendale and a 4H club among youngsters in the area prior to ordination. Foken was a photographer whose work had appeared in *The Challenge*. During the summer they also attended the Preachers' Institute at The Catholic University of America; subsequently they became "interns" in street preaching: McGrath with Steven Leven in Tonkawa, Oklahoma, Smith with Edward Broom, C.S.P. and other Paulists at Winchester, Tennessee, and Foken with Joseph Durick, the head of the Confraternity of Christian Doctrine in Birmingham, Alabama.

During that year (1943–44) when the three priests were attending the mission school at Glenmary, Howard Bishop wrote his first formal mid-winter letter to his confreres. He opened with a commentary on how the ravages of war had "scarred and wounded . . . so many souls" and how "Hearts . . . [were] torn between the call of God to lives of virtue and the call of pleasure made glamorous . . . by an unusually large paycheck." In such a critical condition "the world needs the church of Jesus Christ as never before . . . and here in our beloved America . . . no obstacles are placed by law or custom to prevent the church from . . . doing her utmost to help suffering and sorrowful mankind." The Home Missioners "must be in every sense true ambassadors of Jesus Christ." He reminded them that unlike the ordinary pastor who ministers only to the Catholics in his parish "the missionary includes all human beings within his reach. Protestant, Jew, agnostic, atheist, liberal free thinker, all belong to him. . . ." They should devise special programs for their "separated brethren of

rural America. . . . Let no week pass without some earnest and devoted efforts for the other sheep."

The superior reminded them that "Winter is a time when the poor
suffer very much. Who are the poor in your mission area? Do you
know them? Now is the chance to show them you are their friend. The
most telling approach to the 'other sheep' is by works of charity for
the poor. . . . Christ loved His poor and we are other Christs."[71]

He asked each missioner to submit monthly notes on "your parochial and missionary labors" including reports on conversions and
instruction on the "restoration of fallen-aways," and on "what headway you have made on the sanctification of your flock." He also
wished to know about those programs that were failing and about
prospects and future planning. He considered the home missioners
in the field "as my own beloved sons" for whom he offers "daily
prayers" and asked each of them to keep him informed of "health
and welfare, as well as the personal and missionary needs." He invoked the "intrepid faith and zeal of our beloved Father Sourd" as an
inspiration for missionary activity among the diverse people at the
crossroads of their missions.[72]

When the three young priests had completed the year of mission
school there were seven active home missioners. All but Father Massarella had adjusted well to the pioneer-like condition in the three
mission areas. Through his seminary friendship with Borchers, Massarella had been led to join the Home Missioners. Borchers was from
a farm family and was accustomed to the quiet and the rough social
conditions; Massarella was from Cincinnati. Borchers was self-reliant
while his city confrere tended to be rather dependent. Massarella's
inability to adapt to rural missionary life was exacerbated by a severe
respiratory condition that became acute in the drafty rectories on the
mission.[73]

Because he did not thrive as a missionary and because he had
always tended toward the contemplative life, Massarella left Glenmary to join the Trappist monastery in Gethsemane in 1945. Howard
was agreeable to Massarella's vocation and he considered it to be the
movement of the Spirit. According to his original plan to assign two
priests to work in each mission as a guard against loneliness, Bishop
intended to send the three younger priests to work in established
areas. By September of 1944 Foken was sent to Otway, Ohio while
Smith and McGrath had yet to receive a permanent assignment. Then

on September 14 McNicholas told Bishop that Gerald O'Hara, bishop
of the diocese of Savannah–Atlanta, had sent an "urgent invitation"
to the Home Missioners that they take over a mission in Statesboro
and seven priestless counties in eastern Georgia. Howard's immediate response was that such a venture was "impossible," but McNicholas was so "anxious to help O'Hara that he offered "to lend me a man
[i.e. a priest] to make it possible." Howard consented, "though it
strains our facilities to the cracking point."[74]

Very pleased with the news of Howard Bishop's decision, O'Hara
expressed how "profoundly grateful" he was to McNicholas for
speaking "so favorably of the project" and promising to lend a diocesan priest for the mission. He referred to the prospective Home
Missioners' arrival as beginning "a broad chapter . . . in the history of
the Church here. The territory that will be assigned to Father
Bishop's priests is fertile soil for conversions. . . ."[75] Some three
weeks after O'Hara's invitation Howard Bishop informed the bishop
of Savannah that he had assigned Earl McGrath and Edward Smith to
Statesboro, "two of our best and most promising priests"; he accepted McNicholas' offer of a priest, but assigned him to Otway,
Ohio. He asked the bishop to appoint McGrath a pastor or vicar of
the mission and to appoint Smith as his assistant. Howard explained
the Home Mission strategy. "Our missionary pastors usually are responsible for the Catholics in the area and the missionary assistants
are responsible for making and keeping up contacts and preparing
for instruction of the non-Catholics. At the same time each helps the
other and too rigid lines of demarcation between their work has not
been insisted upon." Bishop contrasted their personalities: Smith was
an extrovert "far more experienced in making contacts and winning
friends. . . ." According to Bishop, McGrath was a "more thoughtful
and studious type and perhaps a little more stable" than Smith.
Bishop told O'Hara that these assignments were only for a year or
two because McGrath was a "future seminary professor" and Smith
was destined for promotional work. Howard Bishop assigned Brother
Vincent Wilmes "to take care of the household problem until another
solution could be found."[76]

Within the seven counties in the Glenmary "parish" there were
100,000 people but only about 100 Catholics: five Catholic adults and
eight children in Statesboro; at Camp Blanding there were about
twenty-five, while at the prisoner of war camps one mile from States-

boro there were some seventy-five German Catholics. Finally there
were some Irish itinerant workers that had settled in the area. Referred to as "Irish travellers," they are still identifiable among the
rural church in Georgia. To help the missioners cover their extensive
parish, Bishop O'Hara gave them a preaching trailer and an automobile. In anticipation of the arrival of Smith, McGrath and Wilmes,
O'Hara had the six-room bungalow, two rooms of which were used as
a chapel, prepared and painted, but it was not until some days after
they arrived that the house was ready. This was by far the society's
most challenging mission. O'Hara was impressed with the two priests
and the lay brother. "They are amiable men, youthful, cheerful and
bubbling with zeal," he wrote to Bishop.[77] Some six weeks later
O'Hara reported that he had attended a housewarming hosted by the
Home Missioners. "The house was filled with people while I was
there . . . your priests have already begun to make their mission
flourish. I met a fallen away family that they brought back to the
Church. Four prospective converts are now under instruction and I
know this number will increase."[78]

The Home Missioners encountered strong anti-Catholic sentiment
in Georgia. Edward Smith noted in an article on his new parish that
"those who misunderstand and malign the Church do so in perfect
faith. . . . When vicious stories had circulated there has been no one
to deny them either in speech or by example." Smith conceded that
there was a great need for priests in the area in order to dispel such
misconceptions.[79] Despite anti-Catholicism the Home Missioners
were generally well received in Georgia. Brother Vincent Wilmes reflected on "those we can never reach except in prayer, wondering if
God may test our good will with apparent failures at times." Though
he was occupied with maintaining the kitchen and the bungalow,
Vincent reported that he "still . . . [had] the knack of befriending the
problem child. . . ." He was particularly concerned with "a scrapper
of ten who picks on smaller kids. I believe he is friendless, untrained,
abnormal (or sub) and lonely."[80]

Edward Smith wrote a weekly column for the *Sylvania Telephone* in
which he announced the Home Missioners' program and presented
"a homily on the Gospel of the week." He also organized a weekly
Friday night meeting at St. Joseph's Church in the Bay Branch mission, where there was a Baptist organist. Smith and McGrath began
the Missa Recitata in English "for the benefit of the non-Catho-

lics . . . and for those Catholics who know little about the Mass." The
Home Missioners' extension into the deep south, 650 miles from
Glenmary, entailed an encounter with a distinctive rural culture, one
that was immersed in racial segregation. One of the first persons to
seek instructions at the Statesboro mission was a black school
teacher.[81]

Howard Bishop was a moderate southerner who saw the evils of
racism, but was a gradualist in remedying those evils. One may recall
that while at St. Louis Parish in Clarksville, the black housekeeper sat
in the gallery of the church rather than downstairs with the other
parishioners. In his 1945 mid-winter letter to the missioners the
founder elaborated on the strategies and tactics proper to those in
the missions. He had consistently stated that blacks "must not, because of local prejudices, be excluded from our love and service.
Encourage kindness and charity between racial groups. This is done
by example as by word." He told his confreres to "avoid controversy"
in general and to particularly stay aloof from movements against
segregation as well as those which promoted racism. "We know that a
certain race is under very severe handicaps. We know that certain
civil rights guaranteed to all citizens in the constitution—as voting—
as that certain others due to them in charity and justice—as adequate
education and health protection—are denied them on purely racial
grounds." In confronting such racial injustice the Home Missioners
should follow the strategies of the foreign missionaries in China and
India; they must be patient and circumspect. "We must do as our
Lord told His apostles, be as wise as serpents and as simple as
doves . . . we must strive to be all things to all people regardless of
their social station. . . . It is not likely that missioners, coming from
other sections, could have a remedy to propose beyond preaching
charity at all times. . . ." He did not expect his confreres to remain
absolutely silent about the injustice but he urged caution. "Among
the native born whom you know well and can trust, open your hearts
only to the broadest, most intelligent and most tolerant. Above all
things, avoid public declaration and harangues against unequal and
unjust race conditions. Avoid everything that should tend to arouse
the rabble, either colored or white and add to their unhappiness by
inciting them to imprudent actions." He reminded them that progress will be accomplished only by a "slow and prudent process of
personal contacts with your own people and with others sufficiently

intelligent and sympathetic to hear you . . . it took Christianity more than a thousand years to eliminate slavery!'' Howard Bishop's mission strategy placed a priority on ''saving souls . . . by winning the love and confidence of all . . . no matter how appalled we may be at public injustice and lack of charity between groups . . . our work is to save souls first.''[82]

The Missioners made friends among the black community. Benedict Wolf, the pastor in Russellville, Kentucky, reported that ''one of my old colored friends passed away last week so I went down to the First Colored Baptist Church . . . where they had his body laid out and said a prayer at the coffin for the repose of his soul. There were quite a few people there and they spread it all over town about 'that there white priest that ain't 'fraid to come down and pay his respecks to a colored man. Father Wolf must have thought lots of the old man.' ''[83] Since Howard Bishop had this letter printed in *The Challenge* he must have been pleased with Wolf's popularity among the black community. From our vantage point Bishop's views appear to have been conservative, but in the context of the mid 1940s they were cautiously moderate. With only a few integrated seminaries there were less than thirty black Catholic priests in the American church. Most religious communities were also segregated. Though the Home Missioners had consistently identified rural black sharecroppers as one of the Lord's neglected, Howard Bishop was too cautious to integrate the Home Missioners. When a black friend of one of the brothers sought information on joining the society, Bishop explained that he could not ''encourage his friend *now*,'' with the obvious implication that he foresaw the time when the Missioners would be integrated in his lifetime.[84]

A year before the Home Missioners entered Statesboro, the founder had promised Bishop John J. Swint that someday the society would take over a mission in the Appalachia area of his diocese of Wheeling. Howard had first encountered Swint during his seminary days when he was a visiting lecturer at St. Mary's. A native of West Virginia and well known for his rural mission efforts before becoming a bishop, Swint was responsible for the entire state of West Virginia and nineteen counties in Virginia. In the autumn of 1945 Howard and Swint arranged for the society to take over St. Anthony's Church in Norton, Virginia and a mission in Appalachia. On December 1, Edward Smith was transferred from Statesboro to become pastor at

Norton, and Joseph W. Dean, who had just completed his year of mission school at Glenmary, was appointed his assistant. Henry Burke, who joined the society as a priest and had also spent a year at the motherhouse, replaced Smith in Statesboro.[85]

Coal mining was the chief industry of the new mission in Virginia. Both churches had a small Catholic community; the Norton church was the base parish. The population was 172,000 in an area of 2,700 square miles; except for the two home missions in Wise county, the six counties were priestless. The Catholic population included Italian, Polish and a few Lebanese families. Within a year after their arrival the Home Missioners built a parish hall at St. Anthony's and St. Patrick's Chapel at Dungannon. Howard Bishop wrote that the "hall will be used for parish purposes and will serve as a lyceum or recreation center for a number of teenage boys of the town, most of whom are non-Catholics." The chapel at Dungannon, located about twenty miles from Norton, served only fifteen parishioners, most of whom "have been either converted to the faith or brought back from virtual apostasy." They donated the logs and much of the labor. Bishop Swint contributed the windows, and there was a $2,000 gift from a friend of Glenmary.[86]

When the Home Missioners were established in Norton in December of 1945 Howard Bishop was thirty years a priest. Glenmary now had thirteen ordained priests, four brothers and seven sisters, while twenty-six men and women were in various phases of preparation as students and aspirants. Nine priests and two brothers were "laboring for the conversion of America in five mission fronts: Otway, Russellville, Sunfish, Statesboro and Norton. In anticipation of his thirtieth anniversary as a priest Howard received a spiritual bouquet of five masses from the "group at headquarters." Brother Vincent Wilmes presented him with the following lines entitled "Blessed Thirty Years."

BLESSED THIRTY YEARS

In the majestic song of a seaboard State
   They sing of "Howard's warlike thrust"
And of gallant things which yet live in memory.
Our thoughts today are with one who loves
   And knows the scenes recalled in the lines

Of "Maryland, My Maryland."
We stand today to cheer the echoing thrust of him,
   Who has grasped anew the pioneer hope
Of "Mary's land."
For thirty years blessed one by one
   In labor and zeal of eternal worth
Another Howard has paced the earth . . .
Earnestly and firmly planting anew The Kingdom
   of the One Who has given him
   These Blessed Thirty Years.[87]

CHAPTER 9

The Women Missioners
1939–1946

Well before the society established its first home missions, Howard Bishop's missionary map was featured in an article in *Time* (October 1941) on the Catholic rural movement.[1] In his comprehensive story of American Catholicity (1942) Theodore Maynard also published the map. He wrote of "heroic enterprise of the Home Missioners of America. . . . A small body of priests, founded by W. Howard Bishop on the outskirts of Cincinnati, are daring to address themselves to the task of rural evangelization with the frank admission at the outset that large sections of the United States have to be approached exactly as a foreign missionary approaches the heathen."[2]

Maynard's book was published in 1942 when there were only five Glenmary priests, one brother aspirant and two sister aspirants. What follows in this chapter is the story of the expansion of the Glenmary community, with particular emphasis on Howard Bishop's role as founder of a community of home mission sisters. Howard Bishop manifested a consistent confidence that the progress of the Home Missioners was according to the design of Providence.

The first woman aspirant to the nascent women's community was Agnes Mahon but, as noted earlier, Howard eventually lost confidence in her vocation to a pioneer society. In 1938 Gertrude Kimmick of Newport, Kentucky became a candidate; without a community she worked as Bishop's secretary at the office on Fifth Street and lived in a rented apartment. In 1940, shortly after Howard and Raphael Sourd moved into the farmhouse in Glendale, Gertrude took up the chores of housekeeping there as well as continuing her work as a secretary fourteen miles from Glendale. When the old granary was renovated into a "respectable little building with living quarters above and office rooms below," the Fifth Street office was closed and Gertrude moved into the apartment in the office building.[3]

On October 15, 1941 Dorothy Hendershot, a nurse from Grand Rapids, Michigan, joined Gertrude Kimmick to form the first women's community. Each of the Home Missioner priests had, by ordination, official status, while Gertrude and Dorothy could only be considered lay volunteers in a nascent community of women religious. Dorothy Hendershot was a rural person who "fell in love with the idea of Glenmary." She was "impressed" with Raphael Sourd, who gave the impression he was the head of Glenmary. Her first meeting with Howard Bishop "was disappointing. He seemed cold and uncommunicative. The only question I can remember him asking me was whether I could bake a pie. I thought that was a good joke, but later learned . . . that Father's 'Pie stands for piety' was more than just a quip. He liked desserts. A couple of hundred pies later, I realized I had been 'conned.' His favorite was apple pie, and we were happy to make it for him . . . as time went on I began to appreciate Father's character more . . . always there was his intense drive."[4]

Dorothy Hendershot and Gertrude Kimmick moved into the old farmhouse after the "motherhouse for the men's community was completed." During the period of 1941–42, when Francis McRae of Maryknoll was helping Bishop in the formation of the three young priests—Massarella, Borchers and Wolf—he was spiritual director of the two women aspirants. A simple rule was composed; they said the Little Office of the Blessed Virgin and received the temporary title, "Women's Missionary Society." McRae, Bishop and occasionally Sourd presented weekly spiritual conferences. Their work was secretarial, housekeeping, and cooking.

In the spring of 1942 Bishop James E. Walsh, Superior of Maryknoll and Francis McRae suggested that Howard Bishop "give up [the] idea of our own sisters' community," presumably because there was a meager number of vocations. Howard told Sourd who in turn told Gertrude. On May 8, 1942 Bishop recorded in his diary: "Sourd and I have more conversation about question: Sisterhood of our own or establish community with our work. In spite of my explanation that no decision has been reached and [that] I broached it for discussion, he is 'still jittery' as he says. To me [Howard Bishop], this is inexcusable in an intelligent, thoughtful man." Bishop concluded with the note: "My weekly talk to Gertrude and Dorothy stresses patience, strong faith, toughness, willingness to endure."[5] These were the very qualities that describe the tenaciousness of the founder and seem to have developed as a result of his faith in his society. The next day Gertrude admitted to Bishop that she told Dorothy about the precarious situation "even though I ordered her not to" lamented Bishop. "A double violation of confidence and obedience."

At first Gertrude seemed "unimpressed" with Howard's views on her "double violation," so he "warned her that if this attitude persisted we could not work together any longer." Later that day Gertrude told him that she had "seen her error,"[6] and the next day Howard recorded in his diary that he reassured "Gertrude [that] the error is not held against her and I still consider her fit for religious life."[7] Since further discussion of the possibility of disbanding the women missioners never surfaced again, the views of McRae and Walsh had no impact beyond this brief crisis in early May of 1942.

To substantiate the permanence of the women's community and to satisfy Archbishop McNicholas' wish that the community be trained by superiors in the religious life, the founder arranged with Mother Stephanie, the mother general of the Dominican Sisters of St. Mary's of the Springs in Columbus, Ohio, to have two of their sisters train the women missioners in the religious life. On September 7, 1942 Sister M. Dorita, assisted by Sister M. Ellen, moved in the old farmhouse to supervise the two candidates, Gertrude and Dorothy.[8] Almost immediately it became evident that Dorita and Gertrude could not easily live together in the same house. On October 5, 1942 Bishop recorded in his diary: "G. Kimmick asks for interview. Impossible to get along with Sr. Dorita who, she says, is unfit to direct women's group. When I refused to take her point of view she announces she is packing to leave. Says she is completely exhausted, tired and incapable of going on. I agree that she is and must at least take a prolonged rest away from here." Sister Dorita denied "persecuting her" and told Bishop that Gertrude was persistently asking her, "Sister, why do you not like me, what have I done to you?" Bishop noted that Gertrude had "troubled me many times with similar queries."[9] Dorita was willing to leave in order to keep Gertrude at Glenmary. However, he insisted that Gertrude leave, and Bishop arranged that she work with the Sisters of Christian Doctrine in New York City. Gertrude's friend and later a sister candidate for Glenmary, Eloise Woodward, traveled with her and worked in Harlem. About six weeks later Gertrude returned to Glenmary. "Apparently she has improved in every way. I made it plain to her that she must toe the line hereafter."[10] By this time a third sister candidate, Opal Simon, had entered the tiny community.

Simon learned of the missioners directly from the founder who celebrated the liturgy in her parish church, the Glenmary mission in Sunfish, Kentucky.[11] It was the feast of Pentecost and Bishop had dinner at the Simon home following mass. "A couple of months later I wrote to Father and told him of my desire to become a member of his infant community," recalled Opal Simon. "He answered my letter with a personal visit to the school where I was teaching. . . . I was very much impressed by Father Bishop the first time I met him. I felt that I could see and feel a universal depth of spirituality in him."[12]

Opal Simon entered the community on November 28, 1942. She and Dorothy Hendershot worked in the kitchen while Gertrude Kimmick worked in Bishop's office. Opal, who later became Sister Frances, said that Sister Dorita "was a very efficient and exacting person. She was a perfectionist about all household duties. . . . Sister Dorita's companion, Sister M. Leonard, was our sunshine in the house. She always had a kind word, a smile, and a joke."[13] Opal reported that even after Gertrude's return from New York she and Dorita "still found it rather difficult to adjust to one another. The clash of personalities naturally influenced all of our lives." Howard Bishop, according to Opal, "used to try to keep us happy by his visits and conferences."[14] Because the founder considered himself responsible for the direction of the sisters, he had conflicts with the Dominican superior. For example, on April 13, 1943, he wrote in his diary: "Went to convent to *direct* Sr. Dorita to omit heavy cleaning of house from girls' program, became involved in spiritual argument, as always happens. She pleaded finally her incapacity for the assignment here and I admitted it was so." He concluded with the remark that Dorita "took it not at all well."[15] At one point Bishop was very upset with Raphael Sourd because he attempted to give him advice on the women missioners. "I had to insist very emphatically that the women's group are entirely my affair and he must not interfere."[16]

Later that spring Howard asked Mother Stephanie to replace Dorita. When she received word of the change Sr. Dorita "seems happy" but Sr. Leonard "sheds tears."[17] A week later Mother Stephanie introduced the newly assigned sisters, Alonso and Charles Edward, to the founder.[18] During her visit, Archbishop McNicholas visited Glenmary. He had "a few words with our girls and a wonderful visit followed by Benediction with women."[19] Opal Simon considered Sister Alonso to have been "more retiring" than Sister Dorita.[20] "Gertrude reports," wrote Bishop, that "the new superior [is] a vast improvement in the way of friendliness and tact." He was also pleased with Mother Stephanie's impressions of the women missioners "She . . . told me [that] the spirit of our girls, mutual helpfulness, friendliness and quiet unassuming piety is splendid."[21]

At Gertrude's suggestion Bishop appointed her "prefect" of the women missioners in late 1943. "She was to work in collaboration with Sister Alonso in executing household affairs," reported Opal Simon.[22] "This set-up, no doubt, was difficult. She was disturbed at what her duties were. After seven months Sister Alonso was recalled and the Dominicans left us on our own."[23] Actually it was in late February that the Dominicans left Glenmary ostensibly because of the needs of their own community. Bishop became concerned that Gertrude was "taking too many exemptions from the rule. A certain number [are] necessary as she is oldest in service and [is] their prefect." However, he reminded her that "she is still, as it were 'in the ranks' and must accustom herself to the same discipline they have." Gertrude agreed but told Bishop that "it will be hard" to just be "in the ranks."[24]

By the winter of 1944 the women missioners numbered five. Eloise Woodward, a graduate of Villa Madonna College in Kentucky, entered in June of 1943, and Joan Wade of Long Island, New York entered in September of the same year. They attended classes in social service conducted by Ruth Fleming of the archdiocesan office of Catholic Charities. They also did home visitation work and observed at the juvenile court. Later they volunteered at the County Home "to comfort and minister to the needs of the sick poor." Several women attended a course in practical nurses' aid at St. Mary's Hospital.[25] (The priests also worked in hospitals during their mission-school year. Three young priests worked for three weeks at the Alexian Brothers' Hospital in Chicago.)

Opal Simon recalled that "Father Bishop tried to keep us happy by his visits and conferences. He talked to us once a week on what he expected us to do when we would finally work in the mission fields."[26]

The earliest conference on record, July 2, 1943, reveals the founder's views on the role of women missioners. "Your work requires special vocation, sympathy and understanding, tact in dealing . . . [with] people." They were to be trained in catechetics, social service and "home arts," i.e. domestic crafts, weaving, sewing, etc. The traditional notion that women belong in the home was transposed to the women missioners' primary mission thrust—"home sharing [and] building. Mary, St. Joseph and Jesus [are] your friends. See Christ in soured, defeated adults and undernourished children." He explained to the sister candidates that through kindness to the children one may "win adults." It was Howard's experience that the mother of the family "readily confides [and] tells her story." As a result of this encounter "a bond of sympathy" is formed between the missioner and the mother and through counseling her the missioner can hope to reach the father. "Become a true big sister to the family,"[27] he said. With characteristic emphasis on practical zeal Howard Bishop outlined ways the women missioners were to evangelize the rural families.

1. Build up confidence in you
2. Build up courage and self-helpfulness in their struggle
3. Build up love of God [and] virtuous lives
4. Gradually, tactfully arouse their interest in the Church
5. If possible, let them take the initiative toward instruction

Don't *condemn* Protestantism, ministers, etc.

Make *them see* by your life and services.

Don't *urge or beg* [them to receive instruction].

Your first object is to save their souls;

go to work on that *at once* by building up courage and natural goodness.

Come to the supernatural message and invitation to Church only gradually—better, let *them* come to it.

Invite but don't press them to missions.

Show kindly interest in them, whether friends or enemies.

. . . Duties of Sister Missionaries

[1] Teaching Children
    Ideal—Bldg. citizens [America] [Heaven]
    Motive—Love of Souls—Image of Christ
    You may be only link between earth and heaven for them.

[2] Contacting adults
   School leads to some Poverty and sickness to others
   Clothing
   Medical Care
   Religious pictures, etc.

[3] Qualifications
   Charity, humility, zeal for souls
   Prudence, tact [getting along well with people]
   (Be kind to *everybody*)
   Spiritual endurance and good nature[28]

The founder stressed the "Dignity of feminine missionary service" and referred to its "Honorable history" by noting such heroic models as Louise de Marillac and Mother Cabrini. A pioneer spirit pervades this conference outline; there is no reference to a rule, to canon law, to the routine of convent life. The character of the missionary presupposed a strong spiritual formation, but the particular qualities of the home missionary were manifested in the evangelization process. Less than a year later, Howard noted in his diary that he had just completed a biography of Louise de Marillac ". . . tremendously edified by joint and separate labors of St. Vincent de Paul and St. Louise de M. It begins to seem to me that our Sisters' program has much in common with the early years of Sisters of Charity. Therefore, *Why* a Constitution? Why a religious costume? Why any of these for years to come? Why a formal habit even?"[29]

In July of 1944, Gertrude Kimmick, Joan Wade and Opal Simon were assigned to three vacation schools with headquarters at Sacred Heart Parish in Russellville, Kentucky, where Benedict Wolf had been pastor since the summer of 1942. It was described by Gertrude in her diary and published in *The Challenge* under a title composed by Howard Bishop, "Our Feminine Missioners Step Out." On the Sunday before their first class at the vacation school the three women walked down to Smoketown: "that is the name of the section of town where the extremely poor colored folks live. We shall have to be very discreet about this though; as we don't want to antagonize our soul-starved white people, some of whom have solemnly warned us to avoid this section. . . . We don't walk very far when we are stopped with the call 'Miss Catlic.' " They responded to the call to find a young boy with an infected leg. After treating him the women missioners found a vacant "shanty"; they immediately thought of converting it into a clinic and a storeroom for distributing second-hand clothing that they had brought with them from Cincinnati; "our founder, Father Bishop, wants us to work in the midst of these people whenever they are in our territory, as well as among the white folk."[30]

At the school the "sisters," who wore a skirt, blouse and veil, found that the thirty-two children, ages ranging from three to sixteen, were lacking the rudimentary knowledge of the Catholic faith. "How sadly these poor youngsters have been neglected and overlooked! And what a pitiable condition of soul starvation the parents, too, are in!" After four weeks in Russellville (morning classes) and Johnstown (twenty-seven miles for afternoon classes) the women moved on to Scioto County, Ohio. They were particularly grateful for the experience in Smoketown where they had established St. Mary's Clinic and Clothing Shop. They sold men's suits for 10 cents, dresses and shoes for 5 cents, and baby clothes for 1 cent, 2 cents and 3 cents.[31]

In Scioto County the children were "more fortunate, they were more familiar with some prayers and hymns." Father Wuest, ordained in 1942, collected many of these children in his pickup truck on his way to a country mission. During recreation period the sisters played softball. "Poor Sister Opal and Sister Joan. Your bodies are worn out running bases and batting for their softball games. Two o'clock finds us driving children home . . . through winding mountainous hills of the Government game preserve. A flash of quick-footed deer, or a glimpse of a bear adds a month or two to our lives. And so, God takes us by the hand and leads us to harvests that are ripe—He looked into our hearts pleading and whispers, GIVE ME SOULS."[32] Thus ends Gertrude's diary.

The second war-time convention of the National Catholic Rural Life Conference was held in Cincinnati, November 10–13, 1944. The Home Missioners were represented by Raphael Sourd on the work of the mission preachers, Clemens Borchers on the mission pastor, and Gertrude Kimmick on the mission sister.[33] Howard had received permission from McNicholas to allow Gertrude "to be referred to as sister when addressing the C.R.L.C. . . . on whose program I have placed her." He also allowed the Home Missioners to have benediction in the trailer-chapel for the C.R.L.C. on November 13.[34] The society had a booth at the conference, and on November 11 Howard Bishop hosted an evening program for the conference at Glenmary;

about eighty priests, sisters and lay people toured the houses and trailer-chapel.[35]

Loveland, where the women of the Grail lived, was also on the program. Bishop was very fond of the Grailville community which was dedicated to the rural ideals and domestic arts and crafts so dear to the superior of Glenmary. He chaired the session of the Home Missioners. "Our missionary meeting a wonderful success . . . Sister Gertrude 'stole the show.' "[36]

During the period when there were no representatives from an established community training the women missioners, Gertrude, the prefect, became de facto the superior but from Howard Bishop's point of view he was still their superior. A complicating factor was the role of Archbishop McNicholas who was superior over all the Home Missioners. In a November 4, 1944 unofficial letter to Rome, which laid the foundation for an official appeal for recognition of the Home Missioners, McNicholas referred to the "sisterhood":

> Without any real encouragement on my part, but rather with constant admonition that I can give no authority to establish a sisterhood, a number of lay women have come here and are eagerly anxious to devote their lives to the poor missions of the United States. It will be very easy, I think, to encourage a good number of women to embrace this apostolate, which needs hundreds of thousands of workers.[37]

Shortly after he wrote this letter, McNicholas told Bishop that "Sisters must be willing to forgo vacations if they want to be Sisters. [They are] on a different basis altogether from [the] priests, who are public persons."[38] Such legal categories seem to have run contrary to Howard's practical views of the public character of women Home Missioners' role in the missions. However, the public priest and the private sister certainly reflected the prevailing patriarchal system in religion and society. Bishop was progressive but within a traditional religious context.

There is "much false sympathy for women these days," said Bishop. "*To remedy drudgery* they take her away from her laboratory workshop [i.e. the home] and send her out in society to live a life of idleness and be a professional vamp to ensnare other women's husbands. *To relieve her pain* they take away [the] function for which God

made her and the glory of motherhood and send her out into the
world to be politician, an athlete or a fancy dancer . . . or to hire out
in an office or factory or store while millions of men with dependent
families are . . . [on relief]." He then elaborated on the role of the
mother as a "homekeeper . . . not a housekeeper." He listed her
domestic duties such as planning meals, cooperating with her husband in his work and he with her "in more important work," parent-
ing children. "But more important, to be a mother as often as God
requires in return . . . [God] bestows privileges and blessings . . .
[upon] her."[39] As noted earlier, a corollary to capitalistic greed that
marked the decay of a just society was birth control, regarded as
synonymous with selfishness and decay of the family. The women
Home Missioners were to be countervailing forces to those twin evils
by building up the sanctity of the home.

The missionary character of the sisters did allow them a great deal
of practical independence; their responsibilities were so distinctive as
to assure them a sense of freedom and self-determination. Bishop
recognized this, in a January 1945 conference he discussed with them
"the situation of Sisters in mission country and their relations with
the Pastor. Their subordination to the Pastor was stressed but at the
same time their independence in their own rule, their convent, their
technic [sic]" was also emphasized.[40]

Some six weeks before the women departed for Kentucky, Gertrude and Howard experienced a critical confrontation on male authority. At a gathering of the men's community and special guests,
the women prepared refreshments in the evening, but when Bishop
suggested that they serve the men, Gertrude "declined in the name of
all." Later that evening Gertrude asked him if the group that goes to
Russellville "must obey [the] pastor." When Bishop said "*yes*," she
replied, "That is something I don't approve of doing." Bishop re-
torted, "Then you don't belong here" and "I made a hasty exit."[41]

Gertrude's experience in the mission and her successful appearance at the November 1944 rural life conference confirmed her leadership ability to Bishop and no doubt to herself as well. Gertrude still
did work occasionally in the office, a place where Bishop's temper was
most likely to explode. He noted in his diary for February 26, 1945:

Most of morning and an hour this P.M. on dictation. Had a spirited
session with Sr. Gertrude because of her fitfulness and whining at

every imaginary slight from me, but I was much too severe and
tonight went over to make amends. However, made it plain to her
she *must* stop taking an offended attitude if she wants to succeed or
even to stay with us.[42]

Troubled by Gertrude's behavior and convinced that it stemmed
from a physical malady, he insisted that she see a doctor and be
thoroughly tested at the hospital. Gertrude struggled against such
demands; according to Bishop she was afraid of an operation. Finally
he ordered her to go. Upon her return she "begged not to be required to go tomorrow." Bishop agreed and in his diary revealed that
the conflict over the hospital was interpreted by him as an authority
struggle. "It was to break down her tremendous resistance to obeying
in things she doesn't like that I had insisted on her going once, even
though unwell."[43] A week later he commented that Gertrude "looks
ill-at-ease and lonesome as well as irreconcilable to hospitals," which
may have meant irreconcilable to obeying Howard. This was followed
a few days later with "a quiet talk" in which he thought he had "at last
succeeded in quieting her fears and misapprehensions."[44]

The conflict temporarily eased. In April Howard noted that Dorothy and Gertrude "returned from a Chicago visit full of enthusiasm
and zeal."[45] By June of 1945 the struggle had rekindled on the issue of
a new sisters' residence some distance from Glenmary.[46] In August
Bishop noted that he had "another argument with Sr. Gertrude
about their getting their own home at a distance." She wished to seek
and purchase property, but Bishop reminded her that he had to discuss the matter with McNicholas. "Then there was a spell of whining
that made me terribly mad and I left. She fears my discussing *her* with
His *Grace*."[47] Characteristic of his remorse over his quick temper,
Howard apologized the next day "for the explosion. It was too cruel
and she had not deserved such punishment." That same day Mc-
Nicholas phoned to inquire about the disagreement. "Unless they get
Sisters (to instruct them) I wash my hands of them," exclaimed Mc-
Nicholas.[48] A few days later the archbishop told Howard that the
sisters "impress me as women who are playing with religious life."[49]
He also informed him that he would appoint Father Edward B. Kot-
ter to act as his liaison with the sisters.

The degree to which this situation grieved Bishop was evidenced in
a severe stomach problem requiring hospitalization. When he did

speak with Kotter he told him of his plan to remove Gertrude as prefect and his hope to get the Maryknoll Sisters to train the sisters. Kotter urged him to remove Gertrude from authority only after the Maryknoll Sisters arrive. "I told him that is too long and uncertain."[50] The following day he informed Gertrude that the "archbishop and I have decided to rotate prefects until formal organization and selection of regular superior—probably some years off. . . ."[51] After polling the sisters on their candidates for prefect—to which he prefaced the conviction that he would not be bound by their vote—he decided to appoint Sister Joan Wade.[52] The decision polarized the community. Over the next two months there were several confrontations between Howard and Gertrude. As early as September 27, 1945 he told her that "as the Archbishop said today we 'may have to get rid of her.' "[53] Two days later he "reproved her for lack of humility."[54] The conflict over a new residence for the sisters was never resolved, but to relieve overcrowding and to separate the aspirants from the older sisters the Home Missioners purchased a house on Oak Street within walking distance of a high school run by the Ursuline Sisters. Gertrude was assigned to live with the aspirants at the Oak Street house. This did not relieve the polarization in the community. When news of this situation reached McNicholas, "It was an occasion of first real show of temperament I have witnessed in him. He is still holding out on what he calls the 'rebellion' among our sisters—chiefly against poor sister G.K."[55]

The following day McNicholas wrote to Bishop indicating that he regretted "very much our interview of yesterday." He told him that he wished to be helpful "to your society" and that because he understands the "basic things about religious life" I must give the directives and make sure that these women are guided and trained in the essentials of the religious life. . . ." McNicholas expressed his doubts that Bishop had "the lights of the special direction of the Holy Ghost for the women's Society that you have for the Society of priests and brothers." He was certain that none of the sisters were directed by the Spirit. His concern for the spirit of the institute led him to conclude, "It is most important that we get a cheerful, cooperative, self-sacrificing spirit among the Missionary Sisters of your Institution."[56]

Bishop's immediate response to McNicholas was to write an apologetic letter which, because a personal interview was arranged, was never mailed. He wrote that he was "most happy that your Grace is so

interested and so generous as to be willing to take personal charge
and to give all directives . . . to our Sisters' group. . . . Just tell me
what part I am to play, as I should like to be somewhere in the picture."[57] The interview with the archbishop was merely a reiteration of
McNicholas' decision "to take over the reins entirely" and of
Bishop's deferential position.[58]

During this same period of late November–early December, Sister
Gertrude wrote to McNicholas a letter (that Bishop paraphrased in
his diary) "asking permission to come and discuss with him a new
community she and other members of our group desire, which would
be free of Fr. Bishop, practice poverty and donate all sums (of money)
received to the poor and be available for social service work under
any priest who wanted them." Bishop reported that McNicholas was
not "sympathetic" and that he seems to have been "fed up on her and
seems disposed to cut her off."[59] Shortly after McNicholas told
Bishop of Gertrude's desires, she "admitted a dislike toward me,"
wrote Howard. "I hinted at the wisdom of her going elsewhere."[60]

The following day McNicholas wrote to Father Kotter, his representative to the "Sisters at Glendale," a response to Gertrude's desire
to form a community; Kotter was instructed to read the contents of
the letter to her. The archbishop would not authorize a new religious
community but "should such a group wish to be merely lay women,
then I would wish to study the plan of such an organization." Mc-
Nicholas was "very much disturbed about the little community at
Glendale. I rather fear that it is the spirit of Sister Gertrude that
prevented this group from seeking the direction of the Church." He
implicitly accused her as a self-serving leader: "Her idea of unity
seems to be that all the Sisters follow her. There is too much Sister
Gertrude in her thinking. . . . She seems to be a useless individual
who wishes to direct rather than be directed." He was particularly
disturbed by the criticism of the Dominican Sister which he blamed
on Gertrude. He considered her influence to be "detrimental" and
he questioned "the advisability of her remaining in the . . . community." McNicholas indicated his conviction that "these candidates at
Glendale do not know the religious life." They must learn not to
criticize those in authority and be able to accommodate themselves
"to every type of superior." Hence they should not be "self-sufficient, making decisions about the proposed organization" but rather

should "give proof of simplicity, humility, and docility, as well as a true spirit of missionary sacrifice. . . ." He seems to have been certain that Gertrude "will find it almost impossible to qualify for the religious life in any community."[61]

Over the next two months the sisters experienced continuous polarization; Gertrude accused Joan Wade, the prefect, of conspiring against her. Forty years later, Joan Wade recalled: "Gertrude continued to undermine Father Bishop at every turn. She tried to turn all the Sisters against Father and me. She did everything she could. I was really no threat. I had no desire to run the order. . . . I had no illusions of grandeur. God had used me to get rid of Gertrude. He hadn't been exactly gentle, but I lived through it. Finally she went to everyone but me and asked if they would leave with her. . . . It was a very painful time for all of us."[62]

Bishop interviewed all the sisters and consulted with Kotter. On February 25, 1946 he told Gertrude that she must leave the community. "She took it more calmly, tho no less sadly, than I had anticipated. Of course, she heaped blame on the community and me. When I saw her again later [that day] she was more kindly disposed, spoke of cooperation with us on the work she is planning to do. Even hinted that I might change my mind, but I had no idea of doing so."[63]

Three days later Gertrude and Eloise Woodward left the community each with a dowry of $200. Sisters were paid $300 a month from which they contributed to a common fund with $200 set aside for each sister's dowry. It was decided to give Gertrude $1,000 for the period of 1938–1942 when she refused to take a full salary. Howard also promised to pay her $1,000 from his personal funds to help her get started. Bishop appears to have been relieved at Gertrude's departure.

Opal Simon, now Sister Frances, recalled that Gertrude's departure "was rather hard for me because Gertrude was hurt. She had worked hard and had put much effort into the community. She had many good qualities and I am sure she felt that what she was doing was the right thing." Sister Frances also noted that Gertrude's mission experience left her dissatisfied with the Home Missioner priests. "She seemed to think that they did not give her enough consideration when planning the work. This made her desire more than ever to have an independent community and now she was heartbroken to have to give it all up. I understood how she felt and really felt sorry for her, but told her when she asked my opinion that I felt it was God's will for her to go . . . now He had work for her in another field."[64]

In the archives of the diocese of Covington there are letters from Gertrude Kimmick. The archivist listed Gertrude as one of the foundresses of the Glenmary Sisters who established a group of lay rural missioners in the diocese of Raleigh who would minister to the people "in cognito." Gertrude, who died in the mid-1980s, proved a successful missioner. She seems to have had inherently strong leadership ability, combined with a deep drive to serve the rural poor. These were the very characteristics that clashed with Howard Bishop's sense of leadership and his tenacious determination to direct the formation of the Home Missioners. Perhaps Gertrude did have at least a half-formed notion that she was the "foundress" of the sisters' community and that eventually Bishop would be won over to her style of leadership and her missionary vision. By appointing her prefect and by not replacing Sister Dorita with another superior from an established community, Howard seemed to raise Gertrude's expectations that at last she had some semblance of independent authority. Had Bishop acted contrary to his character and deferred to her authority in certain areas of responsibility, he may have kept the peace. However, without direction by an established order of sisters, McNicholas would not have petitioned the Vatican for official recognition of the women Home Missioners. It is likely that Gertrude would have been alienated by another Dorita-like superior. Hence, had Bishop been deferential to Gertrude it is unlikely that she would have remained in the community. Of course, one detects a nascent feminism in Gertrude's drive for autonomy, in her desire for a more equitable relationship with the priests on mission, and in her self-styled role as a leader of the women's community. The depth of her religious commitment to poverty and to a life of ministry to the rural poor became quite evident. For her to mediate that commitment in traditional religious-community structures appears in retrospect to have been almost impossible. Howard Bishop's drive was to get the Home Missioners approved in Rome as a viable religious community. Had Gertrude entered after the women's community had been approved, perhaps Howard Bishop would have been more respectful of her gifts and would have tolerated her feminist urgings. However, given the troublesome ways in which he defended his own authority and his short temper in a conflict situation, perhaps qualities of Gertrude as well, one wonders if the latter would ever have persevered under Howard Bishop.

Six months after Gertrude left Glenmary, Sister Kevin of the Adrian Dominicans became superior of the women religious. In his relationship with her and with her successor, Sister John Joseph, Howard experienced several conflicts similar to those he experienced with Gertrude. His self-image as founder and superior gave him authority over all Glenmarians, particularly the women.

CHAPTER 10

Post-War Developments

The Second World War acted as a catalyst in the modernization process. Post-war America was identified with the continuous rationalization of industry, with the dynamic of technological improvement, with centralization and bureaucratization of business and government, with urban growth and suburban sprawl, with the educational opportunities of the G.I. Bill, and with the subsequent expansion of the middle class. There were periods of economic and social dislocation, characterized by strikes and racial tension, but in contrast to the Great Depression of the 1930s, the latter half of the 1940s was a period of prosperity and progress. Post-war foreign policy was preoccupied with the economic and social recovery of western Europe and the containment of Russian expansion in eastern Europe. Portrayed as a cosmic struggle between good and evil the cold war was energized by the fuel of anti-communism, a force that frequently spilled over into a fanatical quest for the "enemies" within American society.

The Catholic community experienced its own modernization; schools, colleges and hospitals proliferated as did Catholic professional societies. There was a significant increase of vocations to the priesthood and the religious life; there were more seminaries built between 1945 and 1965 than between 1791 and 1945. Though the church institutions were Americanized and modernized, Catholics maintained a strong religious separatism characterized by the term "ghetto Catholicism." Fueled by a spirit of triumphalism, the church tended to pride itself on being separate and superior. In retrospect the post-war church, 1945–1960, represents the final flowering of the Catholic ghetto before the inside forces of modernization, higher education, suburbanism and the advance of a critically intellectual

spirit undermined traditional separatism; in hindsight one may conclude that the 1950s represented a transition to many of the changes
associated with the Second Vatican Council and the culture of
the 1960s.[1]

The small home mission society established on the eve of World
War II reflected these trends in society and church. Though Howard
Bishop's agrarianism was in opposition to modernity's penchant for
individualism, he was very modern in his attitude toward professional
training of the priests and sisters (but not the brothers), the centralization of authority, the need for regularizing the society with Vatican
approval, and the need to establish a seminary. Vatican approval and
an independent seminary not only provided the ecclesiastical and
social status that would foster vocations but such institutional growth
would be a symbol of permanence.

In the process of preparing for Vatican approbation Archbishop
McNicholas wrote a formal letter of approval to the Catholic Home
Missioners of America. Though composed in February of 1944 the
letter was dated August 15, 1939 when he gave his tacit approval of the
community by allowing Raphael Sourd to enter the society. Mc-
Nicholas commended the missioners' purpose of serving the poor
and neglected areas of society. Addressed to Howard Bishop, Mc-
Nicholas' letter indicated that the society had only the status of a
"Diocesan character," but the archbishop anticipated a time when
"your Society will merit the approval of the Holy See."[2] Bishop was
grateful for McNicholas' solicitude and his "great care . . . in helping
us to build up our Society" as his seven priest confreres were Cincinnati men ordained by their archbishop.[3]

The following November, McNicholas wrote to the apostolic delegate, Archbishop Amleto Cicognani, an introductory letter on the
status of the Home Missioners. It was merely "an unofficial letter"
which, if it elicited a positive response, would result in the petition to
the Vatican. By this time there were ten priests, eight theological
students, three candidates studying philosophy, two college students,
and one in high school. He informed Cicognani that the society had
vocations from Chicago, St. Paul, Indianapolis, Fort Wayne, Boston,
Milwaukee and Trenton. He was also very optimistic about the
growth of the sisters' and brothers' communities.

In a previous chapter I cited a portion of this letter in which Mc-
Nicholas commented on Howard's character as seemingly "cold and

devoid of emotion." One may recall that the archbishop revealed a keen understanding of the founder: "Interiorly he can be disturbed and experience great enthusiasm." What was most important to both McNicholas and no doubt to Cicognani was that Bishop "thinks clearly and is most anxious to be guided by the Church."[4] One presumes that the delegate responded positively as the process of appealing for Vatican approval progressed albeit at a very slow pace. Some six weeks after McNicholas wrote to Cicognani, Howard proposed that the Home Missioners be named "The Nativity Fathers," but McNicholas did not like the name.[5] Six months later the archbishop asked Howard to consider the title, "Glenmary," a name Howard had considered "years ago" but discarded because there was a Glenmary Street in Cincinnati.[6] On July 6, 1945 Howard noted in his diary that he told the architect of the missioners' new house "to label it *Glenmary*, the Archbishop's choice of a name for our place—and Society."[7]

It was not until the spring of 1947 that Bishop and Sourd made final plans to travel to Rome to seek Vatican approbation. Some few days before their departure Archbishop Curley died. Howard notes that the funeral was "a wonderful and consoling experience. Bp [sic] McNamara preached a powerful and beautiful sermon." He met several bishops at the gathering, and Bishop Ireton of Richmond promised to write a letter of endorsement for him to take to Rome.[8] McNicholas had encouraged him to seek such letters probably because in his letter to the apostolic delegate he had referred to Ireton as an enthusiastic advocate of the Home Missioners' cause. Bishop had received other complimentary letters from Luigi Ligutti and Edwin O'Hara. Cicognani personally presented him with letters to Archbishop Luke E. Posetto, O.F.M. Cap., a member of the Congregation of Religious, and Monsignor Montini (later Pope Paul VI), Vatican acting secretary of state.

On May 28 Sourd and Bishop boarded a plane for Rome with stops in Newfoundland and the Azores, a twenty-six hour trip. The two Glenmary students preparing for seminary faculty posts, Earl McGrath and Howard French, waited at the airport, but since it was not a scheduled flight they left before its late-night arrival. However, as Sourd and Bishop were passing St. Peter's the next day, they spotted French from their taxi. "We found both in excellent health and overjoyed to see us. The mutual happiness of the meeting was worth the journey across," exclaimed Howard Bishop.[9] The four Glenmarians made a pilgrimage on foot to seven churches, including the four major basilicas. They also made a holy hour at St. Peter's on the feast of the Sacred Heart (June 13). In a circular letter to all the Missioners, Bishop said that "we are doing everything we can to move Heaven to bring a favorable decision from the Congregation of Religious." He told them that they had been "only partially successful" with the petition for a "decretum laudis" that would elevate the society to the status of papal congregation. "There is so much for us [Home Missioners] to do, and our maximum success in doing our work in these sorry times that need us *now* depends on the added prestige that will come from Pontifical approval."[10]

Sourd and Bishop called upon friends of McNicholas and Ligutti, all of whom expressed deep interest in the society. Bishop exclaimed in his diary that Cardinal Fumasoni Biondi "remembers me from 25 years ago in Baltimore." At the first meeting with Monsignor Spozette of the Congregation of Religious, the Glenmarians were informed of two negative points against them: "(1) not enough members (100 needed) and (2) we are not yet of Diocesan rite!"[11]

On June 9, 1947 Howard recorded in his diary that Spozette told Sourd and him "that we are approved as a Society of Diocesan Rite, i.e. Abp. McN's [sic] unauthorized act in establishing us as such (by letter of August 15, 1939) has been validated and confirmed [officially referred to as sanctioned] . . . [and] that our petition for pontifical approval is denied." However, they did achieve one concession: the Vatican's requirement for pontifical status was reduced from one hundred to fifty clerics. Spozette was "sympathetic and encouraging." McNicholas had overstepped his authority by approving the society as having diocesan status without the approval of Rome. Bishop cautioned Sourd not to ever "hint to his Grace that we are conscious of an error on his part. He has done too fine a job of backing us for that. Where would we be now but for him?"[12]

Sourd and Bishop visited the acting secretary of state, Monsignor Montini. "We must have waited 2 hours for the very gracious 20 minute interview he gave us," noted Howard. "He is of slight build, serious, of the ascetic type with a graciousness. . . . Characterized our work as 'beautiful.' " They also visited Ottaviani, who "showed eagerness to help. He is close to the Holy Father and powerful." However, later that day, Ottaviani "relieved us of any hope of decretum laudis at this time."[13]

The founder of Glenmary had planned for the Home Missioners to become an international society, one that would train priests from many nations to preach the gospel to fallen-away Catholics and to non-Catholics in the homelands. In his last interview with Spozette, Bishop "startled" him by proposing that he be "allowed to solicit vocations in Italy. 'To take back to the Missions in America?' he asked. 'No, Monsignor. To train for work among the millions of fallen-aways in Italy, chiefly as a means of stemming the advance of Communism.' He wasn't fond of the idea of missions to convert Italy, but I stuck to my point . . . he agreed that the work would be dangerous; 'as missioners we shall have to face danger as we have in the past,' I replied." When Spozette told him that the communists would "heckle and shout when you talk," Bishop replied that "of course as our work organizes in various countries it will have to adapt its technique to the conditions it finds, a different method for each country." The monsignor informed Bishop of the worker-priest movement; the Glenmarian noted in his diary, "I must know more about them."[14] After Bishop had visited a "poverty-stricken" section of Rome he wrote: "a quaint, peaceful people in spite of miserable poverty—apparently they will not yield to Communism if the priests would go to the streets and talk to them."[15]

Midway through their visit in Rome, Sourd and Bishop moved to the Collegio Maryknoll where they felt more at home. Father Skeehan, one of the priests, was "very pleasant" and extended himself beyond "incidental courtesy." Among the many experiences in Rome that was "never to be forgotten" was a canonization at St. Peter's. He recorded the experience in his diary: "When it comes to drama and pageantry and profoundly touching the souls of men by glamorous costume and ceremonial, the Church is master and has no second. The mass, the choir, the silver trumpets, the varied costumes and massive movements of prelates and guards, the bells and, most of all, the Holy Father himself at Mass and being carried high above the crowd in procession all combine to leave an incomparable impression."[16]

A few days before their July 4 departure, Bishop and Sourd, French, and McGrath drove to Assisi, "the quaintest and most beautiful of towns." They spent the night at the hospice of the Sisters of the Atonement founded by Father Paul James Francis in the United States. The next day each celebrated mass at the tomb of St. Francis.[17] The setting with "a rough stone sarcophagus" was, according to Bishop, "very austere but full of inspiration for all missioners. This is a place to visit when courage lags." After visiting several churches this was contrary to his impressions the preceding day: "The Cathedrals and Churches, desolate and forlorn in exterior experience, full of beauty and devotion inside. One almost wearies of saints for the moment."[18]

The day after their return flight home, Sourd and Bishop went to Maryknoll for three days and then traveled to Baltimore and Washington, D.C. to see family and old friends. They arrived at Glendale on July 12 where they received a "hearty welcome."[19] It was not until August 22, 1947 that Bishop received the "Archbishop's Decree of Election and sanction for my document." "Now, for the first time, we exist canonically, though only as a Diocesan Society," exclaimed Bishop in his diary.[20] The Vatican had yet to return the society's constitution, but the society had received Roman affirmation of diocesan status. In Rome the pontifical letter of authorization was dated June 18, 1947 and McNicholas' decree was issued on August 20. Under the title "Rome Ratifies," an article explaining these official actions was published in *The Challenge* (Autumn 1947). Besides the commentary on the decree, the article, probably written by Bishop, noted that Pope Pius XII had "blessed their work and their Society." The concluding remarks illustrated Bishop's intention to "cultivate native vocations in many countries to inaugurate the Home Mission Apostolate. Home Missionaries of many lands and climes and of many tongues, under the influence of enthusiastic America and the safe guidance of Rome, can reap a harvest of countless souls."[21] However, at that time there were only eighteen priests and twenty-two seminarians, far short of the required number of fifty for Rome. Later it was noted that McNicholas had neglected to inform the Sacred Congregation that he did indeed issue the decree of August 20; it was not until November 11, 1949 that he sent a copy of the decree to the Vatican. What may have prompted notice of the missing decree was Bishop's letter seeking Vatican approval for the first rector of the Glenmary seminary, Father Joseph Schneider, who was also rector of Mount St. Mary's Seminary.[22]

While in Rome Howard Bishop received from the Congregation of Religious authorization to borrow $250,000 for the building of a seminary. However it was not until May of 1948 that construction began. Characteristic of the founder's desire to be involved in all facets of the life of Glenmary, Bishop was thoroughly immersed in the seminary from the architect's design to the various stages of construction. It was his idea that the seminary be designed with a southern colonial motif; the building showed a noticeable influence of the Carroll mansion, Doughoregan Manor. The first building to be constructed was the boiler house that was originally planned with only one story to house the boiler, laundry and garage. To change it to a temporary seminary the furnace area was floored over and the space was used for a kitchen, four bedrooms, a small lavatory and two guest parlors. A second floor was to accommodate eighteen priests and seminarians. A construction company owned by a Catholic came with a higher bid than an "outside" contractor. After consulting with his old friend and advisor Mr. Harry Santen and an auxiliary bishop, Howard Bishop decided to go with the outside firm. Though the building was scheduled to be completed by the spring of 1949, it was not ready until late spring of the following year.[23]

The three Glenmarians slated for the faculty were Earl McGrath, Howard French, and John Marquardt, with Benedict Wolf as spiritual director. A tragic interruption of plans occurred on September 29, 1948. McGrath, who had been temporarily assigned to Norton, and a parishioner drove to Statesboro where Edward Smith and Raymond Dehen were stationed. When they were returning to Statesboro their car broke down. Subsequently, as the owner of an auto repair shop was driving them home, the bright lights of an oncoming car obstructed the driver's vision and he ran into the rear of a parked truck. The thirty-two year old Father McGrath died almost immediately; the others were only slightly injured.[24] On October 4, the requiem mass was held at St. Teresa's Church in Cincinnati, the site of McGrath's first solemn mass. There is no extant copy of Howard Bishop's homily on the occasion, but The Challenge contains his reflections on the death of the first seminarian to join the society in 1938.

This death has a strong suggestion of God's providential action. Under the Old Law when God demanded the offering of sacrifices from His people, He asked for the firstlings of their flocks and the first fruits of their harvests. They must give Him of their first and best. It is not surprising that He has demanded of us the first young man to join us, and one of first three set aside and trained for our Seminary faculty.

We shall miss him. But we are consoled by the thought that God will establish him in Heaven as an intercessor before His throne and that rich blessings will flow down upon the earth. Rich blessings will flow to his home and family who have so quietly given him back to God. Rich blessings will come to this diocese to which he originally belonged, whose priests he knew and loved, and which—through our great-souled Archbishop—released him with so many others, to the H.M.A. Rich blessings will flow to our Society which looked upon him as its own and now gives him back to God.[25]

The death of Earl McGrath must have struck Bishop as the passing of the first-born, an experience from which parents seldom survive without permanent psychological scars. Francis L. Cunningham, O.P., who had taught sacred scripture at the Dominican House of Studies in River Forest, Illinois, ultimately replaced McGrath on the faculty.

In October of 1949, just about a year after McGrath died, Our Lady of the Fields Seminary was blessed by George J. Rehring, auxiliary bishop of Cincinnati, with about forty-five priests in attendance. "A Glorious day" exclaimed Howard in his diary, "Bp. Rehring spoke very kindly about our work and Fr. S. to me personally."[26] Because of the growth of the sisters' community Bishop turned over the old motherhouse to them. Bishop and Sourd and two others moved into the seminary along with the nine theologians and the three faculty members. The old convent was transformed into a novitiate for the priests who formed the first formation class under the direction of Father Francis McRae, the Maryknoll priest who had been the first spiritual director of the mission school and unofficial novitiate. Subsequent novitiates were at Milford where the Jesuits provided a building. Concomitant with the opening of the seminary the sisters' community received official status.

On the day of his departure for Rome, Howard wrote to the sisters under the salutation "Beloved Daughters in Christ." Though the sisters did not receive papal approbation until 1952, Bishop viewed papal recognition of the men's community as a "nearer realization" of Vatican approval of the Glenmary Sisters. The remainder of the letter was concerned with the development of a suitable habit.[27] Three days before, he had indicated Sister Dorothy's concern about "Sister Kevin's zeal for Dominican ways & habit."[28] In his 1947 letter he reflected that concern. "It is my hope that by the time Fr. Sourd and I return, you will have picked up a significant number of ideas for the perfecting of your beautiful grey costume. It will of course be substantially the same as it is, as you have developed it to suit the needs of your mission field." He asked them to allow him "the privilege of seeing and passing on your ideas as to head-dress and collar before they become final." After expressing his confidence in Sister Kevin and the Adrian Dominican community, he implicitly charged the Glenmary women to maintain their unique identity, i.e. not to be absorbed into the Dominicans. "Let nothing change you from your steadfast purpose, which God has put in your hearts . . . of keeping the grey habit. . . . You are a pioneer group, doing pioneer work where no community has gone before you. Love and keep the habit that is made for your work and expresses the simple pioneer spirit of your ideal." Knowing full well that Sister Kevin would read the letter, he indirectly informed the sisters that the progress they had made under Sister Kevin's "wise direction is highly gratifying and consoling to your founder."[29]

The following September Sisters Opal, Joan and Bernice were assigned to teach at the new parochial school at Russellville under the pastor, Father Benedict Wolf. Howard Bishop had reluctantly approved Wolf's plan for a school about a year before it opened. He had always envisioned the sisters' mission to be limited to vacation schools and small clinics as well as home visitation to the poor. A few days after the sisters departed for Russellville, Howard received a letter from McNicholas "informing me of his displeasure concerning the present set-up of Sisters' community, accusing me of retarding their progress by insisting upon my authority over him in spite of his repeated advice to the contrary. Also [he] directed that I have no authority over them in the future. . . ."[30]

McNicholas dissolved the office of prefect that allowed one of the Glenmary Sisters to have some authority. Though Opal and others were opposed to Sr. Kevin's introduction of some Dominican customs,[31] it appears that the Dominican superior had considered Howard Bishop to be the primary source of opposition to her authority. Hence, McNicholas told him that Sister Kevin was to have full authority: "[she] may consult with me but not obliged, [she is] free to accept or reject my advice," lamented Howard in his diary.[32] In response to McNicholas' letter, Howard wrote that he "freely and willingly . . . [accepts] your kind and fatherly correction." He informed the archbishop that he had read the letter to Sister Kevin "insofar as they relate to the Sisters' community" and that he requested him "to make whatever readjustments as to community leadership that your Grace's letter may require." He "deeply regretted having disturbed" the archbishop and he explained that his "zeal . . . [had] led me too far occasionally . . . but he doubted that he had been as "imprudent in my zeal as you must now believe. . . ." Howard closed with an expression of concern for the archbishop's health and told him "not to worry any more about my blunders."[33]

McNicholas responded to Howard's letter with his own apology for asserting himself "as strongly as I did. I am too old and, I am sure, too impatient to deal with obstacles that seem to me unnecessary." However, he was convinced that the sisters would make progress when they were no longer under the authority of the founder.[34] According to Howard's diary notation, Sister Kevin expressed her loyalty to him and said that she will "consult [with me] about all important matters."[35]

The issue of the sisters' habit surfaced again in January of 1948. According to his diary Bishop wrote to McNicholas expressing his "regret" to learn that there is a move among the sisters to ask for a Dominican habit, a move that he considered to be in violation of an agreement that he and McNicholas had reached regarding the approval of a "simple habit." If the Dominican habit is adopted, then Howard would refuse to allow "these Sisters on our backwoods rural missions, where the Dominican habit would be impractical." He promised not to interfere with the "internal affairs of the Sisters. . . . But this matter of the habit is one of those fundamental things about which a founder may justly be concerned. . . ."[36] When he was told that McNicholas was unwilling to discuss the matter with him, Bishop "stormed for a while" and even "threatened to ask for my exit."[37] He then consulted with several prominent priests and even Archbishop Cushing. The latter told him that "McN is vindictive. Therefore, let things run their course, don't interfere. He can't live long. Then, I can adjust matters to my ideas.—I replied: dangerous to await anybody's death. I could die first."[38]

Howard adopted a strategy of patient resolve to continue the struggle for the sisters' independence from Dominican customs. In his talks with the archbishop, issues of the habit never surfaced until December 1948. Apparently a compromise had been reached; the sisters would wear the Dominican habit at the motherhouse and their own Glenmary habit in the mission field. McNicholas announced this solution within the context of his stated intention to appeal to the Vatican for papal approval of the sisters' status as a congregation of diocesan right. However, Sister Kevin and Bishop quarreled over the latter's desire "to keep field habit un-Dominican." Though this incident, which occurred on Christmas Eve, ended with mutual apologies, Sister Kevin's behavior toward Bishop remained hostile.[39]

According to Sister Frances' recollection, supported by Sister Dorothy, Howard polled the sisters on the question of the habit and encouraged the majority to tell the archbishop about their opposition to the Dominican habit. On December 29, Sisters Dorothy, Opal and Joan attempted to visit the archbishop but, at the suggestion of Howard Bishop, carried a letter with them in the event they were unable to see him. The letter was couched in respectful terms, but the three sisters very frankly stated their "great disappointment" with the decision that they will not be allowed to wear their "original grey" habit in the motherhouse. "We thought when Your Grace approved our [grey] habit that it was to be permanent and it has become very dear to our hearts—a symbol of Glenmary—our Home Mission field."[40] Though eight of the ten sisters indicated their support of this letter and though Sister Kevin allowed them to express their position, one presumes that McNicholas disregarded their appeal because a week later a minority of two or three Glenmary Sisters expressed their gratitude for his support and their enthusiasm for the Dominican habit. Indeed they stated, "We look forward eagerly to the time when we shall be members of the great Dominican order and pray that we will live up to its magnificent traditions and ideals."[41]

It appeared evident that McNicholas had told Rome that the Glenmary Sisters, on the model of the Maryknoll community, wanted to be trained as Dominicans but with their own missionary identity. The archbishop had become quite weak during the final two years of his life. Shortly after his death on April 24, 1950, Bishop discovered that the request for papal approval of the sisters' community had never been sent to Rome.

In the summer of 1950, when George J. Rehring was administrator of the archdiocese and bishop-elect of Toledo, Mother Gerald Barry, superior of the Dominicans of Adrian, Michigan, notified Rehring and Howard Bishop that she had decided to assign Sister Kevin to Siena Heights College and did not indicate that there would be a replacement. After consulting with Rehring and writing to Mother Gerald, Bishop, accompanied by his secretary James Kelly (ordained in 1948), visited Adrian to discuss Dominican direction of the sisters' community. From his perspective Howard had been respectful to Sister Kevin and could not comprehend the attitude that prompted Mother Gerald's action and Sister Kevin's alienation. He referred to a June 27 conversation during which he said that he would insist that the sisters wear their Glenmary habits even in the motherhouse and even though they followed the plan to become Dominicans. He told Mother Gerald that Sister Kevin said "they ought not become Dominican because it made a confusion of loyalties and tended to cause a divided spirit." "Furthermore," she said, "they don't want to be Dominicans." Though Mother Gerald said she agreed with Sister Kevin, she explained that she removed the sisters from Glenmary "because of your [Bishop's] interference." When sometime later Howard asked to have Sister Kevin reappointed to Glenmary, Mother Gerald "became resentful, accused me of dictating to her." He explained to Rehring, "It was a difficult situation from the *start* . . . after two vain attempts to continue my story and being interrupted each time, it began to look as if I would not have a chance to speak. . . . Her mode of attack had provoked several explosions from me for which I apologized in a night letter before taking my train home." Ultimately Mother Gerald appointed Sister John Joseph as the superior of the Glenmary Sisters. Though she did not attempt to impose Dominican customs, there remained an underlying tension between her and Howard Bishop, particularly because of the latter's conviction that the Dominicans "cannot help but instructing them [i.e. the Glenmary Sisters] in terms of Dominican superiority."[42]

The Glenmary community did its work according to the superior's plan for the division of labor: the priests' sacramental ministry and street preaching; the sisters' catechetical and social work; the brothers' manual labor on the missions and at the motherhouse. Several articles in *The Challenge* were aimed at recruiting brothers. Father William Smith, one of the four Glenmary priests from Chicago, was the director of the brothers during the immediate post-war period. In a 1948 article entitled "Our Brothers," Smith introduced the small community to the readers of *The Challenge*. Brother Thomas Kelly, whose brother James had been ordained for Glenmary that year, had just received his cassock, symbolic of the termination of a six-month postulancy program. Eventually Brother Thomas became Father Sourd's companion and driver on his fund-raising and vocation trips throughout the midwest. Brother Lawrence Jochim of Poseyville, Indiana was a postulant then; he has since served on several missions. Vincent Wilmes, the first brother, was then living at St. Anthony's mission in the Cumberland Mountains of Virginia. "Besides his work with the town boys in the mission recreation center and his indispensable job of keeping the mission well fed, Brother finds time to [be] . . . among the poor folks. . . . So easily he finds people in real poverty, children who need shoes and sweaters and coats [that] he overruns his accounts and ends up in the hole."[43] Brother Anthony Ignatius was stationed at Statesboro and traveled by motorcycle throughout the 900 square-mile parish. Smith seems to have consciously focused on the social ministries of the brothers, perhaps indicating that there was more to their way of life than just manual labor and prayer. In 1948 the brothers initiated a Sunday afternoon program among the poor of Cincinnati. "Armed with boxes of sandwiches, they made off weekly for downtown and their poverty-stricken friends . . . destitute men and women and whole families, hungry, ill housed and thinly clad."[44] In his diary for Easter Sunday, 1949, Howard Bishop proudly notes that the brothers went to town to serve "their dear beggars and bums."[45]

Of all the brothers, Charles Reedy was the most articulate in his concern for the poor. A pacifist and vegetarian he lived alone in a small house on a farm in Blue Creek located in Adams County, Ohio. Bishop recalled that before Reedy "came to us he actually 'deeded it to God,' he says. . . . At least two poor families . . . have occupied it, rent free, since then. While he lived there his sole occupation was to be utterly at the service of his neighbors, especially in time of illness, when he took over their chores for them."[46] In a very real sense Reedy had developed a vision of Christian rural life that was similar to that of Bishop when he was president of the N.C.R.L.C. Reedy wrote that he hoped to spark an "improved social order—voluntary production and consumption, with warehouses, mills, professions, crafts, natural resources, etc. all operative on the voluntary principle coming into service to relieve the congregation of the monetary way of commercial intercourse."[47]

After he joined Glenmary, Brother Charles worked in almost every mission. His skills were so diverse that he could handle almost any task in building and maintaining the church, the rectory and other mission structures. His letters to his superior included reports on construction, reflections on spirituality, and Christian communalism. His radical identity with "the charity of Christ" meant to him "that we can no more contain ourselves than did Jesus. . . . Regardless of what the object is—food, clothing, shelter, fuel, land, property—in the needy man you see Christ and you give to him his needs without restraint."[48]

Howard Bishop admired Brother Charles. He was very pleased that Charles would be attracted to Glenmary. When he indicated a need to live the solitary life, Bishop permitted him to live in a cottage in Buena Vista, and at Otway Charles was allowed to live in a small "lean-to" as Howard called it. By 1947 Charles had developed a plan outlined in a letter to his superior whereby the wealthy would purchase property for the use of poor families. He specifically referred to a family of nine "literally without the means of sustaining natural life—without tenancy or mortgage status" but with the "right to an undisputable spot under the sun." If families abuse their responsibilities, they are to be "crosses" for their neighbors to bear with "Christian patience and fortitude as a means of increasing their own sanctity." The plan established a communal dimension of labor and cooperative agriculture, but it was grounded in the doctrine of the mystical body as the theological basis for "rehabilitating these rundown souls." The rich provide the material aid, and the lay people who live in the community are the "cells of the body, each offering his particular function in the unified operation of the whole." Charles wished to form a volunteer Christian community within Glenmary as central to the functioning of the mystical body of Christ. The brothers would provide "the moral support of their talents for sustaining life in which they direct and teach by example." The sisters' moral support would be expressed in "refinement and inspiration by example," and the priests "are the channels of grace which sustains all these works being the life of Christ continued in contemporary men. . . ."[49] With only a few brief extant letters from Howard to Charles during the period when Charles was striving to find some confirmation of his plan, 1946–1949, we must rely upon Bishop's correspondence to discern his views on Charles' prospective reforms. However, the latter's letters to Bishop reveal that his superior responded consistently with kindness and openness.

In his diary Howard frequently referred to conversations with Charles, to his disagreements with the free-land feature of his plan, and to consultations with Archbishop McNicholas and Bishop Rehring on Charles' vision of a rural community. It became obvious to Charles that if his plan was to materialize he would need to leave Glenmary. He too consulted several people including his spiritual director. While Charles was reflecting on leaving Glenmary, Howard wrote to Bishop Emmet M. Walsh of Charleston. He outlined Charles' plan, expressed his own views, and asked the bishop to grant Charles an interview. Bishop told Walsh of Charles' "humility and selflessness . . . [that] I have not known in any other man. Kindness and charity and service to the poor . . . reminds one of St. Francis." After describing the plan, Bishop said that "the land giving item is one of the points in his plan in which I declined to sponsor him" because of its "limitations and ramifications that render it impractical." The plan's call for a religious community was another point of disagreement: "He can't form a community within ours and he can't take over ours . . . he cannot stay with us and work out his plan too. . . . My own position is this. Charley is highly worth keeping. I want him and he wants us. But I can't persuade him to drop the ideas that he is determined to work out. Recently he has insinuated that I am blocking him although I have repeatedly told him my conclusions."[50]

Howard Bishop's role as founder precluded acceptance of Charles' reforms that symbolized such a radical departure from his own plan. The first two drafts of his plan for the Home Missioners included the desire to establish rural colonies, but these would be based upon small truck farms and cooperative industry rather than Christian communes composed of large farms. It appears that Howard Bishop's anti-capitalist drive had been tempered by the financial considerations of investing the community's funds to finance its missions, seminary and future projects. However, even if he had held fast to his anti-capitalist position of the Depression, Howard Bishop would have been unsympathetic to Charles' plan because its radical Christian character struck him as not only an extreme interpretation of scripture but also contrary to basic principles of rural sociology. It is not surprising that of all of the Glenmarians familiar with the plan of Brother Charles only Gertrude Kimmick found it attractive. However, there was a consensus in the society that Brother Charles was a positive source of sanctity and a skilled craftsman as well.

During the late 1940s when Brother Charles was struggling to implement his plan, two men joined the society as priests. In October of 1947 Patrick T. Quinlan entered Glenmary; he was a rural activist of the archdiocese of Hartford and well known for his statistical work on conversions and his work on behalf of the Catholic Rural Life Conference. He was assigned to a new mission in Kingstree, South Carolina and appears to have been quite effective on the missions. However, he was not willing to make a permanent commitment to Glenmary. Howard Bishop told him that he must either profess the Glenmary oath or withdraw from the society. Quinlan decided on the latter course on November 26, 1948, a little over a year after he had joined Glenmary. In his telephone discussion with Bishop Emmett Walsh of Charleston, Howard strongly recommended that Quinlan remain there as a diocesan priest. "Pat was grateful," noted Bishop in his diary; [Quinlan and Bishop agreed that] "our friendship is not disturbed" by this incident.[51]

Henry Burke, a newly ordained priest of the diocese of Trenton, New Jersey, was assigned to a mission parish in Bennetsville in the diocese of Charleston in February of 1948. Brother Charles Reedy and he formed a Glenmary team in the new mission. Eventually they established their residence in Cheraw. Burke, apparently with some support from the Catholic community, wished to establish a parish school but, as noted earlier, Bishop was opposed to assigning Glenmary Sisters to school work. In his 1951 mid-winter letter the superior elaborated on his policy. Contrary to his strong endorsement of parish schools that formed the base of his League of the Little Flower and to his stated intention in the published plan for the Home Missioners, Howard now considered parish schools to be viable only

when they could be entirely financed by the parishioners. Though the
Sunfish and Russellville missions had schools, he was determined to
draw the line there. He based his position upon two principles:

> *First.* Our services to the people of a mission area should have in
> view the greatest spiritual good of the highest number of people
> that can be reached without undue strain upon our human and
> financial resources, such a strain, I mean, as may retard or even
> defeat our work itself.

> *Second.* We should avoid rendering to one region of a mission area
> a highly specialized service that will be so costly in funds and time
> requirements as to divert us from giving a less costly service to a
> larger number of people elsewhere.

He then listed the costs of providing a modern school that would
tend to "confine schools to the city and town parishes which have a
sufficient number of Catholics to keep such a budget." A country
parish school is an exception. It may only be justified when all the
essential needs of the parish are also satisfied: a C.C.D. program for
non-parish school children and the availability of non-teaching sisters
for home visitation and the C.C.D. program.[52]
The policies governing the Glenmary Sisters were derived from
their general commitment to be a "very mobile group." If they did
become attached to a school, other Glenmary Sisters must serve the
mission by "helping the poor, the sick and the neglected in mind and
body." If they wanted to be attached permanently, he preferred that
it be a small clinic rather than a school. Their service at the clinic or
dispensary would introduce them to the poor and needy people of
the region. In short the sisters were to concentrate primarily upon
catechetical, home-visiting and clinical work.[53] Henry Burke broke
with the society over the school policy and is today a pastor in the
Charleston diocese.
Father Howard French, trained in Rome for the Glenmary seminary, followed Massarella by joining the Trappists of Gethsemane
Abbey in 1952. Two spiritual directors guided him to the Trappists,
but Howard Bishop said to both French and to the Abbot of Gethsemane that if French left before he could train a replacement, "he
must go without my blessing and in disobedience to me."[54] In time, a

replacement was found, and French entered the Trappists with his superior's blessing. Today Father French is a retired diocesan priest of the archdiocese of Louisville. In a recent conversation he told me that his memories of Howard were "kindly and full of respect."[55] He pointed out that the Glenmary superior was approachable but could not engage in small talk. "He was basically shy in a crowd," remarked French. Father Massarella also left the Trappists and is now chaplain at a nursing home in Dayton, Ohio. He agreed that Howard was shy: "he wasn't very sociable among priests of the archdiocese."[56] Both former Glenmarians noted that Howard was fair and compassionate, but also quick-tempered and stubborn. Charles Reedy also left Glenmary; he became a Benedictine priest of St. Benedict's Abbey, Benet Lake, Wisconsin, and ministered to base communities in Mexico for over twenty-five years. In 1990 he is attempting to form a Christian rural community comparable to that envisioned in his plan of the 1940s and to Howard Bishop's design of a colony in Clarksville in the 1930s.

As Howard approached his sixty-fifth birthday in 1950 he began to experience periods of weariness. Though he was pleased with Rome's approval and satisfied with the foundation of the seminary, he experienced several problem situations: the formation of the sisters, the few vocations to the brothers' community (there were only four brothers at the opening of 1950), the challenges of Brother Charles and Fathers Quinlan, Burke and French, and the need to continuously seek funds and promote vocations. Such expressions of weariness were balanced by his strong sense of direction at the hand of providence. He expressed impatience, but that was because he was even less patient with himself. His New Year's maxims for 1950 are illustrative of his self-criticism as a superior.

December 21, 1949 Addendum
    PERSONAL.

Do not "follow up" suspicions of minor violations of rule, etc.

Do your best to prevent, pray, leave the rest to God.

Suspicions of major violations:

Never act until & unless proof is established. Take every prudent means to know facts.

An act of kindness or courtesy is, in the ordinary affairs of life, worth all the inconvenience & delay it may cause.

Even a square peg can be driven into a round hole, but it is not comfortable for the peg—it has to be *driven*.[57]

CHAPTER 11

The Final Years
1950–1953

The founder of Glenmary was well known for his almost fierce attention to every facet of the society's development. His diary notations reveal that no task was too small for him to undertake. A typical day included correspondence; a meeting with architects or contractors; a community lecture on one of several topics such as rural sociology, poetry, history, spirituality or theology; a period of reading, and perhaps an outing to the closing session of a parish forty hours' devotion or a movie. There was also his daily prayer routine beginning with morning prayer and meditation before early mass. He made annual visitations to the missions which would normally include a visit with the bishop. Visits with James E. Walsh of Maryknoll, Archbishop Cushing of Boston, and friends in Baltimore and Washington, D.C. were frequent.

As noted earlier the Santen home was his refuge from the rigorous demands of Glenmary. His visits there were not without their business concerns; Harry was his most trusted advisor on economic and legal matters and Margaret Mary Santen founded the Glenmary Guild that not only acted as a funding arm but also developed widespread interest in Glenmary throughout the Cincinnati area. In 1951 Howard developed a men's counterpart to the Guild, the Lay Associates of the Home Missioners of America with the acronym LAHMAS. It never achieved the strength of the Guild. The Santens introduced Mr. and Mrs. Thomas Bradley of New York to the Home Missioners. In 1961 the Bradleys presented the society with a sizable gift. The Kuntz family of Dayton continued to be very generous, and Father Borchers' family gave an occasional large gift. Of course the

Santens probably matched the Bradley gift over the years and were very generous to Howard personally. Howard's friendship was manifested in several ways. When Margaret Mary was in need of expert medical attention, he arranged for her to be examined by a team of doctors at The Johns Hopkins Hospital where he had contacts from his days in the archdiocese of Baltimore.

In the last three years of his life Howard focused on three major areas: governance, missions and spirituality. Governance entailed the promulgation of the constitution, the first general chapter and the formation of a general council. There was a significant development in the policy directing the missions, one that emphasized indirect evangelization. Howard decided to make a six-month novitiate during that first official novitiate year after the promulgation of the constitution; the year culminated in a thirty-day Ignatian retreat. This focus on governance, mission and spirit clarifies the charism of Howard Bishop as founder of the Home Missioners of America.

The appointment of Karl J. Alter as fifth archbishop of Cincinnati was announced on June 20, 1950. In his years as archbishop of Cincinnati, Alter presided over a building program that entailed 350 parochial and archdiocesan projects at a cost of $60 million. Renovating the Cathedral of St. Peter-in-Chains and the completion of the minor seminary were the two most significant projects.

McNicholas tended to be philosophical and paternalistic; in contrast to his leadership, Alter was a very decisive administrator, one who had been bishop for nineteen years before moving to Cincinnati. No one could have excelled McNicholas as a loyal episcopal patron of Glenmary. Two days after Alter's appointment Howard Bishop wrote to Raphael Sourd that "I think we are safe in his [Alter's] hands."[1] In mid July he informed Sourd of his first meeting with Alter. "I have . . . been very well received" by the archbishop.[2]

It was not until October 3, 1950 that Bishop and Sourd had their first formal interview with Karl Alter. Howard recorded the event in his diary.

1. Grants permission for us to borrow $200,000. . . .
2. Consents to attend our annual spring dinners as a practice but to give the address at our one, *only* . . .

3. My reminder that 18 of our 23 sisters with the habit don't want to become Dominicans brought me a pretty stiff lecture. Two groups *entirely* separate, I have *no* authority, etc. etc. which I, of course, know well. But, his rigid interpretation I did *not* know. We must work toward relinquishing all sisters' services in kitchen and office. He will make a visitation and act according to his findings on [Dominican] affiliation.[3]

Alter's address at the March 1, 1951 banquet with 700 people in attendance was, according to Bishop, "a fine address on anti-Catholic movements in America."[4] According to Alter, the new Dominican superior, Sister John Joseph, and a majority of the sisters were opposed to affiliation with the Dominicans. The archbishop expressed strong interest in applying for Vatican approval to establish the Glenmary Sisters as a congregation of diocesan right.[5]

McNicholas had led the Glenmary men along the path to Vatican approval, but Howard Bishop had to deal with Alter in the final process of approving the constitution for the society. Signed by Alter on March 29, 1951, the document stipulated that the society was ordinarily governed by a superior general assisted by a general chapter. In consultation with Howard, Bishop Alter appointed a temporary council: H. Bishop, Superior General; R. Sourd, Vicar General; C. Borchers, Society Purchaser (Procurator); J. Kelly, Treasurer General; J. Marquardt, Secretary General.

The council's first meeting occurred on May 8, 1951. The major business matters were finances, capital improvements, personnel assignments, and occasionally general policy. The general chapter that would elect officers on a permanent (six-year basis) was scheduled for August 27 after the annual three-day retreat. According to Bishop's diary Alter "invites himself to preside at our election of chapter members preceding Chapter meeting. Will go home immediately. I hesitated, but finally approved 'on condition it be only for election of Chapter.' He iterated it was his right. But all in best of spirit and goodwill."[6]

On August 28, 1951 Howard Bishop was elected superior general by a chapter vote of 10 to 2; Raphael Sourd became the first vicar general, John Marquardt was secretary general, and James Kelly was treasurer general. Clem Borchers and Edward Smith were elected to the council.[7] Bishop's nature almost precluded collegiality. On the contrary he jealously guarded his authority and considered anyone who questioned a particular decision to be impudent and disrespectful. As if to engage in a bit of self-correction Howard copied in his diary a bit of doggerel by Edgar Guest entitled "Thoughtlessness."

He didn't stop to think. He let
Ill temper breed some new regret,
He spoke in anger and in hate,
To wish he hadn't, just too late.
Intelligent and able, too,
The shame of bitter speech he knew.
He also knew when temper flies
No man is either fair or wise,
Or with the morning rises proud
Of conduct arrogant and loud.
Yet none had seen him at his worst
If he had thought it over first.[8]

The minutes of the general council reveal that Bishop proposed and the council disposed, and on certain matters the superior general's proposals were requests for confirmation of his transactions. The first crisis of authority occurred on December 10, 1951 when James Kelly complained that by making all financial decisions and signing checks in his name only, Howard Bishop had unconstitutionally prevented Kelly from fulfilling his position. Kelly, who was also Bishop's private secretary, was aware of Bishop's tendencies to dominate. According to Bishop, he and Kelly had a "spirited discussion" at a council meeting, but Marquardt interfered, and later Bishop and Kelly began to co-sign the society's checks.[9]

The Bishop-Marquardt conflict was acute and chronic. It not only occurred within the council but erupted over Marquardt's rectorship of the seminary. On one occasion, Bishop responded to Marquardt's defense of his autonomy by telling him, "I'm not to be supervised by you but to supervise you."[10] At a day of recollection for the seminary Marquardt seemed to challenge Bishop's authority. The superior general noted in his diary that the rector had made "Rough references to Society and superiors." He quoted Marquardt's lecture. "The Society exists for you, not you for the Society." "The superiors are for

you, not you for them. You are the Society." "Society is a means to an
end, nothing more." "Don't become attached to the Society."
"Danger of community life, one-track minds." "I want you to be
critical. Would hate for you not to be critical."[11] The next day Bishop
interviewed five students about Marquardt's "blast yesterday." They
did not view it as "harmful," but Bishop "explained . . . that the spirit
of criticism must be carefully avoided as destructive of the Society's
peace and unity." He also reported it to Alter who advised him "to do
nothing until after ordination."[12]

Howard had decided to spend six months in the Glenmary "novitiate" (referred to as the Probandate in the constitution) and asked
every priest to follow suit. However, he told Marquardt that he
wanted him to make a six-month novitiate at the same time as he did.
"He bristles, refuses, *unless I commanded* it," wrote Bishop in his
diary. The superior general told Marquardt that he would not command him but that he would like his response after he returned from
his visitation of the missions.[13]

In mid-June of 1952 Howard faced a severe crisis. At the June 16
council meeting Bishop asked Marquardt to resign as rector of the
seminary, to lay aside temporarily his work as secretary general, and
to agree to begin a six month novitiate on September 1, 1952. Marquardt, obviously with great reluctance, accepted these requests.[14] As
he explained two days later, Marquardt consented to the novitiate
"largely in a spirit of obedience." During the council meeting Marquardt had said "our men are treated like pawns on a chessboard," to
which Bishop responded with denial at such a "brash and untrue
comment." He said that he could not "let Marquardt go out on the
mission with such a spirit of criticism." The superior general "made
him promise to build up not tear down home base."[15]

James Kelly was also critical of the superior general. On June 16 he
challenged Bishop's small private fund and suggested that he resign.
The following day Kelly, alienated by Bishop's authoritarian leadership, again asked him to resign. Kelly wrote to Alter and also sent a list
of criticisms to Bishop.[16] Kelly acted as a spokesman for those on the
council who were concerned that Bishop was not governing according to the constitution. He said that Bishop was acting as if he had the
power to dispense with the rule without seeking the council's approval. He intimated that the superior general was interfering with
the officers' responsibility to function as defined by the constitution.

Kelly told Bishop that he could not depose Marquardt as secretary general. Only the Holy See with the general council's recommendations could depose him. If Bishop promised to correct these abuses, then, said Kelly, "the archbishop's concern will be allayed and his confidence in you restored." Bishop said that he adequately answered Kelly's charges and told him that "retiring would not grieve me if Council demands."[7] This disagreement gradually subsided; it did not derive from a fundamental clash of personalities as it did with Marquardt. Indeed Kelly's criticisms were couched in language that was decidedly deferential to the superior general. But the Marquardt–Bishop conflict continued to simmer. When they were in the novitiate together there were periods of reconciliation, but Marquardt never denied his original criticism that Bishop tended to rule by fiat.

In an interview many years after Bishop's death, Marquardt said that in his first year as a priest in Glenmary "he felt totally and completely useless. . . . In Bishop's mind I was not an ordained priest I was just a seminarian."

He was subjected to the rigors of the seminary such as he must be in his room at 7:15 every night; he had to receive special permission to go to town. However, it was not until he was on the council that Marquardt had openly confronted Bishop. "I think I could sum up our relationship on the Council by saying that all the disagreements (practically all of them) were based on this: that it was, and still is, my conviction that Father Bishop was not using the Council to run the Society. He always presented to the Council what he had already decided. . . . I studied Canon Law, and after I came back from Rome, I asked Father one day explicitly, 'Now that you sent me to study and spent all that money do you want me to speak up?' He said of course, that is what you are trained for. One time in a thousand my comment was well received. . . . I think Father Bishop took all disagreements on the personal level, and he saw others as trying to be competitive."[18]

About Bishop's hot temper Marquardt said that there were occasions when he "moved grown men to tears by bawling them out mercilessly in an embarrassing fashion in front of others." Despite all of these adverse characteristics Howard Bishop was, according to Marquardt, "a man of prayer . . . it was probably the one thing that ever let me maintain a basic respect for him. . . . In fact if it had not been true, I would have on occasion opposed him more vigorously than I did.''[19]

Howard Bishop had been very fond of John Marquardt. He was the first Glenmarian from outside Cincinnati and he was specially trained for the seminary with little experience in the missions. In a very real sense Bishop and Marquardt were very much alike; they each held fast to their strong convictions and were sensitive and strongly opinionated. Neither wore authority well; Bishop tended to be coldly objective and jealously guarded his prerogatives; as rector of the seminary Marquardt brooked no interference from Bishop and tended to be protective of his students. But both could be very charming if only they received the respect due to them, the one as founder and superior general, the other as rector, councillor and canon lawyer. Howard Bishop was a professional, but he was impatient with the procedures imposed by canon law. That Howard Bishop could not delegate authority has become an historical truism. He was certainly in the mold of the traditional pastor who ruled the parish, school and rectory with little or no consultation with assistant pastors. As superior general these tendencies were exaggerated because, unlike the pastor, Howard did not have the compensation of a daily ministry in a parish community. Since he tended to be relaxed and very accessible during his visits to the missions, outbursts of temper and authority conflicts were infrequent. Hence, one may conclude that he experienced deep ambivalence in an authority position, particularly that of superior general/founder.

When Howard began his novitiate the Marquardt conflict was temporarily dormant, while the Kelly disagreement was resolved when Bishop successfully withdrew Kelly's letter to Archbishop Alter. Hence, Bishop began his novitiate exhausted by the recent struggle. It is not surprising there was a minor authority crisis and periodic problems related to Bishop's return to the novitiate. At first he was treated just as any other novice. After several weeks he was granted some privileges such as his own prie dieu in chapel and the right to pursue his own schedule.[20] This allowed him to meet in council, continue some correspondence and attend special functions at the motherhouse. Howard also presided at the funeral of a young Glenmary priest, Urban Martin, who suffered a fatal automobile accident. Martin's death was a second tragic blow to the society.

During his novitiate Howard began a series of talks to the novices
that are a commentary on the Glenmary constitution. These were
compiled by James R. Murdock, a young Glenmarian who was in the
novitiate with the founder. Delivered during the last ten months of
his life, these talks represent his final words on the unique character
of the Home Missionary community. He explained the particular
virtues of each of the fourteen patrons of the Society: St. Joseph,
"the *just man*"; St. Paul, "sincerity of conviction"; St. Augustine,
"greatest saint and thinker of his time"; St. Patrick and St. Boniface,
"accomplished great [missionary] work on the national level"; St.
Benedict, "although he remained a *lay brother all his life* he fathered
western monasticism"; St. Francis of Assisi, "the *spirit* of poverty";
St. Ignatius Loyola, "*obedience from the heart*—with a militaristic exact-
ness that is implicit obedience"; St. Francis Xavier, "missionary of
great zeal"; St. Teresa of Avila, "almost a *manly character* [sic] *the mind
of a theologian*"; St. Theresa of the Infant Jesus, "childlike trust"; St.
Isaac Jogues and Companions "the *sporting spirit:* He came back to
this country to work among the Indians even though they cut off his
fingers and although he was sure of martyrdom"; St. Frances Cabrini,
"an American saint—but we want a saint born in this country? How
about one of us? Let's work at it."[21]

The subsequent twenty-three pages were a blend of traditional
maxims for community life and anecdotes derived from Bishop's own
experience. He directly criticized the priests of the society for "failing to promote vocations to the Brotherhood." He reminded them
that brothers may achieve high sanctity and that they must be contemplative. "God grants them amazing 'knowledge' without learning." While the priests were to administer the sacraments and preach
the word of God, brothers, according to Bishop, "must sweat out
their vocations and God loves good sweat."[22]

The Glenmary spirit of poverty permitted the members to receive
personal gifts but the priest was to live on a salary and turn over his
mass stipends to the society, while the brothers also received a
monthly allowance. Bishop said, "God deliver us from being so *poor*
that we cannot give! but deliver us all the more from being so *rich* that
we cannot give." The commentary on celibacy and charity warned of
forming friendships with women, and if such friendships "arise out of
feelings of tenderness, *that is out.* Tender, sentimental thoughts are

ipso facto out of a priest's life, and especially if they are connected with frequent visits."[23]

The comments on obedience, on the exercises of piety and on mortification were conventional, but his remarks on charity and relationships with outsiders entailed a long statement of the need for Christian optimism. "Optimism is distinctly Christian if the soul is penetrated with Christ. . . . Let the Christian say: Let the going be as tough as it may, my God is alive! . . . The antithesis of the beautiful Christian optimism is the habitual growler and grumbler. We are not meant to be cynics—it is bad for the health, especially the spiritual 'health.' "[24]

During his novitiate Howard made an Ignatian retreat. He made two thirty-day Ignatian retreats during his lifetime. His first was in 1941 under T.J. Haggeney, S.J. at Milford. During that experience he wrote that he "had not been favored with any remarkable lights [and that he] had received few [insights] of any kind." He noted that his "dominant fault" was what he called "dissipation of mind," a sort of inability to concentrate and meditate because of his preoccupation with all aspects of his new society. Father Haggeney agreed but said that the dissipation was induced by pride. "Conviction that I am personally indispensable to the solution of each and all of our problems and [I possess] an unwillingness to delegate authority to the extent that I should causes me to carry the whole burden on my mind." A meditation on "Blessed Are the Meek" led him to focus on his "unwillingness to endure opposition or difference of opinion in those with whom I am associated. . . ." He considered this "lack of meekness" to afflict him when confronted with "minor irritations." He pinpointed "definite traces of the infection of tepidity in my spiritual make-up." Such a condition helped explain to him his problem in meditating. "*I do not remember ever meditating well,*" wrote Howard in *his* notes on his first thirty-day retreat. Regarding his commitment to the spirit of poverty, Howard "definitely renounced attachment to worldly goods and pleasures."[25]

In his seven-day retreat in August 1951 Howard noted that he is still struggling against "my *chief* enemy, Pride," particularly manifested in his "sensitiveness and readiness to be offended." He also admitted that this characteristic has led him to "a natural timidity among people."[26] In his diary he occasionally remarked on his shyness, and in my oral interviews with many Glenmarians familiar with the founder, there were frequent references to his shy tendencies, particularly in a crowd of people.

During the second thirty-day retreat that culminated his novitiate Howard was distracted by periodic attacks of rheumatism that left him unable to sit down. He was haunted by his short temper. "Disgraced myself by a show of impatience in refectory at breakfast. My old dominant fault that I had thought I had whipped."[27] In remorse he performed a public culpa or act of penance by kneeling that evening. Though his novitiate and Ignatian retreat were frequently interrupted, the experience had a positive impact upon him. A few weeks after he completed his six-month novitiate Howard noted in his diary: "I have had more and deeper and steadier consolations in prayer during recent weeks, and especially during the Christmas season, than ever before in my priestly life, or during my entire life. Christmas has really been Christ-mass to me this time. I love to visit the manger and meditate long on the unbelievable harmony . . . [between] eternal power and majesty and self-effacing humility in the person of Christ."[28]

Absorbed in traditional spirituality and devotionalism of the day, Howard Bishop frequently spoke on the need for the rosary, morning and evening prayers, and other forms of piety. He was influenced by Ignatian devotions to the Sacred Heart and for many years had experienced a deep dedication to the Little Flower. His own Christian optimism urged him to veer away from rigid Jansenism or a Catholic puritanism. He tended toward a positive anthropology that implied the accessibility of grace in the sacraments and in a proper disposition in prayer. However, as the founder of the Home Missioners he articulated an activist spirituality, one that stressed the Catholic evangelization of rural America. In his own experience Howard said that the country priest may easily suffer from "lonesomeness." Without the easy accessibility of "clerical friends, who are the priests' only companions," the rural pastor may "seek relaxation, recreation and refreshment of spirit among the laity." Though this does not necessarily entail a loss of dignity, it is nevertheless "unfortunate . . . if there is no escape from ennui than the companionship of lay folk."[29] Of course the companionship of lay women was a real danger that could foster "the development of many an unwholesome intimacy between characters of truly noble mold and highest ideals, generally to the serious disadvantage of both."[30] Hence, he did not have a paternalistic attitude toward the laity but rather found himself in easy identification with them. He appears to have been more "at home" with lay people than with priests, while he always felt at ease with Protestants, particularly in a rural context. Such were the appropriate characteristics of the founder of the Home Missioners.

Howard Bishop had consistently urged a gradualist approach in the Missioners' drive for conversions. In his 1952 mid-winter letter Howard Bishop announced a new mission strategy, one that was the result of "some years of thinking. . . . I am convinced that side by side with the great convert making purpose, there is another objective . . . to lift up and improve the moral lives of people around us, regardless of their beliefs or lack of beliefs."[31]

This shift in strategy also entailed a reordering of priorities. Instead of aiming for conversion by a presentation of the Catholic faith, Bishop decided to extend evangelization indirectly by preaching the commandments, the moral virtues and the duties of prayer: "by strengthening their sincerity, improving their lives and drawing down actual graces . . . that can lead to conversion."[32]

The ideal context for such evangelization was not the traditional Glenmary or catechetical sessions as outlined in the 1936 plan for a Home Mission Society but rather a prayer meeting in which moral exhortation and prayer form its core. "Though [you should preach] in strictly Catholic moral teaching as the subject calls for but don't throw the Catholic label at them. They know who you are. . . . Of course the missionaries should continue their Catholic information writings and radio broadcasts and engage in one on one instructions."[33]

Howard admitted that these ideas were not new, and they seemed to have derived from recent experiences in the mission field. Father Ed Smith and Brother Vincent Wilmes had long been involved in youth work without considering conversions. Fathers Robert Berson, Clem Borchers, Robert Healy and several other Glenmarians had responded to the needs of their communities as a major manifestation of their missions. The sisters' clinics and their social work dimension were aimed at elevating the moral climate of the community. Such efforts were more effective ways of reaching non-Catholics than direct evangelization.

In his 1953 mid-winter letter Howard underscored this message of evangelization. The Glenmary Missioners are not only to aim at conversion but "to help our non-Catholics . . . to be better Christians and citizens. . . ." He told his confreres of the need to preach the theological and moral virtues and to urge prayer, self-denial and "remembrance of the presence of God." In accord with the initiative generated by "greater numbers of lay people . . . demanding openings to help" in the pastoral life of the church, Bishop proposed ways to harness this energy. He encouraged his priests to help the laity "feel that the call of Christ to go and teach, addressed primarily to the priest, is also secondarily to the devoted laity as his assistant." He asked them to form small neighborhood groups "for the study of Scripture, of Christian Doctrine or the Liturgy as a means of intensifying their faith and devotion." From this group of activists the pastor would choose "a handful of his best workers to form a Presidium of the Legion of Mary . . . to carry on the missionary work . . . among the fallen aways and non-Catholics."[34]

Howard Bishop's promotion of new developments in church and society extended to his support of a progressive social agenda. On June 1, 1952 he delivered the commencement address at Xavier University in Cincinnati. After an introductory note establishing the theme of saving the world from communism—the mystical body of Satan on earth pitted against the mystical body of Christ—Bishop warned the students not to be duped by the "soft-brained liberals who still believe you can sit down and talk things over and come to an understanding of Communism."[35] He reminded them of their confirmation call to become soldiers of Christ. But rather than focusing on the evils of communism Howard stressed the need to correct the abuses in American society and thus oppose communism. He urged the graduates to struggle against indecent literature and films not by attacking free expression but by moral persuasion. "Christianity is the nurse and guardian of man's civil rights, because God is the author," exhorted Howard Bishop.[36] He then called upon them to address the "grave racial injustices that are so commonplace in America." This open attack upon racism was a strong departure from the slow gradualist approach that he had articulated in the past. "We cannot permanently Jim Crow a whole race of human beings because of the color of their skin." He pointed to the need for government support for housing, education and hospitalization programs and other social benefits "to better the condition of our underprivileged colored brethren."[37] He urged the students to study papal documents advocating the adoption of profit-sharing schemes. The graduates, he said, should demand a new attitude of public service "wherein campaigns can be fought through and decided on a plane of dignity and mutual respect, without mud-slinging, name-calling, slanders and smears." Bishop then quoted from the U.S. bishops' 1951 statement on conscientious public service. He concluded his address by reminding the graduates of the need to struggle for "*moral, racial, industrial, and political reforms* . . . not to make the world safe for democracy but to make democracy . . . God's gift to man . . . true to itself and the means of bringing peace and order to a troubled world."[38]

The commencement address was a combination of moderate social reform and militant anti-communism. As mentioned earlier, he was a Republican convert to the New Deal in the 1930s. Convinced that Harry Truman would be a firm anti-communist he voted Democratic in 1948 but he returned to the Republican Party in the 1952 election. Immediately prior to the Eisenhower election he told the novices of the need for the new administration to put a halt to communist infiltration in government, to corruption, and to the trend toward socialism. He urged his novices to pray for America: "We must put a soul into the soul-less materialism of the West. If the West is saved, it will be by the soul-filled religion brought to us from the East—that of our Lord and Savior, Jesus Christ."[39] In another talk he warned them not to vote "only for Catholics, unless they were better men for the jobs. . . . Watch out for crooked, weak, dishonest Catholics in office."[40] Despite his impassioned anti-communism he never identified with Senator Joseph McCarthy's campaign.

In one of the last talks in the novitiate he reminded the prospective Glenmarians of his three point program "to bring the world to a higher moral conscience."

1. Intensify Faith and Practices.
2. Fire the faithful to zeal and then use them.
3. Address ourselves not merely to Catholics and those of Goodwill, but to all non-Catholics with this Two-Fold aim
   a) to convert them if possible;
   b) to save as many as we can if they cannot be converted.[41]

To encourage lay activism he advocated the Confraternity of Christian Doctrine program and the Legion of Mary. Ever preoccupied with improving the form and content of Glenmary missions, Bishop considered permanent means of incorporating the laity. Four months before he died he visited Grailville to seek recommendations for "an apostolic lay couple to settle in one of our missions, to carry on their avocation of farming and do missionary work for the priest —to be lay catechists."[42] For nearly two years Howard had been working on a paraliturgical service for what he referred to as the "faraways," families who have no Sunday mass in their area; no doubt if the spiritual needs of faraways were not met, then they might become fallen aways. The core of the service was a simple English translation of the mass; a lay leader would read aloud the proper and the community would respond as in the contemporary vernacular liturgies. Howard traveled to St. Louis to consult with the nationally renowned liturgist, Monsignor Martin J. Helriegel. "He likes my Mass for the 'Faraways' . . . and gave me some fine suggestions."[43] As one of the major advocates of mass in the vernacular, Helriegel must have been impressed with the prospect of rural communities reciting the mass in English.

On his last visitation to the mission in Norton, Virginia, he and Father Robert Berson met with a leading layman in the community who had been given a copy of the service. According to Berson's recollections the layman said to Howard Bishop, "Father, I don't think that people will come to be led by a layman through this sort of service. What people want is a priest and Mass."[44] It was Berson's opinion that the man had been concerned with the prospect of being deprived of a priest. He also mentioned other priests who considered the plan impractical. Of course the Norton incident "was a rather severe and obvious disappointment," remarked Berson.[45]

Priestless communities have become a major concern in the contemporary church. In the autumn of 1988 the Vatican Congregation for Divine Worship issued a "Directory for Sunday Celebration in the Absence of a Priest." Contrary to Howard Bishop's "Service for Faraways" that included reading the entire mass without the accessibility of communion, the contemporary Directory divided its service into two parts, the celebration of the word (Sunday's readings) and communion.[46] There are other distinctions in accord with the trends in liturgical renewal over the past twenty-five years. Howard's service may be considered as a precursor to the Directory's celebration, and certainly illustrates his prescience.

Howard Bishop never lived to see his service in action. While visiting the Norton mission he suffered chest pains and was taken to St. Mary's Hospital. Tests revealed inordinately high blood pressure; the next day he suffered a heart attack. Brother Robert Hoffman, who had accompanied Howard on his last series of visitations, was with him throughout the ordeal. Fathers Francis Wuest and Joseph O'Donnell traveled to Norton to be with the founder. Shortly after the coronary, O'Donnell heard his confession and administered the last rites. "Tell Father Sourd that I leave everything in his hands with complete confidence," the founder said with a calm tone. "Give my regards to all the Priests, Brothers and the good Sisters—and the Archbishop. I'm glad I finished my visitation—we've got a good company." With characteristic attention to detail he told Father O'Donnell, "My will is in the top right hand drawer of my desk."[47] A brief period of apparent improvement was followed by violent coughing. A few minutes later at 6:23 A.M. on Thursday, June 11 William Howard Bishop died.

Before he left on his last tour of the missions he and John Marquardt came to a mutual understanding that was as close to a reconciliation as could be achieved by men with such opposing views on authority. Sister John Joseph, the Adrian Dominican in charge of the sisters, had experienced Howard's short temper and his interference in her administration. Shortly before he left Glenmary for the last time he apologized to her for all his blunders and sincerely asked for her forgiveness. She responded asking for his blessing.

He could take pride in the development of the Glenmary community: a seventh mission had just opened in Buffalo, Oklahoma to which Marquardt was assigned; the seminary had just completed its second year; in February of 1953 there were twenty-one Glenmary priests, eleven brothers and fifty-one students; the sisters' community had just begun its first canonical novitiate with sixteen women and twenty-six in the pre-novitiate stages.

In one of his last mid-winter letters Howard Bishop closed with an exhortation that provides us a final glimpse of his practical zeal.

Love the poor, the sick and helpless, and attend to them. They are God's influentials. They are His aristocrats. He loves them. If you are known in your community as the contact man for all the poor and unfortunate of the place, you could not have a more honorable title on earth or one that would make you more welcome in the courts of Heaven. Besides this, you will be a marvelous drawing power for converts.

Our constant solicitude and devoted prayers continue for all our members at home and on our spreading fronts, from our three Wise Men across the sea to the east, to our toiling Shepherds in the southern hills and plains. May God bless you all. Keep in touch with one-another. Keep alive that strong bond of united loyalty which the tie of a common purpose and devotion to our dear Commander, Jesus Christ, has welded for all of us. In these sentiments our beloved pioneer missioner and Assistant Superior [Raphael Sourd] joins me.[48]

Bishop George J. Rehring, bishop of Toledo and former auxiliary bishop of Cincinnati, delivered the eulogy at the founder's funeral on June 16, 1953. With an emphasis upon the Glenmary community as a testimony of his zeal, Rehring made no remarks about his person, his priestly life or his leadership. Of all the statements of sympathy the most significant were penned by those who knew him personally. Luigi Ligutti, executive director of the National Catholic Rural Life Conference, stated that "Father Bishop was a great priest and a great man. I owe to him the inspiration of dedicating myself to the work of Rural Life. . . . It was he who almost singlehanded kept the flame of our organization alive. It was he who saved it from becoming just another economic agency."[49] In a note to Bishop Muench of Fargo, Ligutti remarked on the passing of Howard Bishop, "he was difficult . . . but I shall miss him."[50]

Bishop Raymond A. Lane, superior general of Maryknoll, lamented on the death of the Glenmary founder as "a great shock to all at Maryknoll where he is greatly loved and respected." Archbishop Richard J. Cushing's statement reveals his abiding affection for Howard Bishop whom he encouraged with great enthusiasm. "Father Bishop . . . was one of the country's and the Church's best. I always looked upon him as a man especially chosen by God: simple, humble, full of faith and love for souls. I am confident that he will do more for us in heaven than he could ever do here below."[51]

As his trusted confidant, Raphael Sourd captured the essence of his confrere's character as founder. As one of "total dedication to an ideal . . . Father Bishop was a priest of great foresight, tenacious purpose, extraordinary devotion to duty, zeal and courage."[52]

Devotion, duty, zeal, courage—attributes of his will, appear to be the gifts or charisms of the founder and upon these "living stones" was built the edifice of the Glenmary Home Missioners. Driven to make a strong Catholic mark upon rural America, Howard Bishop continuously expanded his spheres of religious commitment, beginning with St. Louis Parish in Clarksville, then enlarging it to encompass the archdiocese in the League of the Little Flower. Simultaneously, he identified with the national movement in the Catholic Rural Life Conference in 1923, serving as its president from 1928 to 1934. All these efforts were infused with his particular blend of Catholic distributism and rural missionary experience. These forces converged in his "landward" principles and in his attempt to establish a rural colony in Clarksville. His pastoral perspective embraced the entire Clarksville community, not just its small Catholic population. When his major missionary scheme failed, he shifted his focus from a landward movement of unemployed to Catholic rural revivalism in the form of a home missionary society.

Howard Bishop struggled with sermons so frequently that he knew he was no charismatic leader. Indeed he projected a rather formal, shy image, definitely one that did not elicit a strong following. However, he was confident that his organizational abilities, his sincerity, his rural life experience on the parish, archdiocesan and national levels, and his flair for writing provided him with the natural powers and religious grace to gather a community of priests, brothers and sisters committed to implementing his vision of breaking down the walls of anti-Catholic prejudice and building up the Catholic faith in rural America. He understood that he was following along a path formed by the imprints of Isaac Hecker, James F. Price, and James Anthony Walsh, as well as the Josephites and the Missionary Servants. So confident was he that his plan was in accord with the design of providence that he settled in a tiny church in Brown County, Ohio and began to publish *The Challenge,* a publication urging Catholics to respond to the needs of rural America. Its title could apply to how he envisioned his own response to God's call that he form a unique missionary effort.

Howard Bishop had confronted physical, moral and spiritual challenges for a long time, and he worked hard to improve himself. From his home-study programs for efficiency and mental concentration to his spiritual conferences and retreats with the Jesuit fathers at Milford he attempted to deal with his shortcomings. Though he and others focused on his temper, his authoritarianism and his other weaknesses, many of his confreres stressed his kindness, his fatherly tone, and his delight in simple pleasures such as a dish of ice cream or an informal Glenmary gathering for spontaneous entertainment. Some of them remarked on his dignity and his demeanor as a southern gentleman, his broad cultural interests and his inability to participate in small talk. There is unanimity on Howard Bishop's sincere prayer life, his utter lack of pretension, his tendency to avoid talking down to people, and his tenacious will. This latter quality infused with a sense of God's providence is a common characteristic of founders of religious communities as they struggle to respond to a need within the mystical body of Christ. The particular charism of Howard Bishop is that his devotion, duty, zeal and courage were uniquely manifested in a person whose religious spheres were ever expanding outward from St. Louis Parish to wherever there was a need to inflame the home missions with the light of Catholicity. From his boyhood he romanticized the simplicity of rural life. His Catholic distributism and his devotion to the Bethlehem scene as an appropriate setting for the incarnation reveal his deep attachment to what he perceived as building the new Christian commonwealth not in today's urban Babylon but in its rural Palestine. Nowhere were these virtues of nature and the conditions of liberty and the yearning for the supernatural more evident than in rural America. With a clear understanding that the Glenmary lamp was but a flicker of faith on the landscape, Howard Bishop remained undaunted in his commitment to the spread of Catholicity in ever expanding spheres of religious influence in American society.

The Legacy of Howard Bishop

I

Howard Bishop's legacy is woven into the fabric of the Glenmary community. A founder's charism may be viewed as the particular giftedness of the Holy Spirit that forms the original story of a specific community. Because the Home Missioners were founded twenty-three years before the Second Vatican Council, their original story was still unfolding during that period. When most communities were attempting to retrieve their founder's charism, the Glenmary community merely had to reflect on its own lived experiences in the recent past.[1] There appears to be a general consensus that the founder was a rather ordinary man with an extraordinary commitment to a missionary vision. He may not have possessed personal qualities that inspired strong devotion among his followers, but no one doubts his religious commitment to evangelize rural America.

This epilogue is neither biography nor history; rather it is a chronicler's account of the development of the Home Missioners' self-understanding as heirs of Howard Bishop. Future historians may write a full history of the community as it passed through this significant period; as the biographer of Howard Bishop dependent upon only the published articles and official documents, I am seeking to trace the legacy of the founder in contemporary life.

II

The Second Vatican Council initiated profound changes that altered the ways Catholics understand theology, ecclesiology, liturgy, social thought, and social action. The 1950s may be viewed as an era of transition, one that in hindsight prepared the stage for the dramatic action of the 1960s.

The "Catholic ghetto" was a reality in the 1950s; there was a Catholic form for every cultural expression ranging from Catholic art to Catholic etiquette. The walls separating religion from society appeared strong, but in reality there were weaknesses in their foundation. Within the context of religious separatism, Catholic schools, hospitals, newspapers and magazines were becoming increasingly modernized and their personnel, including priests and religious, were becoming professionalized. By meeting the standards established by secular accrediting agencies, Catholic institutions were undermining traditional separatism. Social changes symbolized by the rise of suburban parishes and the increase in first-generation college graduates brought Catholics into various tributaries that eventually led to the mainstream of American pluralism in the 1960s. We now recognize several strands of intellectual life in the church during the 1950s as portending the changes of the 1960s, strands that convey a sense of evolution rather than revolution. By the mid-1950s John Courtney Murray, S.J., Gustave Weigel, S.J., Walter Ong, S.J. and Godfrey Diekmann, O.S.B. were promoting the positive values of pluralism, ecumenism, personalism and liturgical renewal.[2]

The early years of Father Clement Borchers' administration, which embraced the period from Howard Bishop's death to the closing of the Second Vatican Council (1953–1965), reflect the traditions and transitions of the immediate pre-conciliar period. There was a steady rise in vocations, a final wing was added to the seminary, and there was a buoyant optimism, symbolized by the establishment of a new novitiate at Aurora, Indiana. Raised on a farm in Shelby County, Ohio, Borchers had spent several years in the missions; he was well known for his wide-ranging abilities before becoming procurator and director of brothers in 1949. In contrast to Howard Bishop, Clement Borchers was a warm outgoing leader. He shared the founder's original call to convert America, and as a member of the first ordination class of the society he played a vital role in the story of Glenmary. Ordained only thirteen years before becoming superior general, he articulated an understanding of Glenmary that was in the tradition of the founder. Like Howard Bishop, he was continually attempting to improve strategies for evangelizing rural America.

At the 1955 second mission convention of Glenmary, an annual gathering of Home Missioner priests, there was an emphasis on new techniques in outdoor preaching in open air tents. As one illustration of new developments, there was also a report by Father Raymond Dehen on a summer school course at the University of Notre Dame entitled "The Value of Liturgy to Missionaries and Kerygmatic Theology." Dehen's report emphasized liturgical renewal; he explained that the kerygmatic approach to revelation stresses the profound relationship of Christ's message to *a way of life*, in contrast to prevalent catechetical approaches that were based on the doctrines of revelation.[3] Dehen's analysis reflected the traditional missiology of Howard Bishop blended with the traditional but innovative thought of such theologians as Godfrey Diekmann and Gustave Weigel.

Borchers was a practical missioner responsive to contemporary movements. In the 1950s he extolled the "encouraging" developments in the lay apostolate. In the Summer 1958 issue of *The Challenge* Borchers entitled his regular column "Glenmary Comes of Age," a report on the commemoration of the twenty-first anniversary of Howard Bishop's arrival in Cincinnati. He invoked the spirit of the founder when he said that Howard Bishop knew that "the job of converting America 'from the grass roots' . . . wouldn't be easy. Any Glenmarian, Priest, Brother or Sister, who spent a few years in the non-Catholic areas, can tell you of the sweat and fear, and tear-drops. There are truly times of 'roughing it' . . . But then, too, there are times of great consolation for our Missioners who are trying, trying to do God's will . . . [they] foresee that . . . [the] few converts of today will propagate a parish tomorrow."[4]

Reflecting national trends in the increase of vocations and the building of new seminaries (more seminaries were constructed after 1950 than during the entire period from 1791 to 1950), the year 1962 marked the completion of the final wing of the seminary building and the construction of a new national headquarters. Archbishop Karl J. Alter and his auxiliary, Paul Leibold, joined other members of the hierarchy and clergy and lay friends of Glenmary in the dedication ceremonies on May 14, 1962. The festivities climaxed with Archbishop Alter's announcement that the society had received from the Vatican the *Decretum Laudis* raising it from the status of diocesan community to papal rank directly under the authority of the Sacred Congregation for Religious. Borchers reported on these milestones in *The*

Challenge: "With mixed feelings of humility and genuine pride, indeed, we say 'thank you' to all who made this possible."[5]

Symbolic of the community's work on the seminary, a thirty-foot mosaic in the pediment above the main entrance to the colonial-styled seminary building was designed by Fr. Patrick O'Donnell. The mosaic was erected by students, priests and brothers. To honor the founder the society commissioned the sculptor, Ivan Mestrovic, to do a bronze rendering of Howard Bishop. Mestrovic, who had refused commissions from Hitler, Mussolini and Tito, had achieved fame for his work for Pope Pius XII as well as for the American hierarchy at the Shrine of the Immaculate Conception in Washington, D.C. In 1962 he completed a sixteen-foot bronze sculpture of Bishop, his right hand holding a cross and his left hand grasping the Bible close to his heart.[6]

Clement Borchers, who frequently piloted a plane on his annual visitations to the missions, was struck by the "vast differences in resources and culture of one rural area from another though perhaps but fifty miles apart. . . . While not all our mission territory is poor (some of it is fertile, and its people industrious), it is a fact that we are at work in some of the poorest counties in the nation." In an article in *The Challenge* Borchers quoted at length the encyclical of Pope John XXIII on Christianity and social progress, *Mater et Magistra,* and concluded that Glenmary was committed to the alleviation of "illiteracy, poverty and ignorance in culture and religion in these less blessed areas."[7]

During his last year as superior general, Borchers presided over the twenty-fifth anniversary of the foundation of Glenmary, 1939–1964. The most significant growth in vocations occurred among the brothers as the number grew from 5 in 1953 to 42 in 1967. There were also 72 priests, but more importantly there were about 24 in various stages of formation and 33 in the junior house of studies. By 1964 the society had opened its house of studies and prep school at Fairfield, Connecticut, close to the heavily Catholic population of the northeast, and its novitiate overlooking the Ohio River at Aurora, Indiana. It had also established a vocation center in Chicago (Raphael Sourd's base of operations) and operated the Pius XII Pastoral Center and summer camp in Buck Creek, North Carolina. Directed by Father Bernard Quinn, who received his doctorate in missiology from the Gregorian University in Rome, the Pastoral Center provided the

newly ordained Glenmarians with 40 mini-courses in 280 class hours
to prepare the new priests for the rural apostolate. Fathers Raymond
Dehen, Leonard Spanjers and John Barry were faculty members of
the Center.[8]

In 1964 the Glenmarians celebrated regular liturgies in sixty-eight
churches and chapels, a few of which were built by the brothers; over
the twenty-five years priestless counties had been reduced from 1,037
to 800. In an article on the silver jubilee of the community, Father
Patrick O'Donnell, editor of *The Challenge,* noted that "the sleeping
giant of the South is awakening with a burst of new energy brought
through the investment of northern capital," a movement that also
entailed further Catholic migration into the area. These population
trends engendered significant growth in many of the base-parishes.
However, O'Donnell's conclusion was not optimistic: "There remains the misery of depression in vast areas of poverty. . . . Here the
missioner must seek out and soften the suffering of God's poor, must
answer with bread and shoes the daily pain of Christ."[9]

After his twelve years as superior general, Clement Borchers was
ready to return to the missions. He could leave office with a sense of
satisfaction at the completion of many of the projects initiated by the
founder. Spirits were very high during this period, but the Second
Vatican Council was engendering significant reforms that would have
strained Borchers' rather capricious approach to change. He asked
to be assigned to Aberdeen, Mississippi in the northeastern section of
the state. After six years he was assigned to Vidalia, Georgia in 1971. In
eight years his tiny community of 30 Catholics had grown to 135 when
tragedy struck.

Brothers Larry Jochim and Joe Steen were constructing a new
rectory during the summer of 1979; on an excursion to the Florida
beach near Daytona, Brother Larry was drawn into an off-shore
current. Father Patrick O'Donnell described the scene: "While
others ran for the lifeguard, Father Borchers plunged into the waves
and swam to Brother Larry, gave him a push towards the shore and
felt himself caught in the same current. By the time a lifeguard
arrived . . . Father Borchers had overtaxed his heart once too often."
Father Dennis Holly, who was then vice-president of Glenmary, was a
nephew of Borchers and the homilist at his memorial service at his
parish at Vidalia. O'Donnell reported that as a member of the family
Holly thanked Glenmary for providing him with the opportunity to

serve the church, and as a Glenmarian he thanked the Borchers family "for having formed and prepared this warm exuberant personality for his work as a mission priest and superior general at Glenmary."[10]

As the Second Vatican Council was coming to a close, the fourth Glenmary chapter elected Robert C. Berson superior general. The forty-one year old native of Cincinnati had spent his entire mission life in Virginia; his base parish was in Norton and he started new congregations in St. Paul and in Hunter's Valley. He was an active missioner who hosted a Catholic-information radio program. In 1959 he was a special assistant and mission coordinator to Clement Borchers. In the late 1950s he established a summer volunteer program for students.

Of all the documents issued by the Second Vatican Council, those on the church, the missions and the religious life had the most profound impact upon religious communities. Joseph A. Komonchak elaborates on the significance of the Dogmatic Constitution on the Church, *Lumen Gentium.* "It begins with a view of the Church as Mystery, as the community of men and women called together into participation in the triune God. This communion in God produces the communion among the members of the church which makes them the people of God, the Body of Christ, and the Temple of the Spirit." The church is described as sacrament, one of both unity and redemption. From this sacramental character flows the mission of the church; inspired by the Holy Spirit "each disciple of Christ has the obligation of spreading the faith to the best of his [or her] abilities."[11] The Decree on the Church's Missionary Activity, *Ad Gentes,* explored the mission of preaching the gospel and planting new churches among those unacquainted with the gospel. While this reflects Howard Bishop's missiology, the decree went beyond the traditional notion as it referred to "inculturation" of the gospel and the local society. It also emphasized the vital relationship between missionary work and the promotion of human development. In 1975 Pope Paul VI issued the document "Evangelization in the Modern World" which deepened the meaning of *Ad Gentes.* William McConvile, O.F.M. notes: "In its evangelizing mission, the church, empowered by the Spirit, is charged with proclaiming the gospel, but proclaiming it in such a way that the gospel penetrates societies and cultures. . . . This proclamation and penetration demands a linkage between evangelization and liberation. While the gospel offers a salvation that is transcendent and eschatological, evangelization would be incomplete if it is not linked to the political and social orders." *Lumen Gentium* placed the religious life within the "universal call to holiness," thus amending its traditional definition as "a life of perfection."[12]

The Decree on the Renewal of Religious Life, *Perfectae Caritatis*, entailed two major points: "(1) a continuous return to the sources of all Christian life and to the original inspiration behind any given community; (2) an adjustment of the community to the changed conditions of the times." The decree was followed by Pope Paul VI's encyclical *Ecclesiam Suam* of August 1964 in which he stated that the primary sources of renewal are: the gospel, the documents of Vatican II, the spirit of the founder and the contemporary world.[13] *Perfectae Caritatis* and *Ecclesiam Suam* had the most immediate impact upon Glenmary; this became evident in the special chapter of 1968–69 that adopted a new constitution. Prior to that chapter, Robert Berson's administration had established a five-year plan in 1966 that included experimentation in parish structure, ecumenism, clerical garb, the priest-worker program, and the lay apostolate. It also appointed a special liturgical committee. In reviewing the plan in 1967 Berson underscored the importance of maintaining the general policy of the society. "While remaining aware of the trends and initiating experiments, our first concern as a Society of Catholic Missionaries must be the formation of stable Catholic Christian communities, worshipping, working, witnessing. These are our launching pads into evangelism, ecumenism and social action. This is the Church today, and today is when we live."[14]

The Glenmary Town and Country Research Center was established in November of 1966 "to discover, promote and make available theological and scientific information for practical aid in developing the missionary apostolate in town and country, U.S.A."[15] In February of 1967 it affiliated with the Center for Applied Research in the Apostolate (CARA) in Washington, D.C. Father James Kelly was for a time its director, but the driving force was Bernard Quinn who carefully maintained the Center's independence within CARA. Quinn gained national recognition for directing the Center's research into diverse areas of rural life. In 1973 the Center withdrew its affiliation with CARA and gradually moved its offices to Bethesda where it remained until 1982 when it moved to Atlanta. In 1987 Bernard Quinn was replaced by Louis McNeil, a Glenmary priest who had been teaching foundational theology at the Washington Theological Union. Over the years the Center has sponsored many workshops and has published over a hundred studies related to the town and country ministry. The Center certainly represents the charism of the founder as it not only has been responsible for revising Howard Bishop's map, "NO PRIEST LAND," but it also reflects his attachment to the principles of sociology as an essential component of the missioners' training.[16]

Also derived from the 1965 chapter that elected Berson and a new council was the Latin American project. After a preliminary visit in 1966, Fathers Leo Schloemer and Frank Schenk and Brother David Brooks were assigned to Obando, a rural area in the diocese of Cartago, Colombia.[17] Father Ed Smith was assigned to promote a Latin American Home Mission Society and settled in Bogotá. Schloemer and the others were transferred to a parish of eight barrios and some 20,000 people on the west side of Bogotá. As mentioned in the last chapter, Howard Bishop had hoped to see societies established throughout the world on the Home Missioners' model. In 1990 Schloemer and Schenk remain in Colombia.

The most dramatic symbol of post-conciliar change before the renewal chapter was the decision to close the Glenmary theologate and transfer the seminarians first to St. Meinrad Seminary and then in 1968 to the Divinity School at St. Louis University. Father Raymond Orlett, a scripture scholar and the last rector of the seminary, was responsible for research and recommendations to meet the demands of a specialized faculty to teach the proliferation of courses that resulted from the advances of scripture studies and systematic, moral, pastoral and sacramental theology. Small theologates were impractical, and there was also the need to break down the seminary enclosure and to educate Home Missioners in a cosmopolitan and intellectually stimulating setting. Father Charles Hughes was responsible for directing the house of studies in St. Louis located within walking distance of the university. In 1977 it was decided to transfer the theology students to Washington, D.C. where they could pursue theology at either The Catholic University of America or the Washington Theological Union.[18]

In 1967 the house of studies in Connecticut was closed and the undergraduate candidates attended Maryknoll College at Glen Ellyn, Illinois; they later moved to Loyola University in New Orleans and

then to the University of Dayton. There is no pre-novitiate education
program today, but in 1986 a candidacy program was established to
initiate those aspiring to become Home Missioners. The novitiate at
Aurora, Indiana closed in 1967; since then the year of formation
includes a blend of spirituality, counseling, and practical experience
in Glenmary missions. The house of studies in Washington, D.C. also
has a formation program that blends prayer, counseling, and regular
community meetings with graduate education.

III

The women Missioners were also immersed in renewal and reform
during the mid-1960s. One may recall that the Glenmary Sisters had
received official approbation as a community of diocesan right on
July 16, 1952. However, the community marked its origins in 1941 when
Dorothy Hendershot associated herself with Gertrude Kimmick to
form the new society, an association analogous to Raphael Sourd's
decision to join Howard Bishop in 1939. At the close of the first
novitiate in September 1953 the first constitution went into effect. In
the process of composing a rule, Howard Bishop had proposed dele-
tion of all Dominican elements from the original rule, entitled "The
Constitution of the Home Mission Sisters of St. Dominic."[19] In the
1953 document there were no references to Dominican traditions and
St. Dominic was omitted from the title. However, both constitutions
are similar since they followed the norms stipulated by the Vatican
Congregation for Religious.[20]

Karl Alter appointed Mary Catherine Rumschlag as mother general for a two-year term and appointed Sister Geraldine Peterson as
bursar general and Sister Rosemary Esterkamp as secretary general.
With fifteen sisters in vows in 1953 the community entered a period of
expansion. Sister John Joseph, the Adrian Dominican, continued as
novice mistress, and in 1954 the community purchased a home at 4580
Colerain Avenue from the Sisters of Notre Dame de Namur for a new
novitiate. After the general chapter of 1955, which elected Sister Mary
Catherine as mother general, the community purchased property for
a new motherhouse.

Located in Fairfield, just a few miles from Glenmary, the separate
generalate underscored the canonical independence of the women

Home Missioners. In 1958 the generalate moved to Colerain Avenue and the novitiate was transferred to the Springfield Pike property and was eventually purchased by the men in 1971. In 1959 the Sisters of Charity of Cincinnati gave the Glenmary Sisters the vacated military academy in Fayetteville, Ohio. After renovation this became the formation center of the community with many of the young women in various stages of formation attending classes at the Ursuline Teachers' Training Institute sponsored by the Ursuline Sisters of Brown County who welcomed Howard Bishop to Cincinnati. Since 1978 the Glenmary Sisters of Cincinnati have been at Morning Star, a rural oasis where they established their motherhouse.[21]

Mother Mary Catherine did not accept new missions until the sisters received extensive training. She herself attended Sister Formation conferences and encouraged members to attend professional and graduate studies. In 1959–1960 Sister Magdalene Kaercher went to Lumen Vitae in Brussels to prepare for training sisters for catechetical work in the missions. Also in attendance at Lumen Vitae was Sister Dolores Meyer, who focused on religious formation. The following year she spent an additional year at the Formation Institute in Paris.[22] Sister Virginia Trese, with an M.A. in social work from The Catholic University, attended Lumen Vitae in 1960–61.

Reelected for a second term in 1961, Mother Mary Catherine presided over the twentieth anniversary of the community as well as the tenth anniversary of the Vatican's approval of the sisters as a congregation of diocesan right in 1952. By this time there were 73 Glenmary Sisters, some of whom were engaged in catechetical, social service, and clinical and home nursing in seven missions located in five states, with a number of the sisters in temporary vows in studies. Howard Bishop would have been proud of his "grey army" as he called the sisters. Their professional training, their expansion into home nursing and their modernized habit, adopted at the 1961 chapter, would have had his enthusiastic approval.

In the first issue of the Glenmary Sisters newsletter *Kinship*, Mother Catherine told about her visit on a sick call to three elderly people in a one-room mountain cabin. She invoked Howard Bishop, who "had wanted to do 'all that can be done' for the have-nots of our homeland when he laid the foundation of the Glenmary societies."[23] At the Community Institute on August 8, 1962 the Glenmary superior spoke on the "Special End of the Glenmary Sisters." She cited the founder's 1944 mid-winter letter in which he "encourages us to zeal for the conversion of people outside the Fold."[24] Mother Catherine's address stressed the relationship between the sisters' education and orientation and the special missionary character of the order. In juxtaposition to Howard Bishop's 1944 exhortation to conversion was a quote from his 1952 mid-winter letter in which the founder spoke of the need to supplement "convert-making" with the zeal "to lift up and improve the moral lives of the people" regardless of their denomination. She concluded with a commentary on the prescience of the founder when he said that he had "no illusions as to the magnitude of the labors that confront us. It will be of many years, perhaps several generations."[25]

The 1961 general chapter revised the constitution to include a directory which incorporated then current trends in liturgy, ecclesiology, scripture, and spirituality; the chapter also confirmed those customs that stress personal autonomy and new modes of community. Effective in August of 1962, the directory represented a transition from traditional, strongly authoritarian structures to those of a more contemporary and personalistic character. However, the directory was more than transitional because there was a clause for continuous updating.[26]

In 1963 Archbishop Alter authorized such experimentation as the wearing of secular clothing and granted them permission to work in secular agencies. In 1964 the community established an Appalachian Study Center in Chicago. With the help of a social psychologist a group of sisters interviewed urban migrants from Appalachia and studied their needs to prepare for the rural ministry. Mother Catherine spent a three-month period at the Chicago house. Also in 1964 a house of studies was established in Milwaukee to allow the junior sisters to attend Marquette University. With over half of the sisters less than ten years in the community, formation and education were major concerns.

As experimentation and reform gained momentum, criticism from both sisters and outsiders came to the attention of Archbishop Alter, who was the ultimate authority for this diocesan community. In September 1965 he issued directives calling for conformity to traditional constitutions of the community. Though many of those directives restored legal customs, others placed controls upon the sisters' daily schedules, education, contact with lay people, and the stipulation that for a year the community should not accept new members. A year later these directives along with explanatory letters found their way into the press (it is possible that they were intentionally "leaked" as a way of fostering public debate); this exacerbated a situation that was becoming intensely polarized not only between the archbishop and the leadership of the community but also among the sisters themselves. According to Maureen O'Connor, a former sister who wrote an article on the crisis, the publicity "was an embarrassment for all the parties concerned." By this time the sisters were preparing for a general chapter.[27]

At the chapter meeting of December 26–January 1, 1967 the community decided to concentrate its missionary energies entirely on the Appalachian apostolate; this also included an inner city mission to emigrants from the mountains. The chapter adopted a new habit and passed resolutions endorsing continued experimentation. Because the leadership appeared to ignore the archbishop's authority and because experimentation was rationalized on an appeal to Vatican norms, Alter asked Rome to appoint a special religious assistant to guide the community in acceptable lines of formation. No doubt Alter felt that the Glenmary Sisters had rejected him as "superior" of the diocesan community. During this time of crisis fifteen sisters immediately left (March 1967); in late July, Mother Catherine, her entire council, and forty-five other sisters left to form a new group called "Federation of Communities in Service." They planned to carry on the same mission work, but as lay women who would be free from ecclesiastical interference.[28] Catherine Rumschlag noted that the break was not merely in reaction to Alter's directives; it was also engendered by what was perceived as the negative attitude of the institutional church toward sisters.[29] The nineteen sisters who remained issued a statement: "Those remaining as Glenmary Sisters desire to continue in the rural mission areas to which they committed themselves, with the prospect of renewal in the religious life as called for by the Second Vatican Council."[30]

Sister Mary Joseph Wade, who had spent the major part of her Glenmary life in the missions, was elected mother general and immediately proceeded to initiate a healing process. On the first page of *Kinship,* published shortly after her election, Mother Mary Joseph quoted John F. Kennedy: "Our work will not be finished in the first one hundred days nor will it be done the first one thousand days. But let us begin.''[31] Two issues later *Kinship* featured a tribute to the founder on the fifteenth anniversary of his death: "The Glenmary Sister, like her founder, shares the hope of a 'vision of the whole,' the hope that all men will come to the knowledge of Jesus Christ. She knows we are far from Christian Unity. She hopes to open the way for people of differing backgrounds . . . religious, class, racial, educational, cultural or political . . . to come to the fullness of the knowledge of Christ which she believes to be in the Eucharistic community.''[32] Later Sister (the title "Mother" had been eliminated) Mary Joseph recalled that during the years immediately prior to the 1967 crisis she had shifted from a woman of gentleness to one who was "a fighter. . . . More than likely, I would have not remained a Glenmary Sister if I had not allowed myself to fight for my vocation." She explained that in 1967 "we were a residual group of mortally wounded women who had been vowed to Christ and consecrated to the Church to spread the Kingdom in rural America. Through the years of much personal prayer and sacrifice and a continual interest in people rather than self, we have grown into a community of healed missionaries who daily go about the gigantic work of reconciliation in a manner appropriate to our talents and training.''[33] Her emphasis upon the rural apostolate was explicitly intended to reassert a traditional identity, in opposition to Catherine Rumschlag's venture into an inner-city apostolate to migrants from rural America.

IV

The men's renewal chapter opened on May 21, 1968 and closed on August 15, 1969. There were sixty-three sessions, with six society-wide meetings. The formal chapter meeting entailed 2,999.3 man hours of discussion on the floor; with committee and area meetings that figure would probably be quadrupled.[34] It produced 133 documents and 61 resolutions. The major result was the provisional constitution and directory, the latter being a specification of the "general ideals and norms enunciated in the Constitution." For example, a series of articles in the constitution deals with "Our Call," and is divided into the call to community, to service and collaboration; under the same rubric, "Our Call," the directory specifies areas such as experimentation, leadership, relationship to the hierarchy, and ecumenical coop-

eration. The constitution was only eleven pages in contrast to the
directory's forty-five pages.[35]

The constitution was so arranged that the sources of the articles,
i.e. the gospel, the church—particularly the documents of Vatican
II—the founder's spirit, and the contemporary world were featured
on the page directly opposite them. The section, "Our Way of Life,"
elaborates on the commitments to poverty, chastity and obedience,
prayer, the welfare of members, brotherly love and formation; the
sources include twelve citations from scripture and references to six
decrees of the Second Vatican Council. There were three quotations
from Howard Bishop; the one for prayer reads: "In every Mass, in
every morning and night prayer, pray for the salvation of your people, especially for the conversion of the 'other sheep.' " The statement was between a quote from the gospel of Luke and one from the
Constitution of the Church.[36]

Robert Berson recalled the imprint of the founder's legacy on the
chapter:

> Most of all, the Special Chapter acted in the spirit of the Founder
> when it displayed unanimity of over-all purpose, enthusiasm for
> carrying the gospel and bringing all the blessings of the Catholic
> Faith into small town and rural America. We have re-affirmed that
> "the neglected people of rural America" are our people. We have
> done this with the clear vision that government action and the
> attention of universities is focused on urban problems. We have
> done this knowing from our own experience that too many of our
> small town and rural people have un-Christian racial attitudes and
> that frequently they are unwilling to abandon obsolete prejudices
> and patterns of life. The sixty-nine million Americans in town and
> country are not always the most attractive people, yet they are
> redeemed and they do have admirable qualities. One of the graces
> of Glenmary which so obviously first impelled our Founder is that
> we, who as a group yearn for an end to oppression and discrimina-
> tion, remain dedicated to these people who seem least likely of all
> Americans to change in social attitudes. In the spirit of Father
> Bishop, we, in this Special Chapter, have said Amen again to the
> giving of our lives to rural men.[37]

The establishment of a new governance structure, based upon the
principles of collegiality and subsidiarity, was a drastic departure

from the authoritarian government that had been instituted in 1948 according to guidelines from the Vatican. In the spirit of the council, the chapter attempted to balance "a healthy principle of democracy" with the "concept and ideal of religious authority and the evangelical counsel of obedience."[38]

Symbolic of the change was the shift from the title "superior general" to that of "president." The latter was elected by a popular vote of members in perpetual oath instead of indirectly by chapter delegates. The president shared executive responsibility with two elected vice presidents. The executive staff was composed of heads of departments appointed by the president and approved by the general assembly; the treasurer was also an elective office.

"Legislative" responsibility was vested in the general assembly members who were elected every two years. (Because of directives from the Vatican the assembly no longer may legislate; it is only a deliberative body.) The president has veto power but may be overridden by a two-thirds majority of the assembly. Once every four years the assembly acts as a general chapter "with full competence over all matters including the constitutional law of the Society." Hence, only the chapter has canonical authority to legislate; the general assembly passes on new policies that if they are to become law must be approved by a chapter. (This latter provision was an amendment of the ordinary general assembly, June 1971.) Berson later recalled that his most significant contribution to the organization of the society was "to establish the General Assembly. It was an effort to broaden the base of consultation and to share the responsibility for leadership."[39] He also supported the evolution of the brothers from the status of auxiliary lay-religious to that of co-missioners.

As noted previously, Howard Bishop, adopting the model of several communities, had relegated the brothers to inferior status. At the motherhouse priests and brothers dined in separate refectories; the brothers' training was in manual labor to the exclusion of academic studies. At the 1953 chapter the ideal brother was an "all around missioner," still an auxiliary but with some attention to developing his general talents. In 1959 the chapter stipulated that brothers would be trained "in specific fields" at outside institutions.[40] The co-missioner status, enacted at the 1965 chapter, was based upon principles derived from the Second Vatican Council such as the laity's share in the priesthood of Christ. The Congregation for Religious disapproved of constitutional amendments that would have guaranteed the brothers full equality with priests in the governance of the community. Brother Nicholas Scheller was a vice-president in 1979 and in 1987 Brother Terry O'Rourke became second vice-president of Glenmary, the highest position a brother could achieve. However, in terms of equality of opportunity to pursue their potential, brothers and priests are on the same level. An egalitarian spirit prevails today. While several brothers have undergraduate and graduate degrees, manual labor is not disparaged. On the contrary it is highly regarded. Brothers Terry O'Rourke and Paul Wilhelm built twenty houses for low-income families in Dahlonega, Lumpkin County in northeast, Georgia. Under the direction of Brother Lawrence Jochim, a team of brothers constructed the residence building at the new headquarters in 1970–1971. Brothers have entered several professional fields: Brother Charles Kennedy is a music director; Brother William Early has been a youth director in Sylvania, Georgia; Brother Thomas Kelly manages the Glenmary men's residence at the motherhouse; Brother Curt Kedley has been a community developer; Brother Robert Hoffman has been on the training staff and building crew and has been a vocation counselor; Brother Albert Behm, a communications specialist, has been a chaplain in a correctional facility and in campus ministry; Brother Michael Springer is trained in gerontology and Brother Ken Woods in nursing; Brother Francis Sauer has had several positions of responsibility at the national headquarters ranging from purchasing agent to personnel director.[41]

Robert Berson did not wish to be reelected for a second term in 1971. To refer to his administration as one of continuous change would be an understatement. Every facet of community life, e.g. governance, spirituality, and ministry, had been reshaped in accord with the spirit of the times in church and society, and in consonance with the gospel and the spirit of the founder. Berson is generally regarded as a Glenmarian who possessed the intelligence, the administrative qualities, the self-confidence and the ability to deal with controversial issues with a sense of authority and a respect for loyal opposition. He led the society through a period of profound change with a firm grasp of the core of the Glenmary tradition.

Berson was succeeded by Father Charles Hughes, the first president to be elected by a popular vote. He was a native of Brooklyn and entered Glenmary as a seminarian. Ordained by Archbishop Alter in 1954, Hughes received his S.T.D. from the Angelicum in 1959. He had some experience in the missions but he was trained as a seminary professor. He taught dogma at Our Lady of the Fields Seminary from 1960 to 1963 and later was director of the Glenmary house of studies at St. Louis University.[42] Forty-three years old when he was elected president, Hughes' inaugural address stressed the need for affirmation: "I will try to remain happy and joyful because faith must win over confusion, hope over hopelessness, and love over sin. . . . Now as president, I feel obliged to specify the invitation that I think goes out to each of us to be dedicated like Jesus was dedicated, and to point again and again to the mountain top where each of us has an appointment with the Risen Christ."[43] According to Father Leonard Spanjers, a member of his executive council, Hughes' primary goal was "to strengthen, affirm and extend the pastoral ministry of Glenmary's Priests and Brothers who are spending long, hard hours of apostolic labor sharing the Good News of Jesus in small town and rural America."[44]

In his address at the congress of 1971, Hughes underscored the need for affirmation of the Glenmary mission experience. Entitled "Renewal . . . Hope, Peace and Joy," the address was in a real sense a personal statement of commitment. As in most communities that experienced profound changes in the immediate post-Vatican II period, there were those who lamented the departures from tradition and those who regretted the slow pace of progress in renewal and adaptation. Hughes implied that the community included some demoralized priests and brothers. "If, and that is a big if for at least some of us, if we are dissatisfied, disillusioned, unhappy with our present Glenmary life, if some of us are unattractive and unacceptable to others . . . if our life day by day does not have a satisfying meaning to ourselves, if we are not joyful, happy men, even in the midst of struggle, then something should be done to change the situation . . . it is imperative that we experience real meaning, peace, joy and happiness in our life. If this is not our experience, then, as being messengers of the Christian gospel, we are a contradiction in terms."[45] Hughes prescribed personal renewal tailored to the individual's character. As an example he spoke of his own program that entailed daily reading, studying, praying, practicing the guitar and exercising, all of which consumed five hours a day. "All our effort for renewal should be motivated by a desire to be more effective witnesses to the love and goodness of God."[46]

In that section of the address where he focused on pastoral mission, Hughes invoked the spirit of the founder. Father Bishop "wanted and directed us to engage in local parish ministries, but it was to be a specialized parish ministry, in a special locale and with a special quality about it." Hughes also endorsed district and national programs, such as the Regional Workers' Project that included Father Les Schmidt's social justice/liberation ministry among various people in the Appalachian region, and the work of Fathers Frank Ruff, Robert Berson, Wilfred Steinbacher, Joseph O'Donnell, and Robert Dalton in interfaith relations with Southern Baptists. He also supported the Three Rivers Team Ministry in Mississippi that incorporated laity, women religious, and Glenmary brothers and priests in a diversified program to meet the social, economic and religious needs of black and white Catholics in the deep south.[47]

Hughes directly confronted the problem of Glenmarians leaving the society. His strong affirmation of the society's ministry as well as his call for personal renewal within a sense of peace and joy was partially motivated by the need to engender collective confidence in the Glenmary identity as a viable and vital home-mission community.

Hughes' personalist style of leadership was a break from Berson's more structured approach but there was continuity of programs, as well as of principles of collegiality and subsidiarity. Because he was primarily concerned with elevating morale, deepening spirituality, and affirming the community's traditional identity, the presidential term of Charles Hughes may be viewed as a period of nurturing the new growth in the soil of the post-Vatican II field.

In 1975 Robert Berson was again elected president. He had been regional worker with the Southern Baptists seeking greater understanding between Catholics and the thirteen million Christians in that denomination. He was doing graduate work at the Gregorian University in Rome immediately before his election. Reelected in 1979 Berson served a total of fourteen years between 1965 and 1983. He established several special commissions or task forces dealing with social justice and other aspects of the Glenmary ministry. Those qualities that were so apparent in his leadership at the 1967–1968 renewal chapter were evident during his second and third terms as president.

He had known Howard Bishop and visited with him just before his death. Berson focused on Bishop's determination and his tenacity, characteristics that also seem to represent Berson's administrations; he was determined to preserve the Glenmary identity as the society accommodated itself to the spirit of the times. In terms of personality, Bishop and Berson were not cut from the same cloth. The founder was given to impassioned views and periodic explosiveness; the president projected a more restrained image. However, Robert Berson understood his own identity as a Glenmarian within the context of the charism of Howard Bishop.

V

During the late 1970s the women Missioners continued along a course of consolidation and renewal that had begun under Sister Mary Joseph Wade (1967–1975). In accord with the founder's views on mission activity, Sister Michelle Teff, president from 1975 to 1979, stressed the social needs of rural America. In one of her regular columns in *Kinship* she encouraged her readers to consider the issues of hunger, health care, housing, unemployment and public assistance as major priorities.[48] In 1978 the women missioners celebrated the twenty-fifth anniversary of the foundation of the community and in November of that year they moved into a new motherhouse, Morning Star, a rural retreat off Cheviot Road that was sold to them by Mrs. Florence Esterkamp and Mrs. Mabel Coughlin. The architectural style was a blend of traditional material and modern design which, according to Sister Mary Michelle, "is a contemporary expression of the women of Glenmary, serving the Church in today's world . . . while our new headquarters speaks of beauty and vision, it is also designed as an efficient, functional center. . . ."[49]

In 1979 Sister Rosemary Esterkamp was elected president, but as a mark of continuity Sister Michelle was elected to her council. The new president recalled her early days when she worked as part-time secretary to the founder: "I liked Father Bishop, I felt a real kindness from him."[50] Sister Rosemary was opposed to the Glenmary community being incorporated with the Dominican Order and, as mentioned earlier, she and another sister composed a letter to Howard indicating their support for him and a Home Missioner's distinctive habit. In 1953 Alter appointed her as secretary general, and two years later she was elected first councillor (1955–1961). During the early 1960s Sister Rosemary was engaged in graduate studies and formation. When the community experienced the crisis of 1967 she inclined toward the group that wished to form a non-canonical community because it seemed to be more in accord with the founder's vision, but "as summer went on and I heard more, it sounded less and less like what Father Bishop wanted."[51] Hence, Sister Rosemary brought to the office of president a rich experience with the founder and his legacy.

In her correspondence there are frequent references to Howard Bishop's inspiration of the community's missionary character and to the women's desire to implement his plan. Sister Rosemary and her council had periodic meetings with the leaders of the Glenmary men. At the Glenmary Sisters Institute on Mission/Spirituality/Purpose, Robert Berson, John W. Padberg, S.J. and John C. Futrell, S.J. were among the speakers. Held in 1982, this conference had a strong influence on the chapter of 1983 which was to develop a new constitution. Replete with quotations from the founder's mid-winter letters, the new constitution was approved by Archbishop Daniel Pilarczyk of Cincinnati and the ordinaries where the community's missions were located. In his approval Pilarczyk noted that the women's community clearly manifested the inspiration of the founder.[52]

Sister Rosemary's columns in *Kinship* also reveal her dedication to the founder. In her last letter to the community she quoted Bishop on the need to elevate the moral climate of the people served by the Home Missioners. Reflecting on her eight years as president of the women Missioners, Sister Rosemary said that she cherished her many visits to the missions. "If every trip to our missions has emphasized for me the continued need of the home mission efforts of Glenmary Sisters, Brothers, and priests . . . national news and international news emphasizes also for me that there is a dire need for much evangelization . . . in our world today."[53]

VI

In 1983 the men's community elected Francis A. Ruff president. Unlike Berson or Hughes, Ruff was of rural background; his family lived in St. Paul's Parish in Bloomer, Wisconsin located in the diocese of LaCrosse. Forty-seven years old when elected to office, Ruff attended Holy Cross Minor Seminary in his home diocese, and The Catholic University of America for philosophy where he was a Basselin scholar at Theological College. He studied theology at the Glenmary Seminary and was ordained in 1963. After six years as an associate pastor of St. Luke's Parish in Dahlonega, Georgia, he became the Glenmary liaison with the Southern Baptists (1969–1971). He was director of the mission office and director of vocations at Glenmary headquarters from 1971 to 1978. As a pastor of two parishes in Middle Tennessee during the five years previous to assuming office, he had broad mission experience; he had also served in the administrations of Hughes and Berson. With a total of twenty years between ordination and election to president, he had more years in Glenmary than any other superior general or president prior to election to office. Though he was the only leader who had never known Howard Bishop personally, he has absorbed his charism not only by his commitment to the Glenmary way of life but also by serving with Home Missioners who were part of the founding group. For example, James Kelly, treasurer under Howard Bishop, is also treasurer in the Ruff administration; the new president also knew Raphael Sourd.

Ruff's leadership reflects the affirming optimism of Hughes, and the administrative expertise and organizational skills of Berson. However, more importantly, the new president has etched his own style of leadership. He is particularly gifted in expressing his views with unvarnished honesty. He has a fine grasp of counseling skills through which he is able to listen and question within a context of respect. For example, he told the 1987 congress how anxious he had been about the upcoming election; he was enervated in anticipation of the community's possible rejection.

Of the programs, task forces, and projects derived from chapters during his first six years in office, 1983–1989, those dealing with evangelization and the mission statement and with the Glenmary Co-Missioners program with the women Missioners are the most significant. At the 1986 Congress, his presidential address was entitled "Our Identity: Home Missioners of America." He opened with reference to the society's mission statement, the implementation of which was a high priority during his first term in office: "We are called to our specific apostolic ministry and also to be members of our unique

missionary community." Ruff shared with his confreres his former
bias against the term "missionary." To him it had "connoted too
grand an ideal of self-sacrifice. . . . Maybe I felt that missionary signi-
fied a closed-minded zealot bringing the Truth to a benighted people." He then quoted Howard Bishop's remarks on the Home Missioners' training. "Of two things we are sure—have always been sure:
(1) We want in our lives the simplicity of true apostles; (2) We want our
work to remain missionary."[54]

During his commentary on another citation from Bishop, Ruff
pointed out that the founder's view of the church as missionary presaged the models of the church in the 1960s. ". . . the Church can
never rise to its full stature as a spiritual force even in the lives of
Catholics themselves until not only priests and bishops, but the rank
and file come to the realization that we are a missionary Church,"
wrote Howard Bishop in 1940. Ruff was convinced that the founder's
charism and "our charism" is that "we are rural missionaries, not just
rural pastors or rural Church workers." The president viewed missionary as "reaching beyond Church circles" and stressed "outreach
as opposed to nurture. . . . Certainly, we do and should be doing
nurture among the Catholics and training them to be evangelizers.
When I speak of outreach, I intend to be understood inclusively, as
evangelization that includes justice and justice that evangelizes. . . .
Evangelization is conversion of both heart and structures."[55]

To underscore that the founder's charism called Glenmary to engage in cross-cultural work, Ruff quoted Howard Bishop's remarks
on the Home Missioners' concerns for "the most neglected people . . . the sharecroppers, tenant and farm laborers of the cotton
belt, the mountaineers of the South and Negroes everywhere."[56]

Sister Christine Beckett, a native of Milwaukee who had professed
her vows in 1977, was elected president of the women Home Missioners in 1987. As president Sister Christine has injected a strong
theological dimension into her articulation of the Glenmary mission.
In one of her first columns in Kinship, she urged the women Missioners to be "God centered, Person oriented and Spirit-Sent-In-
Community."[57] As a woman religious who spent her adult life in the
post-Vatican II world, Sister Christine has been influenced by recent
trends in scripture studies, in spirituality, and in the cause of justice
and peace. In an article entitled "Encouraging God's Influentials,"
she said that the "Glenmary Sisters are committed to and proclaim by

word, action and life style the Gospel of Jesus Christ." Though she had never met the founder she reflected his legacy by quoting his 1948 mid-winter letter in which he urged his community to "love the poor, the sick, the helpless and attend to them. They are God's influentials. They are his aristocrats. He loves them. . . ."[58]

Of all the projects of the women's community, the co-missionary program is a principal priority derived from previous administrations and established as a primary goal at the 1987 chapter. The program entailed a process of encouraging, preparing and including the laity either directly as "missioners in the field" or indirectly as co-missioners "in other ways to support us in the mission." After consultations with the council which met with a Maryknoll lay missioner, Sister Christine invited Father Frank Ruff to involve the men in the co-missioners program.[59] As of late 1989 this program is in the hands of a joint planning committee co-chaired by Sister Christine and Father Michael Caroline.

The Home Missioners' celebration of the fiftieth anniversary of their foundation featured a symposium on evangelization with a number of prominent speakers, including Joseph Cardinal Bernardin, an old friend of Glenmary from the period when he was auxiliary bishop of Atlanta and later archbishop of Cincinnati. At the 1987 Congress Frank Ruff presented several views on contemporary evangelization that reveal his indebtedness to the founder.

> Let us go to God in prayer now with St. Paul and with the North American martyrs by our side and beg God for the gifts of wisdom, enthusiasm and perseverance. We need the gifts of wisdom to know to adapt the Gospel to the cultures in which we work. We need the gift of enthusiasm as Paul and the North American martyrs had it, and we need the gift of perseverance because the heat of the noonday sun can tire us and we can get discouraged. (The group knelt down, joined hands, and prayed silently and out loud for the three gifts.)[60]

Fifty years before this congress Howard Bishop had just arrived in Cincinnati with a plan; he had found an episcopal patron, and he had a deep sense of the Spirit's movement in his ever expanding spheres of home mission activity. It is apparent that the founder's spirit still animates the ministries of the Glenmary sisters, brothers, and priests.

NOTES

Abbreviations

AAB   Archives of the Archdiocese of Baltimore
AACin   Archives of the Archdiocese of Cincinnati
ACUA   Archives of the Catholic University of America
ADS   Archives of the Diocese of Savannah
APF   Archives of the Paulist Fathers
AMU   Archives of Marquette University
GHMA   Glenmary Home Missioners Archives
GSA   Glenmary Sisters Archives
MA   Maryknoll Archives
NCRLC   National Catholic Rural Life Conference
SAB   Sulpician Archives of Baltimore

Introduction

1. Henri Bremond, *The Mystery of Newman* (London, 1907), p. 13.
2. Quoted by Bremond, p. 291.

Chapter 1

1. *The Catholic Directory* (New York, 1915), p. 34.
2. For background on the church and John Carroll see Joseph P. Chinnici, *Living Stones, The History and Structure of Catholic Spiritual Life in the United States* (New York, 1989), pp. 1–34; James Hennesey, S.J., "An Eighteenth Century Bishop: John Carroll of Baltimore," in *Patterns of Episcopal Leadership*, ed. Gerald P. Fogarty, S.J. (New York, 1989), pp. 5–34; Margaret Mary Reher, *Catholic Intellectual Life in America: A Historical Study of Persons and Monuments* (New York, 1989), pp. 1–27; Thomas Spalding, CFX, *The Premier See, A History of the Archdiocese of Baltimore* (Baltimore, 1989).
3. For information on the life of John England see Patrick Carey, *An Immigrant Bishop: John England's Adaptation of Irish Catholicism to American Republicanism* (Yonkers, 1982); Peter Clarke, "John England, Missionary to

261

America, the Then and Now," in *Patterns of Episcopal Leadership,* pp. 68–84; Peter Guilday, *The Life and Times of John Carroll, 1786–1842* (New York, 1927) 2 vols.

4. Dolores Liptak, R.S.M., *Immigrants and Their Church* (New York, 1989), pp. 57–113; David O'Brien, *Public Catholicism* (New York, 1989), pp. 34–61.

5. John Farina, *An American Experience of God, The Spirituality of Isaac Hecker* (New York, 1981) and *Hecker Studies,* ed. John Farina (New York, 1983).

6. On Americanism see Robert D. Cross, *The Emergence of Liberal Catholicism* (Cambridge, Massachusetts, 1958); R. Emmett Curran, S.J., *Michael Augustine Corrigan and the Shaping of Conservative Catholicism in America* (New York, 1978); Dorothy Dohen, *Nationalism and American Catholicism* (New York, 1967); John Tracy Ellis, *James Cardinal Gibbons, 1834–1921* (Milwaukee, 1952), vols. 1 and 2; Gerald P. Fogarty, S.J., *The Vatican and the Americanist Crisis* (Rome, 1974), and *The Vatican and the American Hierarchy* (Stuttgart, 1982); Andrew M. Greeley, *The Catholic Experience* (New York, 1967); James Hennesey, S.J., *American Catholics* (New York, 1982), pp. 184–203; Christopher J. Kauffman, *Tradition and Transformation in Catholic Culture: The Priests of St. Sulpice in the United States* (New York, 1988), pp. 153–78; Thomas McAvoy, *The Great Crisis in American Catholic History* (Chicago, 1957); James J. Moynihan, *The Life of Archbishop Ireland* (New York, 1953); William Leroy Portier, "Providential Nation: An Historical Theological Study of Isaac Hecker's Americanism" (Ph.D. diss., University of Toronto, Saint Michael's College, Canada, 1980); also by Portier, "Isaac Hecker and *Testem Benevolentiae,*" in *Hecker Studies,* ed. John Farina (New York, 1983); Margaret Mary Reher, "The Church and the Kingdom of God in America: The Ecclesiology of the Americanists" (Ph.D. diss., Fordham University, 1972), and "Leo XIII and Americanism," in *Theological Studies* 34 (1973), 679–689; Thomas E. Wangler, "The Ecclesiology of John Ireland" (Ph.D. diss., Marquette University, 1968); Joseph M. White, *The Diocesan Seminary in the United States* (Notre Dame, 1989), pp. 165–266.

7. "Sermons of James Gibbons," RG 26, Box 1, Sulpician Archives of Baltimore (hereafter cited as SAB).

8. Ibid.

9. Ibid.

10. Felix Klein, *Americanism, Phantom Heresy* (Atchison, Kansas, 1951).

11. John Ireland in "The Introduction to Walter Elliott," *The Life of Father Hecker* (New York, 1894), p. xxi.

12. Chinnici, *Living Stones,* pp. 135–72.

13. Kauffman, *Tradition and Transformation,* pp. 153–78.

14. John Tracy Ellis, *James Cardinal Gibbons 1834–1921.* 2 vols.

15. James Gibbons, *The Ambassador of Christ* (Baltimore, 1892), p. vi.

16. Ibid., pp. vii–viii.

17. Ibid., p. ix.

18. Ibid., p. 171.

19. Kauffman, *Tradition and Transformation,* p. 288.

20. Quoted by Spalding, *Premier See,* p. 335.

21. Ibid.

Chapter 2

1. Howard Bishop, newspaper cuttings. Glenmary Sisters' Archives (hereafter GSA).

2. Transcript of interview with Grace Bishop, Glenmary Home Missioners' Archives (hereafter GHMA).

3. Ibid.

4. *The Catholic Directory* (Baltimore, 1892).

5. Interview with Grace Bishop, GHMA.

6. Historical files, W.H.B. (i.e. William Howard Bishop), "The Western Central Debate," *The Review* 11 (April 11, 1906), 159, GHMA.

7. Ibid., "School Honesty," *The Review* 17 (May 16, 1906), 186–87.

8. Ibid., "Editorials," *The Review* 17 (June 13, 1906), 209.

9. Quoted in "Father Bishop, The Man and His Work," *The Challenge* XVI (Autumn 1953), 3.

10. Transcript of interview with Harry Bishop, GHMA.

11. Historical files, newspaper cuttings, GSA.

12. Folder of historical photos, GSA.

13. Historical files, Harvard College Alumni Report, class of 1910, third report, March 1917. This portion was written by Howard Bishop, GHMA.

14. Historical files, "By and about Howard Bishop." This was an anonymous report on autobiographical reflections of W.H.B., GHMA.

15. Howard Bishop to Dr. Dyer, August 11, 1909, student files, SAB.

16. Ibid., Bishop to Dyer, August 11, 1909.

17. Catalogue of St. Mary's Seminary, 1909–1910, p. 9, SAB.

18. Ibid., pp. 147–148.

19. Howard Bishop, academic record, student files, SAB.

20. Ibid.

21. Catalogue of St. Mary's Seminary, 1910–11, p. 44, SAB.

22. Howard Bishop student files, SAB.

23. Ibid.

24. Ibid.

25. Bishop to Dyer, April 2, 1914, SAB.

26. Dyer to Bishop, November 1, 1914, SAB.

27. Bishop to Dyer, November 2, 1914, SAB.

28. Bishop to Dyer, March 15, 1915, SAB.

29. Howard Bishop's sermons 000527-24, GHMA.

30. "Diary of W. Howard Bishop," typed transcripts of manuscript copies (hereafter cited as Diary), August 2, 1915, GHMA.

31. Ibid., August 6, 1915.

32. Ibid., September 23, 1915.

33. Ibid., January 4, 1916.

34. Ibid., January 9, 1916.

35. Ibid., March 27, 1916.

36. Ibid., February 8, 1916.

37. Ibid., January 16, 1916.

38. Ibid., January 21, 1916.

39. Ibid., January 30, 1916.

40. Ibid., February 25, 1916.

41. Ibid., March 27, 1916.

42. Ibid., May 15, 1916.

43. Ibid., June 8, 1917.

44. Howard Bishop's sermons 000532, GHMA.

45. Diary, April 29, 1916, GHMA.

46. Ibid., May 2, 1916.

47. Howard Bishop file, newspaper cuttings, GSA.

48. Diary, July 18, 1916, GHMA.

49. Ibid., December 31, 1916.

50. Ibid., March-December 1916.

51. Ibid., December 2, 1916.

52. Ibid., December 2, 1916.

53. Ibid., December 18, 1916.

54. Ibid., February 2, 1917.

55. Ibid., September 8, 1916.

56. Transcript of interview with McAdams, GHMA.

57. Diary, September 9, 1917.

58. Ibid., September 10, 1917.

59. For a pattern of his expenses see Diary, 1917–1918.

60. Howard Bishop's sermons, 000531, GHMA.

61. Ibid., 000579.

62. Ibid.

Chapter 3

1. Michael Gannon, *Rebel Bishop: The Life and Times of Augustine Verot* (Milwaukee, 1964).

2. Carl J. Liljencrants file, student files. Also see *100th Anniversary of St. Louis Parish* (privately published, October 3, 1955), pp. 46–73, SAB.

3. Charles Carroll to Cardinal James Gibbons, August 2, 1917. Chancery parish files, St. Louis Parish, Clarksville. Archives of the Archbishop of Baltimore (hereafter cited as AAB).

4. Ibid., same to same, September 4, 1917.

5. Diary, September 17, 24, 1917, GHMA.

6. Ibid., November 2, 1917.

7. Ibid., November 27, 1917.

8. Ibid., December 26, 1917.

9. Ibid., April, May and June, 1918.

10. Ibid., April 9, 1922.

11. Ibid., April 10, 1922.

12. Ibid., April 11, 1922.

13. Ibid., April 28, 1922.

14. Annual reports, Chancery parish files, St. Louis Parish, Clarksville, AAB.

15. Transcript of oral interviews with Mrs. Jones, GHMA.

16. Ibid.

17. "Veteran Retires," *The Little Flower* III (June 1929), 5, AAB.

18. Diary, December 13–20, GHMA.

19. Ibid., January 3, 1918.

20. Ibid., February 8, 1918.

21. M.V. Kelley C.S.B., "Attending Scattered Missions," *The American Ecclesiastical Review* LVIII (February 1918), 177.

22. Annual Reports, Chancery parish files, St. Louis Parish, Clarksville, AAB.

23. Diary, November 8, 1918, GHMA.

24. Transcript of oral interview with R. Hewitt Nichols, January 3, 1969, GHMA.

25. Ibid., Joseph Thompson, January 3, 1968.

26. Ibid., Mary Smith, December 29, 1968.

27. Diary, Memoranda, December 25, 1918, GHMA.

28. "Clarksville, A Sociological Study" (M.A. Thesis, The Catholic University of America, 1935).

29. Diary, November 4, 1919, GHMA.

30. Chancery parish files, Bishop to Gibbons, December 11, 1920, AAB.

31. Annual report, 1921, Chancery parish files, AAB.

32. Ibid., annual report, 1922.

33. Ibid., annual report, 1923.

34. Diary, March 24, 1922, GHMA.

35. Ibid., April 12, 1922.

36. W. Howard Bishop, "Letter to the Editor," *The Baltimore Catholic Review,* April 15, 1922, p. 4.

37. W. Howard Bishop, "Country Parochial Schools," *The Baltimore Catholic Review,* April 22, 1922, p. 4.

38. W. Howard Bishop, "Country Parochial Schools," Part II, *The Baltimore Catholic Review,* April 29, 1922, p. 4.

39. Records of the League of the Little Flower, AAB.

40. W. Howard Bishop, "Old Friends," *The Little Flower* 1 (July 1926), 4, AAB.

Chapter 4

1. For background on The Catholic Rural Movement see Colman Barry, O.S.B., *The Catholic Church and German Americans* (Milwaukee, 1953); David S. Bovee, *The Church and Land: The National Catholic Rural Life Conference and American Society, 1923–1985* (Ph.D. diss., University of Chicago, 1986); Timothy Michael Dolan, *To Teach, Govern and Sanctify: The Life of Edwin Vincent O'Hara* (Ph.D. diss., The Catholic University of America, 1985); Philip Gleason, *The Conservative Reformers: German-American Catholics and the Social Order* (Notre Dame, 1968); James P. Gaffey, *Francis Clement Kelley* (Bensenville, Illinois, 1980), two vols.; Philip Witte, S.M., *Twenty-Five Years of Crusading: A History of the National Catholic Rural Life Conference* (Des Moines, 1948). Also see "Rural Life," *U.S. Catholic Historian* 8 (Summer 1989).

2. Gaffey, I, p. 80.

3. Francis Clement Kelley to Romanus Bastion, June 9, 1916. Simon A. Baldus Papers, The Archives of the Catholic University of America (hereafter cited as ACUA).

4. John LaFarge, S.J. to Right Rev. Francis C. Kelley, December 4, 1922. Extension Papers RGI, Box 2. Archives of Loyola University of Chicago.

5. Dolan, *To Teach, Govern and Sanctify*, pp. 25–63.

6. Bovee, *The Church and Land*, pp. 102–03.

7. Edwin V. O'Hara, "The Church and the Rural Community," *The Catholic Charities Review* VI (April 1922), 115.

8. Ibid., p. 116.

9. Bishop to O'Hara, May 9, 1922, Edwin V. O'Hara Papers. Microfilm copy of the papers located in the Archives of the Archdiocese of Kansas City, ACUA.

10. O'Hara to Bishop, November 6, 1922, ACUA.

11. Bishop to O'Hara, August 23, 1923, ACUA.

12. Ibid.

13. O'Hara to Bishop, August 28, 1923, ACUA.

14. Bishop to O'Hara, September 14, 1923, ACUA.

15. Ibid.

16. Quoted by Bovee, *The Church and Land*, p. 189.

17. Ibid., p. 133.

18. James A. Madison, "Reformers and the Rural Church, 1900–1950," *Journal of American History* (April 1987), 646.

19. Ibid.

20. *St. Isidore's Plow* II (January 1924), National Catholic Rural Life Papers, Archives of Marquette University (hereafter cited as AMU), 1.

21. Files of the League of the Little Flower, *The Little Flower* I (April 1926), 1, AAB.

22. W. Howard Bishop to "Reverend and Our Father," February 23, 1924. Copy, O'Hara Papers, ACUA.

23. *The Little Flower* (January 1927), 1, AAB.

24. Papers of the National Catholic Rural Life Conference, Archives of Marquette University (hereafter cited as AMU), Papers, *Catholic Rural Life*, 3 (March 25, 1925), 2.

25. Bishop to O'Hara, August 20, 1924, O'Hara papers, ACUA.

26. Bishop to Father Carey, July 14, 1924. Copy, O'Hara papers, ACUA.

27. Bishop to O'Hara, January 27, 1925, O'Hara papers, ACUA.

28. "The Rural Conference," *The Baltimore Catholic Review*, October 17, 1925, p. 4

29. "Advance Made at Congress on Rural Life," *The Baltimore Catholic Review*, October 31, 1925, 5.

30. Ibid.

31. Bovee, *The Church and Land*, pp. 138–140; Witte, p. 144.

32. Files of the League of the Little Flower, annual reports, 1928, AAB.

33. Transcript of oral interviews with R. Hewit Nickols, December 29, 1968, GHMA.

34. Ibid., Paul Thompson, January 3, 1969, GHMA.

35. Ibid., Sister Mary Bernard, C.D.P., December 18, 1968, GHMA.

36. Ibid., Sister Mary of Providence, C.D.P., December 17, 1968, GHMA.

37. Ibid., Sister Mary Bernard, C.D.P.

38. Ibid., Thelma Gatton.

Chapter 5

1. Frank O'Hara. "The Catholic Rural Life Movement," *Commonweal* XV (January 20, 1933), 324.

2. Reverend William Howard Bishop, "Putting Romance into Farming," *Catholic Rural Life* VI (November 1927), 1–2, papers of the NCRLC, series 6, box 23, AMU.

3. Reverend William Howard Bishop, "Aim of the C.R.L.C.," *Catholic Rural Life* VII (October 1928), 5, papers of the NCRLC, AMU.

4. Ibid.

5. Ibid.

6. Reverend W. Howard Bishop, "A Christmas Message," *Catholic Rural Life* VII (December 1928), 1, copy in GHMA.

7. For historical background on the Klan see David M. Chalmers, *Hooded Americanism: The First Century of the Ku Klux Klan: 1865–1965* (New York, 1965); Kenneth T. Jackson, *The Ku Klux Klan in the City 1915–1930* (New York, 1967).

8. Quoted by Michael Williams, *The Shadow of the Pope* (New York, 1932), p. 193.

9. W. Howard Bishop, "The Lesson of Intolerance," *The Little Flower* III (November 1928), 1, AAB.

10. Ibid.

11. W. Howard Bishop, "Intolerance in Rural Communities. How to Meet It," *American Ecclesiastical Review*, Ninth Series, I (LXXXI) (December 1929), 593.

12. Ibid., 596.

13. Ibid., 599.

14. Ibid., 593.

15. Ibid., 590–593.

16. A copy of this circular letter, dated February 19, 1930, is in the John LaFarge papers, Box 1, Folder 54, Archives of Georgetown University.

17. Ibid.

18. Presidential Address, Eighth Annual Catholic Rural Life Conference, Springfield, Illinois, August 25–28, 1930. Also see 34106–34113, GHMA, papers of the NCRLC, series 8, box 1, AMU.

19. Presidential Address, Wichita, Kansas, October 18, 1931, AMU.

20. Ibid., Presidential Address, Dubuque, Iowa, October 19, 1932, AMU.

21. Ibid.

22. "Landward," *The Little Flower* VI (April 1932), 1, AAB.

23. *Landward* I (Spring 1933), papers of the NCRLC, series 6, box 3, I (Spring 1933), AMU.

24. Witte, pp. 159–162.

25. W. Howard Bishop, "Dear Board Member," May 26, 1933, NCRLC papers of the series 13, box 3, AMU.

26. *Landward* I (Spring 1933), AMU.

27. Minutes of the Board of Directors, October 17, 1933. Papers of the NCRLC, series 10, box 1, AMU.

28. Ibid., *Landward* 1 (Spring 1933), 3.

29. Diary, January 27, 1933, GHMA.

30. *Landward*. For background on Catholic rural leaders and the New Deal, see David O'Brien, *American Catholics and Social Reform: The New Deal Years* (New York, 1968); Edward S. Shapiro, "Catholic Agrarian Thought and

The New Deal," *The Catholic Historical Review* 65 (October 1979), 583–99; "Catholic Rural Life and the New Deal Farm Program," *American Benedictine Review* 28 (September 1977), 307–32; "Decentralist Intellectuals and the New Deal," *Journal of American History* 58 (March 1972), 938–57; also see papers of the NCRLC, series 6, box 3, AMU.

31. Luigi G. Ligutti, "A Rural Industrial Colony Proposed for the Bituminous Coal District of Southern Iowa," *Landward* 1 (Winter 1934), 5, papers of the NCRLC, series 6, box 3, AMU.

32. W.H. Bishop to L.G. Ligutti, October 3, 1933, general correspondence, Ligutti papers, AMU.

33. Ligutti to Bishop, November 27, 1933, Ligutti papers, AMU.

34. Bishop to Ligutti, January 9, 1934, Ligutti papers, AMU.

35. Diary, January 16, 1934, GHMA.

36. *Landward* 11 (Spring 1934), 4, papers of the NCRLC, series 6, box 3, AMU.

37. W.H. Bishop to M.L. Wilson, February 15, 1934, GHMA.

38. "The Clarksville Rehabilitation Farm Project" (Tentative Plan), GHMA.

39. Revised Tentative Plan, GHMA.

40. Diary, February 28, 1934, GHMA.

41. *Landward,* papers of the NCRLC, series 6, Box 3, AMU.

42. Dorothy Day to Donald Powell, October 30, 1934, Dorothy Day/Catholic Worker collection, series W2, box 1, AMU. This letter concluded with the remark "yours for the Revolution in Christ."

43. W. Howard Bishop to Donald Powell, November 21, 1937, series W2.1, box 1, AMU.

44. Dorothy Day to Father Bishop, December 7, 1934, series W.2, box 1, AMU.

45. Diary, December 9, 1934, GHMA.

46. Ibid., December 14, 15, 1934.

47. Bishop to Dorothy Day December 12, 1934, Catholic Worker collection, W2.1, Box 1, AMU.

48. W. Howard Bishop, "Canada Rural Movement," *The Little Flower* IX (Summer 1934), 1, 8, AAB.

49. Ibid.

50. Bishop to M.M. Coady, August 4, 1934, GHMA.

51. Diary, August 28, 1934, GHMA.

52. Henry H. Ourings to Bishop, January 19, 1935, GHMA.

53. John W. Magruder to Bishop, January 31, 1935, GHMA.

54. Diary, September 18, 1933, GHMA.

55. Minutes of the Board of Directors, October 18, 1933, papers of the NCRLC, series 8, box 1, p. 90, AMU.

56. J.M. Campbell to W. Howard Bishop, September 4, 1934, GHMA.

57. J.M. Campbell to James Burns (sic), September 4, 1934. Copy, GHMA.

58. Ibid.

59. Diary, September 27, 1934, GHMA.

60. Diary, November 5, 1934, GHMA.

61. W. Howard Bishop, "Agrarianism: The Basis of a New Order," papers of the NCRLC, series 5, box 2, AMU.

62. R.P. Walsh, "Distributism," *The Catholic Encyclopedia* (New York, 1907), IV, p. 962.

63. Bishop to Byrnes, February 17, 1936, GHMA.

64. Edgar Schmiedler, O.S.B., "Herbert Agar, Land of the Free," *Landward* IV (Spring 1936), 6, papers of the NCRLC, series 6, box 3, AMU.

Part II: Introduction

1. John W. Kuykendall, *Southern Enterprise: The Work of Evangelical Societies* (Westport, 1982), pp. 16–17.

2. John Farina, ed., *The Diary of Isaac Hecker* (New York, 1988); also John Farina, *An American Experience of God: The Spirituality of Isaac Hecker* (New York, 1981).

3. John Farina, ed., in *Hecker Studies* (New York, 1983).

4. Thomas F. Price, "Localized Work in Country Districts," *Proceedings of the Winchester Convention,* 1901 Supplement to *The Missionary,* p. 127.

Chapter 6

1. W. Howard Bishop. "Country Parochial Schools," *The Baltimore Catholic Review,* April 29, 1922, p. 5.

2. Diary, Pentecost Sunday, 1935, GHMA.

3. *Landward* III (Summer 1935), papers of the NCRLC, series 6, box 3, AMU.

4. James A. Walsh to W. Howard Bishop, August 28, 1935, Maryknoll Archives (hereafter cited as MA), W. Howard Bishop File.

5. Bishop to Walsh, September 4, 1935, MA.

6. "A Tentative Plan for an American Society of Catholic Rural Missions," MA.

7. Ibid.

8. Ibid.

9. Ibid.

10. Howard Bishop papers, Retreat Notes, 1952, 1154, GHMA.

11. M.E. Williams, "Catholicism," *The New Catholic Encyclopedia* (New York, 1967), Vol. 3, p. 338.

12. Herbert Thurston, "Catholic," *The Catholic Encyclopedia* (New York, 1908), Vol. 3, pp. 449–52.

13. G. Thiels, "Catholicity," *The New Catholic Encyclopedia* (New York, 1967), Vol. 3, p. 339, ibid.

14. Bishop to Walsh, September 26, 1935, MA.

15. Curley to Bishop, September 23, 1935, AAB.

16. Walsh to Bishop, October 2, 1935, GHMA.

17. Bernard F. Meyer, "Regarding a Society in the United States to Train and Send Priests to Poor Dioceses," GHMA.

18. Bishop to James A. Drought, November 23, 1935, GHMA.

19. Myer to Bishop. undated, ca. October 1935, GHMA.

20. W. Howard Bishop, second draft, "A Plan for an American Society of Catholic Home Missions to Operate in the Rural Sections of the United States," MA.

21. W. Howard Bishop, first draft, "For the Missions of Rural America, A Tentative Plan for An American Society of Catholic Rural Missions," MA.

22. Second draft, MA.

23. Ibid.

24. Bishop to Amleto G. Cicognani, December 3, 1935, GHMA.

25. Same to same, December 7, 1935, GHMA.

26. Cicognani to Bishop, December 11, 1935, GHMA.

27. Bishop to Cicognani, April 8, 1936, GHMA.

28. Cicognani to Bishop, April 9, 1936, GHMA.

29. Curley to Bishop, September 23, 1935, AAB.

30. Curley's circular letter; March, 1936, AAB.

31. Diary, February 26, 1935, GHMA.

32. Notes on Father Bishop's autobiographical reflections, n.d., ca. January 1952, GHMA.

33. Diary, February 28, 1935, GHMA.

34. Michael Irwin to Bishop, March 28, 1935, GHMA.

35. Ibid.

36. Diary, February 28, 1935, GHMA.

37. Ibid., June 21, 1935.

38. Ibid., April 15, 1935.

39. Ibid., May 25, 1935.

40. Ibid., June 22, 1935.

41. Ibid., June 27, 1935.

42. Most Reverend John B. Morris, "An Open Letter," *Extension Magazine* XXXI (September 1936), 3. I am indebted to Brother Michael Grace, S.J., archivist, Loyola University Archives, for providing me with a copy of this "open letter."

43. Ibid., p. 4.

44. Ibid., p. 32.

45. Diary, October 8, 1936, GHMA.

46. Bishop to the Most Reverend John B. Morris, September 8, 1936, copy, GHMA.

47. Diary, April 17, 1936, GHMA.

48. Joachim V. Benson, M.S.SS.T., "The Missionary Councils and Rural Missions," *American Ecclesiastical Review* 94 (June 1936), 618–623.

49. Ibid., 619–21.

50. Eugene J. Brennan, M.S.SS.T. to Bishop, September 1, 1937, GHMA.

51. Bishop to Thomas O'Keefe, February 24, 1953, GHMA.

52. Diary, March 19, 1936, GHMA.

53. Ibid., June 13, 1936.

54. Ibid., October 19, 1936.

55. McAdams to Bishop, April 7, 1936, GHMA.

56. Bishop to McAdams, April 13, 1936, GHMA.

57. "Considering the Other Sheep," *Landward* IV (Summer 1936), 2, GHMA.

58. Campbell to Bishop, July 3, 1936, GHMA.

59. Byrnes to Bishop, September 30, 1936, GHMA.

60. McGinn to Bishop, April 4, 1936, GHMA.

61. Bishop to McNeill, October 1, 1936, GHMA.

62. Bishop to Malloy, October 1, 1936, GHMA.

63. Bishop to McGinn, October 1, 1936, GHMA.

64. Copy of McGinn's address at the 1936 convention in Fargo, N.D., papers of the NCRLC, series 81, box 2, AMU.

65. Diary, October 14, 1936, GHMA.

66. Minutes of the Board of Directors, October 13, 1936, papers of the NCRLC, series 81, box 2, AMU.

67. Ibid.

68. Diary, October 15, 1936, GHMA.

69. Ibid., January 4, 1937.

70. Ibid., March 9, 1937.

71. Ibid., March 27, 1937.

72. Ibid., April 14, 1937.

73. Ibid., April 16, 1937.

74. Ibid., April 17, 1937.

75. Ibid., April 22, 1937.

76. "Practical Preliminary Step," April 23, 1937, GHMA.

77. Diary, April 22, 1937, GHMA.

78. Bishop to Curley, April 27, 1937, AAB.

79. Diary, April 28, 1937, GHMA.

80. Ibid., May 3, 1937.

81. Ibid.
82. Curley to Bishop, May 4, 1937, AAB.
83. Diary, May 5, 1937, GHMA.
84. McNicholas to Bishop, June 5, 1937, GHMA.
85. McNicholas to Curley, May 29, 1937, copy GHMA.
86. Curley to McNicholas, June 1, 1937, copy, GHMA.
87. Ibid.
88. Diary, June 6, 1937, GHMA.
89. Bishop to McNicholas, June 4, 1937, GHMA.
90. Diary, June 16, 1937, GHMA.
91. Ibid., June 20, 1937.
92. Ibid., June 27, 1937.
93. Ibid., July 6, 1937.
94. Ibid., July 7, 1937.
95. Ibid., July 10, 1937.
96. Ibid., July 12, 1937.

Chapter 7

1 Steven M. Avella, "John T. McNicholas in the Age of Practical Thomism," *Records of American Catholic Historical Society* (1987), 16–22.
2. Quoted by Thomas Spalding, *The Premier See,* p. 335.
3. Transcript of oral interview of George H. Rehring, February 22, 1969, GHMA.
4. Avella, 20.
5. McNicholas remarked that "Floersch is a saintly prelate but I am convinced has the mind of a seminarian"—quoted by Avella, "John T. McNicholas," 27.
6. "Problems of Agriculture, From the Standpoint of Catholic Principles," McNicholas Papers, Archives of the Archdiocese of Cincinnati (hereafter cited as AACin).
7. W. Howard Bishop to the Most Reverend Archbishop and Bishops of the Province of Cincinnati, circular letter, June 23, 1933, McNicholas Papers, AACin.
8. John T. McNicholas to "Your Excellency," November 5, 1944, AACin.
9. Diary, July 23, 1937, GHMA.
10. Bishop to Curley, October 21, 1937, AAB.
11. Ibid.
12. Transcript of oral interview of Sister Aloysius, March 13, 1969, GHMA.
13. Diary, July 27, 1937, GHMA.
14. Transcript of oral interview, Most Reverend John S. Spence, January 4, 1969, GHMA.

15. Diary, July 1, 1937, GHMA.

16. Ibid., July 27, 1937.

17. Oral interview of Spence, GHMA.

18. Diary, September 8, 1937, GHMA.

19. Michael J. Curley to Austin G. Healy, November 27, 1937. Monsignor Healy kindly provided me with this letter.

20. Healy to Kauffman, December 30, 1986.

21. Curley-Bishop correspondence, October 1937, AAB.

22. Telephone interview: C. J. Kauffman with Agnes Mahon, October 4, 1990.

23. Ibid.

24. Diary, January 31, 1938, GHMA.

25. Telephone interview: C. J. Kauffman with Agnes Mahon, October 4, 1990.

26. Diary, January 31, 1938.

27. Personal interview: C. J. Kauffman with Paul Thompson, December 18, 1988.

28. W. Howard Bishop, "Our Frontier Mission," *Landward* (Summer-Autumn 1937), 4. Papers of the NCRLC series 6, Box 3, AMU.

29. William Howard Bishop, "The Organization of Catholic Resources in the Hinterlands," in *Catholic Rural Objectives* (St. Paul, 1938), p. 171.

30. Ibid., p. 172.

31. Ibid., p. 173.

32. Diary, November 9, 1937, GHMA.

33. Ibid., November 7, 1937.

34. William Howard Bishop, "The Organization of Catholic Resources in the Hinterlands," p. 170.

35. Diary, February 22, 1938, GHMA.

36. Ibid.

37. Ibid., March 22, 1938.

38. Transcription of oral interview of Luigi Ligutti, May 21, 1972, GHMA.

39. Byrnes to Bishop, April 7, 1938, GHMA.

40. W. Howard Bishop, Letter to the Editor, *Catholic Rural Life Bulletin* 1 (May 1938), 24.

41. *The Challenge* I (February 1938), 1.

42. Ibid.

43. Ibid., 4.

44. Ibid.

45. Ibid., 5.

46. Diary, July 23, 1938, GHMA.

47. Ibid., July 24, 1938.

48. Ibid., August 1, 1938.

49. For background on the Catholic Evidence Guild see Debra Campbell, "The Heyday of Catholic Action and the Lay Apostolate," in *Transforming Parish Ministry,* ed. Jay P. Dolan (New York, 1989), pp. 235–236, 241.

50. Stephen A. Leven, *Go Tell It on the Mountain* (published by his nephew, Reverend Marvin Leven, Edmund, Oklahoma, 1984), pp. 23–36.

51. Bishop to Leven, March 28, 1938, GHMA.

52. Leven to Bishop, April 12, 1938, GHMA.

53. Bishop to Leven, May 7, 1938, GHMA.

54. Leven to Bishop, June 10, 1938.

55. Diary, September 26, 1938, GHMA.

56. Leven, *Go Tell It on the Mountain,* p. 59.

57. Leven to Joseph Gartner, February 11, 1972, GHMA.

58. Diary, October 31, 1938, GHMA.

59. Ibid., October 30, 1938.

60. Ibid.

61. Ibid., January 5, 1939.

62. Ibid., January 8, 1939.

63. Ibid., January 19, 1939.

64. Ibid., January 21, 1939.

65. Ibid., January 22, 1939.

66. "Skirmishing on the Mission Front," *The Challenge* II (Spring 1939), 2.

67. Diary, April 19, 1939, GHMA.

68. Ibid., May 2, 1939.

69. Ibid., June 13, 1939.

70. "Preaching Christ on the Wayside," *The Challenge* II (Summer 1939), 1.

71. Ibid.

72. James P. Kelly "Notes on Interview with Father Raphael Sourd," August, 1970, GHMA.

73. "The First Roll Call," *The Challenge* II (Summer 1939), 4.

74. Francis Massarella, "Community Life Begins," *The Challenge* II (Summer 1939), 6.

75. Diary, June 29, 1939, GHMA.

76. Ibid., July 1, 1939.

77. Ibid., July 2, 1939.

78. Benedict Wolf, transcript of oral interview, GHMA.

79. Diary, July 30, 1939, GHMA.

Chapter 8

1. John T. McNicholas to W. Howard Bishop. August 15, 1939, GHMA.

2. Diary, March 15, 1941, GHMA.

3. Raphael Sourd, "Highlights from the Missions," *The Challenge* II (Christmas 1939), 3.

4. W. Howard Bishop, "The Conquest of No Priest Land," *The Challenge* II (Christmas), 4.

5. W. Howard Bishop, "Home Mission Vocation," *The Challenge* II (Christmas 1939), 6.

6. Ibid., 8.

7. Edward Smith, "Crib Carriers," *The Challenge* II (Christmas 1939), 8.

8. Francis A. Wuest, "Rural Family and Family Life," *The Challenge* III (Spring 1940), 5.

9. W. Howard Bishop, Speeches, etc., GHMA.

10. Ibid.

11. Ibid.

12. Cornelius Collins to W. Howard Bishop, October 22, 1941, GHMA.

13. Excerpts from the *New York Times*, November 18, 1941, GHMA.

14. Thomas J. McDonnell, November 21, 1941, GHMA.

15. Bishop to McDonnell, November 27, 1941, GHMA.

16. Ibid.

17. Diary, November 25, 1941, GHMA.

18. Heykar to Bishop, May 4, 1940, Home Missioners Files, AACin.

19. Bishop to McNicholas, July 1, 1940, AACin.

20. Diary, June 1, 1940, GHMA.

21. "Living in 1840 During A.D. 1940. *The Challenge* III (Summer 1940), 2.

22. "At Last We Have a Motherhouse," *The Challenge* III (Christmas 1940), 3.

23. Ibid., 5.

24. Transcript of oral interview of Vincent Wilmes, April 9, 1968, GHMA.

25. Diary, December 25, 1940, GHMA.

26. Ibid.

27. Ibid., January 21, 1941.

28. Ibid.

29. Ibid., June 8, 1941.

30. Ibid., June 15, 1941.

31. Bishop to Ignatius Smith, O.P., May 13, 1941, GHMA.

32. Smith to Bishop, May 19, 1941, GHMA.

33. Arand to Bishop, May 31, 1941, GHMA.

34. Bishop to Arand, June 3, 1941, GHMA.

35. Diary, August 13, 1941, GHMA.

36. W. Howard Bishop, "The Home Missioners Fund New Fields," *The Catholic Life Bulletin* 3 (August 20, 1941), 16.

37. Personal interview: C. J. Kauffman with Benedict Wolf on November 11, 1988.

38. Diary, August 13, 1941, GHMA.

39. Diary, June 29, 1941, GHMA.

40. Bishop to Walsh, April 20, 1941, Howard Bishop files, MA.

41. Walsh to Bishop, May 15, 1941, Howard Bishop files, MA.

42. Diary, May 15, 1941, GHMA.

43. Bishop to Walsh, May 22, 1941, Howard Bishop files, MA.

44. Diary, May 27, 1941, GHMA.

45. Bishop to Walsh, December 9, 1941, Howard Bishop files, MA.

46. "At Home," *Field Afar* (November 1941), 1.

47. Bishop to Walsh, December 9, 1941, Howard Bishop files, MA.

48. "We Take On a Pilot," *The Challenge* IV (Christmas 1941), 4.

49. Diary, October 3, 1941, GHMA.

50. Mid-Winter Letter, 1942, located in the bound volume of *The Challenge* 1938–1946, GHMA.

51. W. Howard Bishop, "On the Firing Line" *The Challenge* V (Summer 1942), 2.

52. Ibid.

53. Sourd to Bishop, June 28, 1942, Sourd papers, GHMA.

54. Ibid., same to same, August 6, 1942.

55. Diary, July 19, 1942, GHMA.

56. Ibid.

57. Sourd to Bishop, July 31, 1943, Sourd papers, GHMA.

58. Brother Charles Reedy to the community, *The Challenge* IV (Summer 1943), 8.

59. Diary, April 1, 1942, GHMA.

60. Bishop to Cotton, March 26, 1942, GHMA.

61. Ibid., same to same, May 27, 1942, GHMA.

62. Same to same, May 29, 1942, GHMA.

63. Cotton to Bishop, June 18, 1942, GHMA.

64. Bishop to Cotton, June 16, 1942, GHMA.

65. "Sunfish," *The Challenge* V (Summer 1942), 2.

66. Diary, June 17, 1942, GHMA.

67. "Russellville" *The Challenge* V (Christmas, 1942), 2.

68. Oral interview of Benedict Wolf, November 11, 1988.

69. "Russellville–Ottway," *The Challenge* V (Christmas 1942), 2–3.

70. Ibid.

71. Mid-Winter Letter, 1944, GHMA.

72. Ibid., 8.

73. Oral interview of Francis Massarella, 1988. Also see "Father Massarella to the Trappists," *The Challenge* VIII (Christmas 1945), 3, 7.

74. Diary, September 15, 1944, GHMA.

75. Gerald O'Hara to John T. McNicholas, September 18, 1944. Archives of the diocese of Savannah (hereafter cited as ADS).

76. Bishop to O'Hara, October 4, 1944, ADS.

77. O'Hara to Bishop, October 30, 1944, ADS.

78. Same to same, December 12, 1944, ADS.

79. Edward William Smith, "Marching Through Georgia," *St. Anthony Messenger* (July 1945), 8–9.

80. Brother Vincent Wilmes, "Mission Letters," January 25, 1945, *The Challenge* VIII (Spring 1945), 8.

81. Father Edward Smith, "Mission Letters," February 2, 1945, *The Challenge* VIII (Spring 1945), 8.

82. Howard Bishop, "Mid-Winter Letter," 1945, GHMA.

83. Father Benedict Wolf, "Mission Letters," *The Challenge* VIII (Summer 1945), 3.

84. Diary, January 30, 1945, GHMA.

85. "New Frontier," *The Challenge* VIII (Christmas 1945), 3.

86. Howard Bishop, "Mid-Winter Letter," 1947, GHMA.

87. Diary, February 15, 1945, GHMA.

Chapter 9

1. W. Howard Bishop, Mid-Winter Letter, 1942, GHMA.

2. Theodore Maynard, *The Story of American Catholicism* (New York, 1942), p. 455.

3. W. Howard Bishop, "Announcing Our Women Missioners," *The Challenge* VII (Summer 1944), 2.

4. Transcript of an oral interview, Sister Dorothy Hendershot, GHMA.

5. Diary, May 8, 1942, GHMA.

6. Ibid., May 9, 1942.

7. Ibid., May 10, 1942.

8. "Archives and Memories," April 8, 1981, p. 21, Glenmary Studies No. 3, GSA.

9. Diary, October 5, 1942, GHMA.

10. Ibid., November 16, 1942.

11. Sister Mary Frances Simon, "Father Bishop As I Knew Him," Glenmary Studies, No. 5, October 1981, p. 1, GSA.

12. Ibid.

13. Ibid., pp. 3–4.

14. Ibid., p. 3.

15. Diary, April 13, 1943, GHMA.

16. Ibid., October 8, 1943.

17. Ibid., June 17, 1943.

18. Ibid., June 24, 1943.

19. Ibid., June 25, 1943.

20. Sister Mary Frances Simon, p. 4, GSA.

21. Diary, June 27, 1943, GHMA.

22. Sister Mary Frances Simon, p. 4, GSA.

23. Ibid.

24. Diary, January 29, 1944, GHMA.

25. "Archives and Memories," pp. 3–4, GSA.

26. Sister Mary Frances Simon, p. 3, GSA.

27. W. Howard Bishop, "Talk to the Sisters' Community," October 2, 1943, Speeches, etc., GHMA.

28. Ibid.

29. Diary, April 15, 1944, GHMA.

30. W. Howard Bishop, "Our Feminine Missioners Step Out," *The Challenge* VII (Autumn 1944), 4.

31. Ibid., 8.

32. Ibid.

33. John J. Marquardt, "The Catholic Rural Conference," *The Challenge* VII (Christmas 1944), 3.

34. Diary, October 31, 1944, GHMA.

35. Ibid., November 11, 1944.

36. Ibid., November 19, 1944.

37. John T. McNicholas to "Your Excellency," November 5, 1944, Glenmary Files, AACin.

38. Diary, November 23, 1944, GHMA.

39. W. Howard Bishop, "Talk to Women Missioners," Speeches, etc., n.d., GHMA.

40. Diary, January 24, 1945, GHMA.

41. Ibid., May 18, 1944.

42. Ibid., February 26, 1945.

43. Ibid., March 8, 1945.

44. Ibid., March 13, 17, 1945.

45. Ibid., April 11, 1945.

46. Ibid., June 19, 20, 1945.

47. Ibid., August 19–20, 1945.

48. Ibid., August 21, 1945.

49. Ibid., August 23, 1945.

50. Ibid., September 10, 1945.

51. Ibid.

52. Ibid., September 11, 1945.

53. Ibid., September 27, 1945.

54. Ibid., September 29, 1945.

55. Ibid., November 23, 1945.

56. McNicholas to Bishop, November 24, 1945, GHMA.

57. Bishop to McNicholas, November 26, 1945, GHMA.

58. Diary, November 27, 1945, GHMA.

59. Ibid., December 6, 1945.

60. Ibid., December 8, 1945.

61. McNicholas to Kotter, December 9, 1945, AACin.

62. Joan Wade Markey, "Recollections of an Early Glenmarian," Glenmary Studies, No. 8, May 1986, GSA.

63. Diary, February 25, 1946, GHMA.

64. Sister Mary Frances Simon, p. 6, GSA.

Chapter 10

1. For background on the 1950s see Jay P. Dolan, *The American Catholic Experience* (New York, 1985); James Hennesey, S.J., *American Catholic: A History of the Roman Catholic Community in the United States* (New York, 1981).

2. McNicholas to Bishop (February 15, 1944), August 15, 1939. A handwritten copy of this letter is in the Sourd papers, GHMA.

3. Bishop to McNicholas, February 28, 1944, GHMA.

4. McNicholas to Cicognani, November 5, 1944, AACin.

5. Diary, January 19, 1945, GHMA.

6. Ibid., June 19, 1945.

7. Ibid., July 6, 1945.

8. Ibid., May 22, 1947.

9. Bishop to "Glenmarians," June 1, 1947, GHMA.

10. Same to same, June 14, 1947, GHMA.

11. Diary, June 3, 1947, GHMA.

12. Ibid., June 9, 1947.

13. Ibid., June 16, 1947.

14. Ibid., June 9, 1947.

15. Ibid., July 3, 1947.

16. Ibid., June 22, 1947.

17. Ibid., July 2, 1947.

18. Ibid., July 3, 1947.

19. Ibid., July 12, 1947.

20. Ibid., August 22, 1947.

21. "Rome Ratifies," *The Challenge* X (Autumn 1947), 2.

22. *The Official Catholic Directory*, 1950 (New York, 1950), p. 52.

23. "Groundbreaking," *The Challenge* XI (Summer 1948), 2; also see Diary, May 21, 1948 and *The Challenge* XII (Summer 1949), 2.

24. Copy of a newspaper article found in Bishop's diary, September 30, 1948, GHMA.

25. W. Howard Bishop, "Death Visits Glenmary," *The Challenge* XI (Autumn 1948), 7.

26. Diary, October 23, 1949, GHMA.

27. Bishop to "Beloved Daughters in Christ," May 21, 1947, GHMA.

28. Diary, May 18, 1947, GHMA.

29. Bishop to Beloved Daughters in Christ, May 21, 1947, GHMA.

30. Diary, September 9, 1947, GHMA.

31. Sister Mary Frances Simon, p. 10, GSA.

32. Diary, September 9, 1947, GHMA.

33. Bishop to McNicholas, September 10, 1947, GHMA.

34. McNicholas to Bishop, September 14, 1947, GHMA.

35. Diary, September 10, 1947, GHMA.

36. Ibid., January 13, 1947.

37. Ibid., January 15, 1948.

38. Ibid., February 4, 1948.

39. Ibid., December 24, 1948.

40. Sisters Dorothy, Opal and Joan to McNicholas. December 29, 1948, GHMA.

41. Glenmary Sisters (no signatures) to McNicholas. January 5, 1949, GHMA.

42. A record of the visit signed by Father Kelly was included in Bishop to Rehring, August 20, 1950.

43. William Smith, "Our Brothers," *The Challenge* XI (Christmas 1948), 6.

44. Ibid., p. 8.

45. Diary, April 17, 1949, GHMA.

46. Bishop to Most Reverend Emmett M. Walsh, Charleston, NC, July 23, 1949, GHMA.

47. Reedy to Bishop, October 14, 1941, GHMA.

48. Ibid., same to same, July 15, 1946, GHMA.

49. Ibid., same to same, April 13, 1947, GHMA.

50. Bishop to Walsh, July 23, 1949, GHMA.

51. Diary, November 27, 1948, GHMA.

52. W. Howard Bishop, *Mid-Winter Letter,* 1951, GHMA.

53. Ibid.

54. Diary, November 29, 1949, GHMA.

55. Personal interview: C. J. Kauffman with Fr. Howard French, March 1988.

56. Personal interview: C. J. Kauffman with Fr. Massarella, March 1988.

57. Telephone interview: C. J. Kauffman with Rev. James Reedy, O.S.B., October 3, 1990.

58. Diary, December 31, 1949, GHMA.

Chapter 11

1. Bishop to Sourd, June 22, 1950, Sourd Papers, GHMA.

2. Ibid., same to same, July 16, 1950.

3. Diary, October 3, 1950, GHMA.

4. Ibid., March 1, 1951, GHMA.

5. Ibid.

6. Ibid., August 18, 1951.

7. Minutes of the General Chapter, 1951, Chapter files, GHMA.

8. Diary, June 21, 1950, addendum, GHMA.

9. Ibid., December 10, 1951.

10. Ibid., March 31, 1952.

11. Ibid., April 4, 1952.

12. Ibid., April 5, 1952.

13. Ibid., June 4, 1952.

14. Ibid., June 16, 1952.

15. Ibid., June 18, 1952.

16. Ibid., June 16, 1952.

17. Kelly to Bishop, July 1, 1952—Kelly's private file.

18. Transcript of oral interview of John J. Marquardt, November 24, 1968, GHMA.

19. Ibid.

20. Diary, September 22, 1952, GHMA.

21. W. Howard Bishop, "Commentary on the Constitution of Glenmary," September 1952–June 1953 as compiled by James Murdock, pp. 1–2, Constitution files, GHMA.

22. Ibid., p. 3.

23. Ibid., chapter IV, 12; and chapter VII, 11.

24. Ibid., p. 23.

25. "Retreat Notes," January 1–30, 1941, 1097–1140, GHMA.

26. "Retreat Notes," August 20–27, 1951, 1147, GHMA.

27. Diary, December 14, 1952, GHMA.

28. Ibid., January 3, 1953.

29. "Retreat Notes," 1941, 1114, GHMA.

30. Ibid., 1117.

31. W. Howard Bishop, Mid-Winter Letter, February 1952, GHMA.

32. Ibid.

33. Ibid.

34. W. Howard Bishop, Mid-Winter Letter, February 1953, GHMA.

35. Howard Bishop, Writings, Homilies, etc., Xavier University, June 1, 1952, GHMA.

36. Ibid.

37. Ibid.

38. Ibid.

39. Quoted by Murdock, "Commentary on the Constitution . . ."

40. Ibid.

41. Ibid.

42. Diary, February 13, 1953, GHMA.

43. Ibid., March 29, 1953.

44. Transcript of oral interview of Robert Berson, April 10, 1968, GHMA.

45. Ibid.

46. "Directory for Sunday Celebration in the Absence of a Priest," *Origins* 18 (October 20, 1988), 301–07.

47. Brother Robert Hoffman "Father Bishop, The Story of His Death," *The Challenge* 16 (Autumn 1953), 14.

48. Howard Bishop, Mid-Winter Letter, January 1948, GHMA.

49. "Condolences," *The Challenge* 16 (Autumn 1953), 15.

50. Ligutti to Bishop Muench, June 1953, Muench Papers, ACUA.

51. These were quoted in "Condolences."

52. "Father Sourd Speaks," *The Challenge* 16 (Autumn 1953), 2.

Epilogue

1. Charles E. Bouchard, O.P., "The Charism of the Community," *Review for Religious* 37 (April/May 1978), 350–56; Daniel T. Dorsey, *Reverend William Howard Bishop, Toward an Understanding of His Charism as Founder of the Glenmary Home Missioners* (S.T.L. thesis, The Gregorian University, Rome, 1983); John Carroll Futrell, "Discovering the Founder's Charism," *The Way Supplement* 14 (Autumn 1971), 63; Bernard J. Lee, S.M., "A Socio-Historical Theology of Charism," *Review for Religious* 48 (January/February 1989), 124–35. John Manuel Lozano, CMF, "Founder and Community: Inspiration and Charism," *Review for Religious* 37 (January–February 1978), 214–36.

2. For background of the immediate pre-Vatican II church in the United States, see "Transitions in Catholic Culture: The Fifties," *U.S. Catholic Historian* 7 (Winter 1988).

3. Raymond Dehen's report to the Glenmary Congress, 1955, Congress files, GHMA.

4. Clement Borchers, "The Lay Apostolate," *The Challenge* XX (Spring 1958), 3.

5. Clement Borchers, "Our Gratitude," *The Challenge* XXIV (Autumn 1962), 7.

6. "Mestrovic," *The Challenge* XXIV (Autumn 1962), 6.

7. Clement Borchers, "Mater et Magistra," *The Challenge* XXIV (Autumn 1961), 6.

8. "Pastoral Center," *The Challenge* XXV (Summer 1963), 5.

9. Patrick O'Donnell, "25 Years," *The Challenge* XXV (Spring 1964), 4.

10. Patrick O'Donnell, "Gone to Glory," *The Challenge* XLII (Christmas 1971), 3.

11. Joseph A. Komonshak, "Vatican Council II," *The New Dictionary of Theology,* eds. Joseph Komonshak, Mary Collins, Dermot Lane (Wilmington, 1987), 1074 (hereafter cited as NDT).

12. William McConville, OFM, "Mission," NDT, 665–66.

13. Quoted by Juliana Casey, I.H.M., "Religious Life," NDT, 871–72.

14. Robert Berson, Superior General's Report to the Glenmary Congress, 1967, Congress files, GHMA.

15. Ibid., 1970.

16. See Louis McNeil's reports of the Glenmary Research Center, 1987–89, GHMA.

17. See Robert Berson's reports of the President to the Glenmary Congress, 1965–70.

18. Reports of the Education Committee, 1965–70. Berson papers, GHMA.

19. "The Constitution of the Home Mission Sisters of St. Dominic, 1950," GSA.

20. "The Constitution of the Home Mission Sisters, 1953," GSA.

21. Sister Rosemary Esterkamp, "Pictorial History of the Glenmary Sisters," GSA.

22. Sister Rosemary Esterkamp's historical notes, *Memorandum,* June 1989, GSA.

23. Mother Mary Catherine, Superior General's letter, *Kinship* I (February 1962), 2.

24. Mother Mary Catherine, "Special End of the Glenmary Sisters," Report to the Institute, September 8, 1962, GSA.

25. Ibid.

26. Constitution and Directory, 1962, GSA.

27. Maureen O'Connor, "The Glenmary Crisis," *St. Anthony Messenger* 75 (September 1967), 22.

28. Ibid., pp. 22–23.

29. Quoted in *The National Catholic Reporter,* June 1967, a cutting, GHMA.

30. Ibid.; also see Sister Rosemary Esterkamp, "Reflections," in *Glenmary Studies* 6 (December 1982), GSA.

31. Mother Mary Joseph, "Let Us Begin . . ." *Kinship* (Winter 1967), 1.

32. "Father William Howard Bishop, December 19, 1885–June 11, 1953, Founder of the Glenmary Sisters," *Kinship* 7 (Summer 1968), 1.

33. Sister Mary Joseph's report to the chapter, 1975, GSA.

34. Robert Berson's report to the Glenmary Congress, 1969. Congress files, GHMA.

35. Constitution, 1969, GHMA.

36. Ibid., Directory, pp. 2–3.

37. Robert Berson's report to the Glenmary Congress, 1969, GHMA.

38. Constitution, 1969, 11, GHMA.

39. Quoted by Dennis Holly, "To Father Robert Berson: Recognitions, Congratulations, Best Wishes," *The Challenge* XXVI (Autumn 1983), 4.

40. Brother Robert Hoffman, "The Historical Development of the Glenmary Brotherhood," June 1982, GHMA.

41. Ibid.

42. John A. Rausch, "Jubilee," *The Challenge* XLIII (Autumn 1971), 5.

43. Leonard Spanjers, "Our New President," *The Challenge* XXXV (Spring 1977), 3.

44. Ibid., pp. 2–4.

45. Charles Hughes' report to the Glenmary Congress, 1971. Congress files, GHMA.

46. Ibid.

47. Ibid.

48. Sister Mary Michelle, "President's Column," *Kinship* 16 (Spring 1977), 1.

49. Ibid.

50. Sister Rosemary Esterkamp to Christopher Kauffman, June 6, 1989, copy GSA.

51. Ibid.

52. Ibid.

53. Sister Rosemary, President's Column, *Kinship* 27 (Summer 1987), 4.

54. Frank Ruff's report to the Glenmary Congress, 1987. Congress files, GHMA.

55. Ibid.

56. Ibid.

57. Sister Christine Beckett, "God Centered, Person Oriented and Spirit-Sent-in-Community," *Kinship* 27 (Winter 1988), 3.

58. Sister Christine Beckett, "Encouraging God's Influentials," *Kinship* 27 (Spring 1988), 3.

59. Co-Missioner documents, 1988–89. Also see Missionary Statement, 1987 Chapter, GSA.

60. Frank Ruff's report to the Glenmary Congress, 1987. Congress files, GHMA.

INDEX

Ad Gentes, 242
Agar, Herbert, 98–99, 128
Agrarianism, 75
Agricultural depression, 76, 84
Agricultural reforms, 135–136
Alonso, Sister, 188
Aloysius, Sister, 137–138
Alter, Karl J., 220–221, 239, 245, 247–248
The Ambassador of Christ (Gibbons), 14–15
American Country Life Association, 65–66, 67
Americanism, 12–14, 41–42, 66
American Protective Association, 14
Anti-Catholicism
    Bishop on, 80–82
    and Catholic Church, 10, 14–15
    and Curley, 16, 81
    and Home Missioners of
        America, 179
    in rural areas, 145
Antigonish, 92, 123
Athenaeum of Ohio, 134
Atkinson, Alphonsus, 152

Back-to-the-land movement, 87–88, 98
Baker, O.E., 98, 128
Baltimore church
    Anglo-American minority in, 9–10
    under Carroll (John), 10
    under Curley, 16–17
    under Gibbons, 11–12, 14–16
    and preservationists, 10–13
    and transformationists, 10, 13
Bankhead amendment, 88–89
Barrett, John I., 70
Barry, John, 241
Barry, Mother Gerald, 211
Beckett, Christine, 258–259
Behm, Albert, 252
Belloc, Hilaire, 98
Benson, Jochim V., 120–121
Bernard, Mary, 72–73
Bernardin, Joseph Cardinal, 259
Bernice, Sister, 208
Berson, Robert C., 242, 243, 250, 252, 254, 256
Beruatto, Louis, 174
Biondi, Fumasoni, 203
Bishop, Eleanor Knowles, 21–22
Bishop, Francis, 18–19, 34
Bishop, John Knowles, 18, 19, 22
Bishop, Mary Edna, 18, 21
Bishop, William Howard. *See also*
    Home Missioners of
    America; St. Louis Parish;
    Legacy of Bishop;
    N.C.R.L.C.
on agricultural depression, 76, 84
on anti-Catholicism, 80–82
anti-urban expressions of, 79
back problems of, 32, 34, 121–122
and back-to-the-land movement, 87–88

and Bankhead amendment, 88–89
and Benson, 120–121
Bernard on, 72–73
birth of, 18
and Byrnes, 95–96, 96–97, 123
on capitalism, 85, 97–98
and Carroll (Charles), 45–46
Catholic identity of, 38–39
at Catholic University, 26, 29
and *The Challenge*, 145–147
character of, 20–21, 31, 37–38
childhood illness of, 19
childhood parish of, 19
and Clarksville picnic, 51–53
commencement address of, at
    Xavier University, 230–231
on communism, 98
and Conte, 47–48
on conversion to Catholicism, 40
and Corrigan, 32–33
and country life, view of, 107
and Craig, 29–30, 31, 32–33, 35–37
criticism of, by Craig, 30–31
and Curley, 45–46, 54–55, 57,
    130–131
and Day, 91
on devotionalism, 228
diary of, 29–30, 31–32, 34–35
ecclesiology of, 29
editorials of, school, 19–20
education of, 19–20, 22, 29
educational degrees of, 29
eulogies of, 234–235
evangelization of, 103
family background of, 18–19
on fascism, 98
father of, 18–19, 34
first sermon of, 27–28
focus of, in last three years of life,
    220
Gatton on, 73

and home missioners, view of,
    103, 107–109
and Homestead Colony at
    Clarksville, 90–91, 92–93
homilies of, 24–25, 39–40
hospitalization of, 26
Ignatian retreat of, 165–166, 227
ill health of, 22, 25–26
and Irwin, 116–117
and *Landward*, 86–87
last letters of, 233–234
on lay apostles, 41–42
and League of the Little Flower,
    58, 67–68, 71
lecture series of, 149–151
and Ligutti, 89–90, 144
and Liljencrants (John), 44
and Mahon, 140–141
and Marquardt, 222–223, 224–225
and McAdams, 122, 127
and McGinn, 123–124, 124–126
and McNicholas on, 132, 136–137
memory training of, 30
and Morris, 118–120, 124
mother of, 21–22
New Year maxims for 1950s,
    217–218
nickname of, 20
in Nova Scotia, 92
and O'Hara (Edwin), 62–64
ordination of, 27
and Ourings, 93
on parish schools, 55–56
preoccupations of, 22
and Price, 116
on priesthood, power of, 40–41
professional qualities of, 73–74
as public speaker, 25
refuge of, 219
request for ordination by, 26–27
resignation of, from St. Martin's,
    163

retreats of, 165–166, 227–228
on rural development, Catholic
    Church's role in, 76–77, 78,
    84
on rural movement, new order
    of, 98
on rural parishes, 56–58
as rural pastor, 46–47, 48–50,
    56–58, 73, 105
rural reform of, 66
at Sacred Heart Parish, 29–36
and Schmiedler, 94–95
sculpture of, 240
self-consciousness of, 31
self-image of, 75–76
self-improvement by, 35, 51
in seminary, 23–26
siblings of, 18, 19, 21, 22
social life of, 21
and Sourd, 157–160
strengths of, 235–236
and summer vacation school at
    Blanchester, 138
theology of nature and rural life,
    77–78
and Thompson, 141–142
transfer of, 36
transformationist position of,
    83–84
on tribal twenties, 79–80
and Vincent, 164
on vocation, early experiences of,
    22–23
and Walsh (James Anthony), 103,
    137
weariness of, 217
work ethic of, 50–51
on World War II, 170
writing style of, 73–74
zeal of, practical, 233–234
Blacks, 47, 103, 145–146. *See also*
    Racism

"Blessed Thirty Years" (Wilmes),
    182–183
Borchers, Clement
    background of, 177
    death of, 240–241
    early years of, 238
    at Glenmary, 152, 164, 166, 176, 221,
        240–241
    and poverty, 240
    and rural movement, 239
    and seminaries, 239–240
Borsodi, Ralph, 98, 128
Bowers, William L., 66
Bradley, Thomas, 219
Brooks, David, 244
Bruneau, Joseph, 24, 25
Buckey, Edward L., 19, 23
Burke, Henry, 182, 215–216
Byrnes, James, 95–98, 123, 144

Cahill, D.P., 70
Campbell, Joseph M., 95, 123, 128
Capitalism, 85, 97–98
Carey, Thomas R., 68
Carroll, Charles, 43, 44, 45
Carroll, John, 10, 11, 14
Catholic Church
    and American experience, 13
    Anglo-American minority in, 9–10
    and anti-Catholicism, 10, 14–15
    Gibbons on, 11, 15
    identities with, 9
    immigrants in, 11–12
    modernization of, 200–201
    and preservationists, 10–13
    priests in, decline in number of, 9
    separatism in, 10, 105, 134, 238
    and transformationists, 10, 13
Catholic Church Extension Society,
    59–60, 119
Catholic Evidence Guild, 140,
    147–148

Catholic Foreign Mission Society, 101

"Catholic ghetto," 238

Catholic Information Center, 168

"Catholicity," 111

Catholic Land Movement in America, 85

Catholic Missionary Union, 102

The Catholic Rural Life Bulletin, 96, 144, 145

Catholic Rural Life Bureau, 60, 64

Catholic Rural Life Conference, 84, 122–123, 167

Catholic Rural Life Convention (1923), 63, 148

Catholic rural movement. *See* Rural movement

The Catholic University of America, 10, 27, 29, 166, 244

Catholic Worker, 91

Center for Applied Research in the Apostolate (CARA), 243

Central Bureau of the Verein, 59

Central Verein, 59

The Challenge, 145–147, 152, 170

Chesterton, G.K., 97, 98

Cicognani, Amleto G., 114–115, 201, 202

Cincinnati archdiocese
  and agricultural reforms, 135–136
  and home missioners, 128, 129–133
  and Home Missioners of America, 154
  and McNicholas-Curley conflict, 134–135
  size of, 134

Clarksville parish school, 53–54, 57

Clarksville picnic, 51–53

Clergy. *See* Priests; specific names of

Coady, M.M., 92, 123

Co-missionary program, 259

Communism, 98

Conference of Missionaries, 102–103

Confraternity of Christian Doctrine (C.C.D.), 83, 84, 161, 232

Conroy, P.J., 69–70

Conte, "Aunt" Nancy, 47–48

Conversion, to Catholicism, 39–40, 229

Convert program, 160

Cooperatives, 85, 92

Corrigan, Michael Augustine, 11, 32–33, 136

Cotton, Francis R., 172–173

Coughlin, Mabel, 255

Craig, Francis E., 29–30, 31, 32–33, 35–37

Cronin, John, 111

Cunningham, James, 167

Curley, Michael J.
  and anti-Catholicism, 16, 81
  background of, 16
  Baltimore church under, 16–17
  and Bishop, 45–46, 54–55, 57, 130–131
  death of, 202
  and home missioners, 116, 130–131
  and McNicholas, 134–135
  and N.C.R.L.C. conference of 1924, 70
  priorities of, 17

Cushing, Richard, 172

Dalton, Robert, 254

Daniel, John W., 21

Day, Dorothy, 91

Day, Victor, 65

Dean, Joseph W., 182

Decretum Laudis, 239

Dehen, Raymond, 239, 241

Devotionalism, 228

Diekmann, Godfrey, 238

Divinity School at St. Louis University, 244

Dominicans, 208–211, 245
Dorita, Sister, 186, 187
Dorothy, Sister, 208
Dougherty, Cardinal, 118
Doyle, A.P., 102
Drought, James A., 113
Duffy, John A., 151
Dungannon, 182
Dyer, Edward R., 23, 27–28, 33

Early, William, 252
Ecclesiam Suam, 243
Ellen, Sister, 186
Elliot, Walter, 102
England, John, 10, 59
Ernst, Loretta, 172
Esterkamp, Florence, 255
Esterkamp, Rosemary, 245, 255–256
Evangelization
    Bishop's strategies of, 103
    contemporary, 259
    of Glenmary, 189–190
    Hecker's program of, 102
    and Home Missioners of
        America, 160–161,
        163–164, 229–230
    ideal context of, 229–230
    open-air, 160–161, 163–164
    and women missioners, 189–190

Fallon, Lester J., 128
Fascism, 98
Fenlon, John, 28, 138, 139
Floersch, John, 135
Foken, Herman J., 176, 177
Formation Institute, 246
Frances, Sister. See Simon
French, Howard, 202, 216–217
French liberal Catholics, 13–14
Friends of the Rural Mission, 146
Furfey, Paul Hanley, 114
Futrell, John C., 256

Gaffey, James, 59
Gallicanism, 13–14
Gatton, Thelma, 73
German-American Benevolent
    Societies, 59
Gibbons, James
    on Americans, 15
    Baltimore church under, 11–12,
        14–16
    and Bishop's request of
        ordination, 28
    and Bishop's transfer, 36
    book by, 14–15
    Carroll's influence on, 11, 14
    Carroll's letter to, 44
    on Catholic Church, 11, 15
    on conversion to Catholicism,
        39–40
    on immigrants, 11–12
    on priests, American, 15–16
    style of, 39
Gibbons' church, 14, 41, 43
Glendale
    building of, 168–169
    first Christmas at, 165
    first mission of, 172–173
    and Maryknoll, 169
    men missioners at, 164–165
    Owensboro mission, 172, 174–175
    and poor, 177
    second mission of, 174–175
    secretarial help at, 172
    study and travel by missioners of,
        166–168
    Sunfish mission, 172–174
    and World War II, 170–171
Glenmary Guild, 219
Glenmary Home Missioners. *See also*
    Men missioners; Women
    missioners
    Borchers at, 152, 164, 166, 176, 221,
        240–241

Burke at, 215–216
closing of theologate at, 244
division of labor at, 211–212
evangelization of, 189–190
faculty at, 206, 207
fiftieth anniversary of, 259
French at, 216–217
Hendershot at, 185, 186
income of sisters at, 197
Kimmick at
    acceptance into community, 186
    and Bishop, conflict with,
        194–197
    early duties of, 172, 184–185
    as prefect, 188, 192
    at Russellville parish, 190–191
    superior of, 192
legacy of, 237, 241–242, 244,
    244–249
and Levin, 149
liturgies at, 241
Mahon at, 184
and McGrath, 176
in 1944, 188
in 1945, 182
1955 mission convention of, 239
and obedience, 227
parish, 178–179
polarization of sisters at, 197–199
and poverty, 226–227
Quinlan at, 215
Reedy at, 171–172, 212–215
seminary of, building of, 206
Simon at, 187, 188–189, 190, 197,
    208–209
Smith at, 153, 176, 177, 178
Sourd at, 149, 152, 164
thirtieth anniversary of, 182–183
training at, 186–187, 189
twenty-fifth anniversary of, 240
Wade at, 188, 190, 197, 208

Woodward at, 188, 190, 197
and World War II, 175–176
Glenmary Guild, 219
Glenmary Sisters, 216, 245–249. See
    also Glenmary Home
    Missioners; Women
    missioners
Glenmary Sisters Institute on
    Mission/Spirituality/Purpose
    (1982), 256
Glenmary Town and Research
    Center, 243
Grailville community, 192
Granger settlement, 89
Guest, Edgar, 222

Habit of sisters, 209, 210
Hafey, William J., 116
Halloran, Thomas, 167
Hayes, Cardinal, 118
Healy, Austin, 133, 138, 139–140
Hecker, Isaac, 10, 101, 102
Hellriegel, Martin, 164
Hendershot, Dorothy, 185, 186
Heyker, Mathias F., 163
Hoffman, Robert, 252
Hogan, John, 14
Holly, Dennis, 241–242
Home missioners, 101–102. See also
        Glenmary Home Missioners;
        Home Missioners of
        America; Men missioners;
        Women missioners
    Bishop's idea of, 103, 107–109
    call for, 106–107
    and Catholic Rural Life
        Conference, 121–123
    and Cicognani, 114–115
    in Cincinnati archdiocese, 128–
        129, 133
    and Curley, 116, 130–131

earliest documentation of,
    105–106
first draft of plan for, 107–111
history of, 101–102
and Irwin, 116–117
and Ligutti, 144–145
and McNicholas, 128
meeting of priests to advance
    plan of, 127–128
and N.C.R.L.C., 123–127
opposition to, 118–121
and Protestantism, 101
rural context of, 108
second draft of plan of, 113–114
specifics of, 108–110
support of, 117–118
tours to promote, 116–118
and Walsh, 106–107, 112–113
Home Missioners of America. *See
    also* Glenmary Home
    Missioners; Home
    missioners; Men missioners;
    Women missioners
and Alter, 220–221
and anti-Catholicism, 179
beginning of, official, 156
and Burke, 215–216
and *Catholic Rural Life Bulletin,*
    145
and *The Challenge,* 145–147
and Cincinnati archdiocese, 154
constitution of, 221
and conversion, approach to, 229
council on, 221–223
establishment of, 136–137, 154
and evangelization, 160–161, 163–
    164, 229–230
fiftieth anniversary of, 259
first campaign of, 150
first meeting of, 153
first missioners of, 152–153
first motherhouse of, 164
first sermons of, 153–154

focus of, in final years, 220
and French, 216–217
international vision of, 204
in Latin America, 244
and lay activism, 219, 232–233
and Marquardt-Bishop conflict,
    222–223, 224–225
Maynard on, 184
McDonnell's criticism of, 162–163
and McGrath's death, 206–207
and McNicholas, 156–157, 201–202
and N.C.R.L.C., 142–145
national attention to, 161–162
national vision for, 140
and "new social order," 161
by 1950, 217–218
novitiate year in, 168
priest recruitment for, 137, 138–
    139, 157
and Quinlan, 215
and racism, 230–231
and Reedy, 212–215
and retreats, 227–228
second meeting of, 160
seminaries, building of, 206–207
support of, 201–203
and talks to novices, 226–227, 231
and Vatican appropriation,
    202–205
Vatican approval of, 207–208
violence against, 171
and women missioners, 208–211
and World War II, 170–171, 175–
    176, 200–201
Homestead Colony at Clarksville,
    90–91, 92–93
Homilies, 24–25, 39–40
Hoover, Herbert, 79, 85
Hughes, Charles, 244, 252–254

Ignatius, Anthony, 212
Ignatius, St., 165–166
Immigrants, 11–12, 13, 38–39

"Immigrant style," 39
Industrial Recovery Act, 88
Institutum Divi Thomae, 134
Ireland, John, 11, 12, 24, 39, 39–40, 59
Ireton, Peter L., 117
Irish Catholic Colonization Society,
    59
Irwin, Michael, 116–117, 118
Isrod, Henry, 65

Jesuits, 68
Jewish Agricultural Society, 67
Jochim, Lawrence, 241, 252
John Joseph, Sister, 199
John XXIII, 240
Johnson, Joseph, 69
Josephite Fathers, 103
Judge, Thomas Augustine, 120

Kaercher, Magdalene, 246
Keane, John J., 11, 12
Kedley, Curt, 252
Kelley, Francis Clement, 59–60, 81
Kelly, James, 221, 223–224, 243
Kelly, John T., 70
Kelly, Thomas, 212, 252
Kenkel, Frederick P., 59, 64
Kennedy, Charles, 252
Kennedy, John F., 248–249
Kevin, Sister, 199, 209
Kimmick, Gertrude
    acceptance into community, 186
    and Bishop, conflict with, 194–197
    early duties of, 172, 184–185
    as prefect, 188, 192
    at Russellville parish, 190–191
    superior of, 192 172
Kinship, 246–247, 249, 256, 258
Kirsch, Felix M., 69
Knights of Labor, 10
Komonchak, Joseph A., 242
Ku Klux Klan, 145

LaFarge, John, 60, 68–69, 88,
    126–127
Landward, 86–87, 98, 106, 144
Lane, Raymond A., 234
Latin America project, 244
Lay activism, 13, 219, 232–233
Lay apostles, 41–42, 228–229, 239.
    See also Home missioners
Lay Associates of the Home
    Missioners of America
    (LAHMAS), 219
Lay women, 228–229
League of St. Louis, 58, 67–68, 71
League of the Little Flower, 58,
    67–68, 71
Leary, Joseph J., 132
Lee, Thomas Sim, 19
Legacy of Bishop
    and Ad Gentes, 242
    and Borchers, 238–241
    CARA, 243–244
    and Ecclesiam Suam, 243
    and Glenmary, 237, 241–242, 244
    Latin America project, 243
    and Lumen Gentium, 242–243
    men missioners, 249–255, 256–258
    and Perfectae Gentium, 243
    research center, 243
    and Second Vatican Council,
        237–238
    and seminaries, building of,
        239–240
    women missioners, 244–249, 255–
        256, 258–259
Leibold, Paul, 239
Leo XIII, 12, 98, 136
Leonard, M., 187
Leven, Stephen A., 147–149, 167
Ligutti, Luigi G., 68–69, 89–90, 96,
    144–145
Liljencrants, Carl J., 43, 44–45
Liljencrants, John, 36, 43
The Little Flower, 67–68, 86, 92

Liturgies, 241
Loyola University, 244
Lumen Gentium, 242–243

Madison, James A., 66
Maes, Camillus, 24
Magnien, Alphonse, 11, 14
Mahon, Agnes, 140–141, 172, 184
Malloy, William T., 124, 126
Manor chapel, 44–46
Marquardt, John, 221, 222–223, 224–225, 233
Martin, Urban, 225
Maryknoll, 169, 205
Maryknoll College, 244
Maryknoll Sisters, 195
Massarella, Francis, 152–153, 164, 166, 175, 176, 177
Maurin, Peter, 91
Maynard, Theodore, 184
McAdams, Edward P., 122, 127
McAuliffe, Maurice F., 117–118, 127
McConvile, William, 242
McDonnell, Thomas J., 162–163
McGinn, John T., 123–124, 124–126
McGrath, Francis Earl, 152, 176, 177, 178, 202, 206–207
McGuinness, Monsignor, 128
McNabb, Vincent, 98
McNeil, Louis, 243–244
McNeill, Leon A., 95, 124, 148
McNicholas, John T.
  and Bishop, 132, 136–137
  and Curley, 134–135
  and home missioners, 128
  and Home Missioners of
    America, 156–157, 201–202
  and rural movement, 65
  and women missioners, 192, 196–197, 208–209
McQuaid, Bernard, 11
McRae, Francis, 169, 185

Men missioners. *See also* Glenmary;
    specific names of
  Borchers, 164, 166, 167
  Foken, 176
  at Glendale, 164–165
  Massarella, 164, 166, 167
  McGrath, 176
  1953 renewal chapter, 251
  1959 renewal chapter, 251
  1965 renewal chapter, 251–252
  1968 renewal chapter, 249–251
  in 1970s, 252–255
  in 1980s, 256–258
  at Preachers' Institute, 166–167
  Reedy, 171–172
  under Ruff, 256–258
  Smith, 160, 176, 177
  Sourd, 157–160
  Vatican approval of, 207–208
  Wilmer, 164–165
  Wolf, 164, 166, 167
  Wuest, 160, 176
Mestrovic, Ivan, 240
Meyer, Albert, 149
Meyer, Bernard, 117
Meyer, Dolores, 246
Michelle, Mary, 255
Missionary Servants of the Most
    Holy Trinity, 120
Mission school, 168, 169–170
Modernization, 200–201
Morris, John B., 118–120, 124
Mosaic, 240
Motry, H. Louis, 129
Mount St. Agnes Convent, 30
Muench, Bishop, 144
Mundelein, Cardinal, 118
Murdock, James R., 226
Murray, John Courtney, 127, 238

N.C.R.L.C. (National Catholic
    Rural Life Conference)

and American Country Life
    Association, 65–66
and Bishop
    agricultural reforms, 136
    financial crisis, 96–97
    first meeting, 65
    home missioners, 142–143
    Landward, 86–87
    League of the Little Flower, 68
    1938 board of directors
        meeting, 143–144
    as president, 74, 80
    vision of, 74
and Byrnes, 95–97
constitution-revision committee
    of, 95–96
and Curley, at 1924 conference, 70
first meeting of, 64–65
and home missioners, 123–127
and Home Missioners of
    America, 142–145
and League of the Little Flower,
    68
News Service of, 68
1924 conference, 68–70
1926 conference, 71
1928 conference of, 78–79
1929 conference of, 81
1930 conference of, 83
1932 conference of, 85–86
1934 conference of, 96
1937 conference of, 142–143
1938 conference of, 148
1944 conference of, 191
National Catholic Rural Life
    Conference. *See* N.C.R.L.C.
National Catholic Welfare Council
    (N.C.W.C.), 13, 60, 61, 63
National Child Labor Committee, 26
National Farm Organization, 85
Nativism, 16
Navagh, James J., 151

Nester, Frank J., 126
Niebuhr, H. Richard, 102
Nikols, R. Hewitt, 71
Noll, John, 127
Norton mission, 182
Nova Scotia, 123

Obedience, 227
O'Brien, David, 39
O'Brien, W.D., 118
Ong, Walter, 238
O'Connell, Denis, 11
O'Donnell, Joseph, 254
O'Donnell, Patrick, 240, 241
O'Hara, Edwin Vincent
    and C.C.D., 83
    and rural movement, 60–66
O'Hara, Gerald, 178–179
Orlett, Raymond, 244
Ottaviani, 203–204
Otway parish, 175
"Our Call," 249–250
Ourings, Henry H., 93
O'Rourke, Terry, 252
Our Lady of Lourdes Parish, 175
"Overchurched," 66
Owensboro mission, 172, 174–175

Padberg, John W., 256
Paul VI, 243
Paulists, 10, 101, 102, 167
Perfectae Caritatis, 243
Peterson, Geraldine, 245
Pilarczyk, Daniel, 256
Pius XI, 98, 136, 158
Poverty, 160, 177, 226–227, 240
Powell, Donald, 91, 98
Preachers' Institute, 166–167
Preservationists, 10–13, 83
Price, Thomas F., 24, 101, 102, 103,
    116, 146

Priests, 9, 15–16, 30, 40–41. *See also* specific names of
Progressive movement, 66
Propagation of the Faith, 105
Protestant Extension Society, 59
Protestant rural reformers, 66
Protestantism, 101
Pupett, Raymond, 72

Quadrigesimo Anno, 158
Quebec, 92
Quinlan, Patrick T., 215
Quinn, Bernard, 240, 243

Racism, 145, 180–181, 230–231
Reedy, Charles, 171–172, 212–215
Rehring, George J., 135, 211, 234
"Republican style," 39
Retreat movement, 13
Rice, Charles Owen, 111
Roosevelt, Franklin D., 85
Roosevelt, Theodore, 64
Ruff, Francis A., 254, 256–258, 259
Rumschlag, Mary Catherine, 245–247
Rural movement
   and anti-Catholicism, 80–82
   Bishop's new order of, 98–99
   Bishop's theology of, 78–79
   and Borchers, 239
   Catholic Church's role in, 76–77, 78, 84
   colonization efforts of, 59
   and Kelley, 59–60
   and McNicholas, 65
   in 1900s, early, 59–60
   and O'Hara, 60–66
Russellville parish, 175, 181, 208
Ryan, Edward F., 43
Ryan, James A., 118
Ryan, James H., 134–135
Ryan, John A., 60, 61

Sacred Heart Parish, 30–36
Santen, Margaret Mary, 219
Sauer, Francis, 252
Schenk, Frank, 244
Schloemer, Leo, 244
Schmeidler, Edgar, 94–95, 96
Schmidt, Les, 254
Schneider, Joseph, 205
Schrembs, Joseph, 118
Second Vatican Council (1962–1965), 237–238, 241, 242
Seminaries, 239–240
Separatism, 10, 105, 134, 238
Shahan, Thomas J., 28
Sheed, Frank, 140, 147
Simon, Opal, 187, 188–189, 190, 197, 208–209
Sisters of Mercy, 30
Sisters of the Divine Providence, 70
Smith, Albert E., 69
Smith, Edward
   assignment of, 178
   on council, 221
   at Glenmary, 153, 176, 177, 178
   in Latin America, 244
   at Norton, 181–182
   and poverty, 160
   responsibilities of, 179–180
Smith, Ignatius, 166–167
Smith, Mary, 52
Smith, William, 212
Society of Missionary Priests of St. Paul the Apostle, 101, 102
Sourd, Raphael
   and Bishop, 157–160
   on council, 221
   and eulogy of Bishop, 234–235
   at Glenmary, 149, 152, 164
   preaching by, 166
   violence toward, 171
   writings of, 157–160, 164
Spalding, John Lancaster, 59

Spanjers, Leonard, 241
Spence, John, 133, 138, 139
Sperti, George Speri, 134
Spirituality, 16, 228
Spozette, 203
Springer, Michael, 252
St. Isidore's Plow, 63, 66–67, 86
St. Louis Parish
  background of, 43
  under Bishop
    achievements of, 75
    arrival of, 43–44
    building fund, 54–55
    conflicts at, 44–45
    finances of, 51–52
    goals of, 53–54
    and Manor chapel, 44–46
  Bishop's transfer to, 36–37
  blacks in, 47, 180
  finances of, 51–52
  immigrants in, 38–39
  picnic of, 51–53
  school of, 53–54, 57
St. Louis University, 244
St. Martin's Parish, 153, 163
St. Mary's Seminary, 23–26, 27
St. Mathew's Parish, 19
St. Meinrad Seminary, 244
Stang, William, 102
Statesboro mission, 178
Steen, Joe, 241
Steinbacher, Wilfred, 254
Stephanie, Mother, 187–188
Sulpician Seminary, 27
Summer vacation school at
    Blanchester, 138
Sunfish mission, 172–174
Swint, John J., 24, 181

Teff, Michelle, 255
Testem Benevolentiae, 12–13
Theological College, 27

Thomasino, Sister, 54
Thompson, Joseph, 72
Thompson, Paul, 141–142, 152
"Thoughtlessness" (Guest), 222
Transformationists, 10, 13, 83–84
Trese, Virginia, 246
Tribal twenties, 79–80, 82

University of Dayton, 245

Verot, Augustin, 43
Vieban, Anthony, 139
Vincentians, 167–168

Wade, Joan, 188, 190, 197, 208
Wade, Mary Joseph, 248–249, 255
Wallace, Henry, 93
Walsh, James Anthony, 101, 103, 137
  and Bishop, 103, 137
  and Bruneau, 24
  and Catholic Foreign Mission
    Society, 101
  and home missioners, 106–107,
    112–113
Walsh, James E., 132, 146, 168, 185
Ward, Maisie, 140, 147
Washington Theological Union, 244
Weigel, Gustave, 238
Wilhelm, Paul, 252
Williams, Michael, 88
Wilmes, Vincent, 164–165, 178, 179,
    182, 212
Wilson, M.T., 89, 90
Wolf, Benedict, 153, 164, 166, 174,
    175, 181
Women missioners. *See also*
    Glenmary Sisters; specific
    names of
  under Beckett, 258–259
  dress of, 209, 210
  under Esterkamp, 255–256
  and evangelization, 189–190

Hendershot, 185, 186–187
and Home Missioners of
    America, 208–211
independence of, from
    Dominicans, 208–211
and Kimmick-Bishop conflict,
    194–197
Kimmick
    acceptance into community, 186
    and Bishop, conflict with,
        194–197
    early duties of, 172, 184–185
    as prefect, 188, 192
    Russellville parish, 190–191
    superior of, 192
Mahon, 184
and McNicholas, 192, 196–197,
    208–209
missionary character of, 193

in 1944, 188
in 1950s, 245–247
in 1960s, 247–249
in 1970s, 255–256
and patriarchal system, 192–193
permanence of, substantiation of,
    186
polarization of, at Glenmary,
    197–199
Simon, 187, 188–189, 190–191
Vatican approval of, 207–208
Wade, 188, 190–191
Woodward, 188
Woods, Ken, 252
Woodward, Eloise, 188, 190, 197
World War II, 170–171, 175–176,
    200–201
Wuest, Francis A., 160, 176